D0845175

GOVERNING MEXICO

Governing Mexico

The Statecraft of Crisis Management

John J Bailey

Associate Professor of Government
Georgetown University, Washington, D.C.

St. Martin's Press New York

 For information, write:
Scholarly and Reference Division,
St. Martin's Press, Inc., 175 Fifth Avenue, New York, NY 10010

First published in the United States of America in 1988

Printed in Hong Kong

ISBN 0-312-01209-8

Library of Congress Cataloging-in-Publication Data
Bailey, John J
Governing Mexico, 1976-88: the statecraft of crisis management
by John J Bailey.
p. cm.
Bibliography: p.
Includes index.
ISBN 0-312-01209-8: $39.95
1. Political participation—Mexico. 2. Mexico—Politics and government—1970- 3. Industry and state—Mexico. 4. Political parties—Mexico. 5. Mexico—Economic conditions—1970- I.Title.
JL1281.B34 1988
320.972—dc19
87-28479
CIP

For my parents,
Farrell and Betty Bailey,
and
Barbara Ward

Contents

Acknowledgements

Over the years I have accumulated many debts in preparing this book, and I am pleased to acknowledge them here. The US Department of Education awarded me Fulbright–Hays Faculty Study Abroad grants in 1979 and 1985, and Georgetown University provided sabbatical support and funds for travel and research on different occasions. In Mexico I found supportive research havens in the Instituto Nacional de Administración Pública (1979) and the Centro de Estudios Internacionales of the Colegio de México (1985). The Colegio de Sonora also granted me library privileges.

Many Mexicans shared their perspectives on contemporary politics and provided helpful advice on how to do research. Lic. Juan José Rodríguez Prats contributed a good deal of his own scarce time to support and encourage the study. Dr Jorge Carpizo, Lic. Esteban Garaiz, Lic. Víctor González Avelar, Lic. José Roberto Mendirichaga, Lic. Javier Moreno Toscano and Lic. Ignacio Pichardo Pagaza all made special efforts to facilitate the research.

Delal Baer (Center for Strategic and International Studies), Roderic Camp (Central College of Iowa), Wayne Cornelius (University of California – San Diego), John Link and Donna Roberts (US Department of Agriculture), Catherine Thorup (Overseas Development Council) and Jay Van Hueven (US–Mexico Chamber of Commerce) allowed me to participate in conferences and meetings on a number of occasions that helped inform my views. My efforts to understand the border and politics in northern Mexico were much helped by Dudley Althaus, *The Brownsville Herald*, Marjorie Miller, *The San Diego Union*, Kieth Rosenblum, *The Arizona Daily Star* and William Waters, *The Arizona Republic*.

Several colleagues gave an extra measure by commenting on the entire manuscript: Roderic Camp, George Grayson, Daniel Levy, Gabriel Szekely and Sidney Weintraub. And for reading chapters or fragments, I thank Manuel Barquín, Bruce Bagley, Jorge G. Castañeda, Guy F. Erb, Louis Goodman, Soledad Loaeza, Jeffrey Needell and Jorge Pinto.

Rainer Godau, much missed since his death in 1984, helped at several points along the way, especially with respect to Mexican bureaucracy.

Westview Press of Boulder, Colorado, kindly permitted me to

quote from my chapters published in Roderic Ai Camp (ed.), *Mexican Political Stability: The Next Five Years* (1986), and Judith Gentleman (ed.), *Mexican Politics in Transition* (1987).

It goes without saying that I bear full responsibility for the final product. In fact, several who facilitated the research and commented on drafts disagreed with parts or most of the analyses that follow.

Leopoldo Gómez, Rafael Fernández de Castro, Jorge Molina and Mary Kay Loss assisted the research.

The several scores of US foreign service officers who participated in my area seminar at the Foreign Service Institute made the subject constantly fresh and enjoyable, as did my Georgetown students. And Sandy, Paul and Meryl endured and encouraged me throughout the project.

JOHN J BAILEY

List of Tables

List of Figures

List of Abbreviations

ALFA – Industrial Group ALFA
AMIS – Mexican Association of Insurance Institutions
ANIERM – National Association of Importers and Exporters of the Republic of Mexico
APRA – American Popular Revolutionary Alliance
BCN – Baja California Norte
CAMCO – American Chamber of Commerce of Mexico
CANACINTRA – National Chamber of Transformation Industries
CCE – Business Coordinating Council
CCI – Independent Peasant Confederation
CDE – State Directive Committee (PRI)
CEN – National Executive Committee (PRI)
CEESP – Center for Private Sector Economic Studies
CEPES – State Commission for Political, Economic, and Social Studies (PRI)
CES – Center for Sociological Studies
CFE – Federal Electoral Commission
CMHN – Mexican Council of Businessmen
CNC – National Peasant Confederation
CNG – National Confederation of Cattlemen
CNPC – National Confederation of Small Merchants
CNOP – National Confederation of Popular Organisations
CNPP – National Confederation of Small Farmers
CONASUPO – National Staple Products Company
CONCAMIN – National Confederation of Chambers of Industry
CONCANACO – National Confederation of Chambers of Commerce
CONCANACOMIN – National Chambers of Commerce and Industry
COPARMEX – Mexican Employers' Confederation
COPLAMAR – Coordinating Commission for the National Plan on Deprived Zones and Marginal Groups
CROC – Revolutionary Federation of Workers and Farmers
CROM – Regional Federation of Mexican Workers
CT – Congress of Labor
CV – variable capital (form of incorporation)
CTM – Mexican Workers Confederation

CUC – Single Coordination Agreement
CUD – Single Development Agreement
FERTIMEX – Mexican Fertilisers Company
FSTSE – Federation of Public Sector Unions
GATT – General Agreement on Tariffs and Trade
GDP – Gross Domestic Product
GSP – Generalised System of Preferences
IEPES – Institute for Political, Economic and Social Studies
IMCE – Mexican Institute for Foreign Commerce
IMF – International Monetary Fund
IMSS – Mexican Social Security Institute
INFONAVIT – Workers Housing Institute
IPN – National Politechnical Institute
ISI – Import-Substituting Industrialisation
ISSSTE – Institute of Security and Social Services for State Employees
JPRS – Joint Publications Research Service
LOPPE – Law of Political Organisations and Electoral Processes
MAP – Popular Action Movement
MAUS – Action Movement for Socialist Unity
NAFINSA – National Finance Bank
NOTIMEX – Mexican News Agency
OECD – Organisation for Economic Cooperation and Development
OPEC – Organisation of Petroleum Exporting Countries
PAN – National Action Party
PARM – Authentic Party of the Mexican Revolution
PCM – Mexican Communist Party
PDM – Mexican Democratic Party
PEMEX – Mexican Petroleum Company
PIDER – Integral Rural Development Program
PIRE – Immediate Program for Economic Recovery
PMT – Mexican Workers Party
PNR – National Revolutionary Party
PPS – Popular Socialist Party
PRI – Institutional Revolutionary Party
PRM – Party of the Mexican Revolution
PRT – Workers' Revolutionary Party
PSR – Socialist Revolutionary Party
PST – Socialist Workers' Party
PSUM – Unified Socialist Party

SA – incorporated, limited liability
SAHOP – Secretariat of Human Settlements and Public Works
SAM – Mexican Food System
SARH – Secretariat of Agriculture and Water Resources
SCGF – Secretariat of the Controller
SDN – Secretariat of National Defense
SECOFIN – Secretariat of Commerce and Industrial Promotion
SECTUR – Secretariat of Tourism
SEDUE – Secretariat of Ecology and Urban Development
SEMIP – Secretariat of Energy, Mines and Parastatal Industry
SEP – Secretariat of Public Education
SEPAFIN – Secretariat of Patrimony and Industrial Promotion
SEPANAL – Secretariat of National Patrimony
SEPESCA – Secretariat of Fisheries
SG – Secretariat of the Interior
SHCP – Secretariat of the Treasury
SIDERMEX – Mexican Iron and Steel Company
SNTE – National Union of Educational Workers
SP – Secretariat of the Presidency
SPP – Secretariat of Programming and Budget
SRA – Secretariat of Agrarian Reform
SRE – Secretariat of Foreign Relations
SSA – Secretariat of Health and Welfare
STRPRM – Union of Revolutionary Petroleum Workers of the Mexican Republic
STPS – Secretariat of Labor and Social Welfare
UAM – Autonomous Metropolitan University
UIA – Iberoamerican University
UNAM – National Autonomous University of Mexico
VISA – Industrial Values Company
VITRO – Industrial Group VITRO

United States of America
San Antonio
Brownsville
Laguna Madre
Matamoros
Nuevo Laredo
Rio Grande
Piedras Negras
Rio Bravo del Norte
El Paso
Ciudad Juárez
Rio Grande
Mexicali
Nogales
Hermosillo
SONORA
Chihuahua
CHIHUAHUA
Jiménez
COAHUILA
Saltillo
Monterrey
NUEVO LEON
Torreón
Durango
DURANGO
Culiacán
SINALOA
Mazatlán
Tepic
NAYARIT
Zacatecas
ZACATECAS
AGS
Aguascalientes
SAN LUIS POTOSI
San Luis Potosí
Cuidad Victoria
TAMAULIPAS
Tampico
Guadalajara
JALISCO
León
GUANAJUATO
Querétaro
QUERETARO
HIDALGO
Pachuca
MEXICO CITY
MEXICO
Morelia
MICHOACAN
Colima
COLIMA
Toluca
MOR
Puebla
PUEBLA
TLAXCALA
Jalapa
VERA CRUZ
Vera Cruz
Oaxaca
OAXACA
Acapulco
Chilpancingo
GUERRERO
Rio Balsas
TABASCO
Villahermosa
CHIAPAS
Tuxtla Gutiérrez
Tapachula
Campeche
CAMPECHE
Mérida
YUCATAN
Santa Cruz
QUINTANA ROO
Belize
Guatemala
El Salvador
Honduras
Nicaragua
Gulf of Mexico
Gulf of California
BAJA CALIFORNIA NORTE
BAJA CALIFORNIA SUR
La Paz
PACIFIC OCEAN
0
400 kilometres
0
250 miles
N

1 Introduction: Perspectives on the Mexican Crisis

In contrast to the majority of Latin American countries in the post-Depression era, Mexico has shown remarkable success in constructing resilient political institutions. While many other nations have experienced military interventions, sporadic violence and ephemeral authoritarian or democratic governments, Mexico has appeared stable. Throughout much of the region, the late 1970s witnessed the onset of a cycle of democratisation following a cycle of authoritarianism that was ushered in with the Brazilian coup of 1964. Yet despite the apparent renaissance of democracy in several Latin American countries during the 1980s, the economic crisis of the region as a whole has deepened, surpassing even the intensity of the early 1930s.

Mexico has not escaped this regional and global crisis. The depression of the 1980s has been so severe that – in the unlikely event of a strong recovery – it will require several years to return to the average living standard of the late 1970s. The political forms that worked so well in the past are under considerable strain, and many observers are returning to examine this remarkable system. How resilient is it? What are the possibilities for change?

In 1985 Mexico celebrated 175 years of political independence and the seventy-fifth anniversary of the Revolution. That year also marked at least a decade of crisis. While the term 'crisis' is vague and over-used, it is clear that the massacre of several hundred mostly young people near the centre of Mexico City on 2 October 1968 struck a deeply ominous note. The turbulent government of Luís Echeverría that ended in 1976 with extensive land expropriations in Sonora and Sinaloa, the subsequent capital flight and a traumatic currency devaluation after 22 years of stable exchange with the dollar marked the passing of an order. The oil boom and inflation of the José López Portillo government (1976–82) that ended in two devaluations and the bank nationalisation and currency controls of 1982, gave many Mexicans the sensation of a country reeling out of control. And the wrenching stabilisation programmes under President Miguel de la Madrid (1982–88), with continuing inflation, devaluation and austerity has eliminated one of the main legitimating claims of the regime: a record of constant economic growth since the Great Depression.

With the crisis, the so-called Revolutionary Family, that congeries of political alliances, tacit agreements and practices that have given Mexico significant stability and progress, is undergoing stress as basic pacts are being challenged.[1] Foremost among these disputed pacts is that between government and business. Some members of the business–financial community express profound dissatisfaction with the direction of government policy since the early 1970s. Symptoms of discord include the continued haemorrhaging of capital from Mexico, the harshness of the charges exchanged between government and business leaders and the decision by business groups to become more active in civic life, with some businessmen entering the National Action Party (PAN) to contest elections in key northern states. A related area of renegotiation involves the enormously complicated relationship between Mexico and the United States, a relationship strained by differing interpretations of the turmoil in Central America and the problems of illegal migration and drug trafficking. The Mexican Catholic Church also seeks to renegotiate its political status, in this case to regain a legal standing lost in the Constitution of 1917. On the occasions when the government seeks support from its labour, nationalist and anti-clerical bases, it casts its putative antagonists, that is, business, PAN and the Catholic church, in terms of a 'reactionary trilogy' bent on subverting the Revolution. Since 1983 some elements of the government and official party began to add the United States to this rogues' gallery, and the rhetorical mix has evolved subsequently in complicated and changing ways.

Of course, one might argue that such rhetoric has served as a standard legitimating technique for the regime and is the symbiology to be expected as the government struggles to confront its worst crisis since 1929. Certainly these symbols remain potent to many Mexicans. However, it is unarguable that the postwar confidence has been shaken. Many Mexicans, especially among the emerging middle sectors, have been disturbed by what they perceive as arbitrary and extreme decisions by public authorities, as exemplified in the bank nationalisation. Shaken confidence is especially important, because earlier studies on Mexican political culture stressed optimism about the future as a key ingredient of the legitimacy of Mexico's aspirations for democracy.[2] More difficult to discern in the haze of rhetoric is how the government will respond in order to preserve its hegemony, because in the short term, despite the impressive pressures it must endure, the regime has the capacity to survive. Thus, Mexico differs from other countries in the region. Its response to crisis has not been to open toward democracy in the sense of electoral competition. Rather, Mexican leaders have sought survival in the reaffirmation of fundamental principles and pragmatic adjustments of policies and practices.[3]

INSTITUTIONAL, STRUCTURAL AND POLICY PERSPECTIVES

What is the nature of the crisis Mexico presently confronts? On the political front, the regime faces pressures to accommodate itself to a transformed socioeconomic order. The structures and practices that once worked well to maintain control and generate support now encounter resistance. On the economic front, the postwar strategy of import–substituting industrialisation (ISI) encounters barriers to continued growth. After successive episodes of populism and oil-fuelled growth, no viable alternative model has emerged. With respect to demography, the absolute size, high growth rate and urban concentration are of unprecedented dimensions. This, with the previous record of economic growth, lends special urgency to the age-old problems of inequality and unemployment. One might object that Mexico has never enjoyed untroubled tranquility, but previous crises were limited to party oppositions (1952), labour (1958–59), or students (1968). After 1976, a generalised crisis increasingly encompassed the entire system.

Efforts to accommodate the old political order to a changing context lead to a variety of reform initiatives, which – if really implemented – would have the effect of undermining important interests as presently constituted. Political authorities face the tricky issue of what to change, in what sequence and to what degree in order to regenerate growth and confidence, but without alienating critical support. This theme of tensions between preservation and adjustment runs throughout the discussion.

This book analyses three central political institutions and two areas of public policy in Mexico during 1976–86 in order to portray how practices have evolved and to identify types of changes needed to cope with the deepening crisis. Chapter 2 provides historical background and characterises the nature of Mexican statecraft. With regard to institutions the presidency, discussed in Chapter 3, is the keystone of the political order. The presidency in turn manages an extensive government administrative apparatus and the dominant Institutional Revolutionary Party (PRI), considered in Chapters 4 and 5. The three institutions are so closely intertwined that, following common practice, I employ the term PRI–government from time to time to denote the complex of actors and organisations taken as a whole.[4]

Since I believe the renegotiation of the government–business accord to be the foremost domestic issue, I devote Chapter 6 to interest group politics and policies affecting the private sector. I focus on this issue because rapid sustained growth is the *sine qua non* of a governable society, and a new form of mixed economy is evolving. And since political reform provides clues about the regime's survival strategy, the record of electoral politics is considered in Chapter 7.

The book considers politics in two senses: the nature of power in Mexican society and the formal and informal rules that govern its use; and the consequences of choices taken by the Mexican government for its society. For those primarily interested in the logic and functioning of Mexican statecraft taken on its own terms, I try to assemble a rather detailed description of how pivotal institutions operate in Mexico's strong presidential system. The description is useful because elements of this regime changed rapidly after 1970 and the scholarship has not quite caught up. Also, an understanding of the institutions is needed to grasp how the Mexican presidential system achieved stability in the past and what changes are needed to confront the future. I would hope also that students of authoritarianism, democratisation and dependent development will find interesting case material as well.[5]

The principal focus throughout is institutional analysis, the traditional concern in political science with describing and evaluating beliefs and practices according to criteria of their relative 'fit' with constitutional prescriptions. Following Samuel Huntington, I employ the term institution broadly as valued recurring behaviour. Institutions may include concrete organisations such as associations and bureaucracies, but they comprise as well valued predictable ways of doing things. Presidentialism is a set of institutions, as are civilian supremacy, one-party dominance, anti-clericalism, centralisation and statism. With relatively continuous evolution over the past half century, Mexican politics has developed complex institutions.[6]

Interesting in this approach is how organisations and practices create incentives that shape individual and group behaviour. Individual rationality, after all, depends on goals and opportunities in specific settings. The nature of the Mexican presidency, its relations with the bureaucracy and PRI and the multiple connections between government and civil society are examined in search of clues about their capacity for change. My basic premise is that a case marked by a powerful state and a relatively weak society warrants a close examination of government institutions.[7]

Institutions must be examined in their setting. In order to grasp the origins and nature of the present crisis, we need to consider Mexican internal politics in the context of the regional and global political economy. As a dependent country, much of Mexico's politics is conditioned in a variety of ways by external forces. In this respect, I employ a structuralist approach in an eclectic way. It is not a systematic application of one or another school, be it neo-Marxist or dependency; rather, it is the recognition that the Mexican polity is thoroughly penetrated by international economic forces that set the parameters for action.[8]

The third perspective is another oft-tilled field of political science: decision making. Here the subject is the decisions taken by public authorities that in turn have consequences for the whole polity.[9] Concretely, I focus on the Mexican policy process and the critical decisions taken with respect to economic policy and electoral politics during 1976–86. The approach is to characterise the decision setting, describe the course chosen and offer reasons why certain choices were adopted while others were foregone.

If these perspectives are successfully integrated, the institutional analysis, taken separately and applied to selected areas of public policy, will show something about the limits and possibilities of change. The structuralist approach will alert us to the internal/external dynamics and boundaries for political choice. But that perspective should not 'force' the analysis. That is, individuals and organisations enjoy varying degrees of political space in which to operate, and various avenues of choice are open to actors. Used in complementary fashion, these perspectives can help decipher the nature of Mexican statecraft.

A note on method. My data come from the public record and conversations with individuals with one or another degree of knowledge and participation over roughly an eight-year period. This included extended stays in Mexico City in 1979 and 1985, involving a consultation on budgetary practices with the Secretariat of Agriculture and Water Resources (SARH), and working visits to nine states. Some of the interviews were formal, with a semi-structured questionnaire and an effort to record the results; most were informal conversations with Mexican scholars, bureaucrats and politicians. With only a few exceptions, I have resisted the temptation to use quotes, and even so I paraphrase. As much as possible, the analysis stands on the public record.

ARGUMENTS: IDEOLOGICAL CONTRADICTIONS AND SOCIAL CHANGE

In simplest terms, I shall argue that the current political crisis stems from the growing tensions between the ideological justifications of the Mexican regime and its real structures and practices. Part of the tension derives from the contradictions inherent in the justifications themselves, and part from the inability of the regime to sustain the image of progress, which had helped to paper over contradictions in the past. At base, the PRI–government was painstakingly constructed to maximise control from Mexico City to the remotest village, and from the government through virtually all social sectors. Control was necessary for various ends: to impose order after the revolutionary turmoil of 1910–29, to mobilise and modernise an agrarian society and to protect national sovereignty, especially from pressures from the United States. As we survey the varieties of forms and techniques that comprise the PRI-government, one impressive recurring theme is the logic of control.

The Mexican Constitution of 1917 sets out three basic projects: the liberal project, involving themes such as rule of law, effective suffrage, individual rights and anti-clericalism; the social welfare project of protecting the weak and improving living standards, especially for the poor; and the nationalist project of the state as rector of society and defender of national patrimony. These goals constitute the legitimacy that has served to justify political practices, especially as judged by elites. Elite support in turn helped the PRI–government to rely more on inducements than on coercion in the mix that any political system employs in order to reproduce itself and advance projects. Legitimacy reinforces the claim of *right* to rule. It distinguishes a movement of tough-minded revolutionaries, struggling to govern in difficult times, from a band of lucky bureaucrats enjoying a *sexenio* (sexennium) of power. Much of the art of Mexican statecraft involves the constant reformulation of these projects to legitimate public policies and the system that produces them.

The party–government has long experienced tensions between its ideological statements and its behaviour, and these tensions have increased as society experienced modernisation and more individuals, especially of the middle sectors, began to hold government to more exacting standards of effectiveness and democratic practice. The tensions were managed in good part by the cultivation of a political class drawn from various social strata and renewed with regular presidential successions, a class steeped in the arts of negotiation, persuasion and – where necessary – of force. The tensions have become acute, however, with the domestic and global economic crisis since the 1970s. The demographic explosion in the midst of enduring scarcity and the continued pursuit of development policies that have tended to concentrate wealth have left some elites sceptical about the future and many of the poor desperate about the present.

The regime's pragmatic justification for authoritarianism stressed results: stability, material progress, proven leadership. However, the erratic performance of the Echeverría government, followed by the impressive corruption of the López Portillo *sexenio* have jeopardised such claims. The De la Madrid government has been fully occupied with financial survival. Thus, basic pacts are being questioned. Some private sector interests have intensified their demands for a reduced government role in the economy, albeit with continued government protection of business interests; and the question of Mexico's posture toward the regional and global economy has returned to the top of the policy agenda.

What kinds of changes are indicated by present circumstances? With respect to institutions, reforms that reduce corruption and promote decentralisation, greater popular participation and increased efficiency in both government and private enterprise would contribute toward restoring a degree of confidence in the political class. With regard to policies, changes that reduce inequalities of access to income, education, housing, health care and the like, would reduce scepticism about the revolutionary projects. These are not, I should stress, the pious hopes of a foreign academic; rather they are the stated goals of Mexican leaders since at least the Revolution.

With respect to the logic and sequence of change, economic and political policies are closely interconnected, and choices about one set of policies imply directions for the other. Given the logic of

Mexican institutions political choices take priority. The stark reality is that such external variables as debt, world oil prices and business cycles strongly influence Mexican macroeconomic policy. Another reality is that incumbent elites will seek to survive in as close to present form as possible by making minimum necessary adjustments.

At least three directions for change might be envisaged. First, a response that preserves the system's political base fairly intact in the short term is to revive somehow the nationalist development project, and to make the necessary adjustments to improve the performance of the existing system. This implies reducing corruption to something on the order of pre-Echeverría levels, when it promoted stability, reducing the worst abuses of police brutality and corruption, fielding better candidates and making incremental adjustments toward decentralisation and administrative reform. This direction would not call for a qualitative change of the PRI-government. It would remain centralised, hierarchical and the dominant social institution. Reasserting the nationalist development project might, if implemented in certain ways, help restore the image of progress toward the nationalist and welfare goals of the Revolution. However, a more likely and less benign variant of the nationalist route is the continued concentration of development efforts on the more privileged elements of Mexican society, that is, agri-business, protected industry, the heterogeneous middle sectors and urban areas generally.

A second option is to do basically nothing: the government can muddle along and hope for uncommon luck. Circumstances might permit this administration to scrape by, leaving the difficult choices to the successor, which takes office on 1 December 1988.

A third route is economic opening. This implies renegotiating a pact with the private sector in its national and international forms and pursuing a policy of attracting foreign investment and encouraging exports. This has been the stated goal since the mid-1970s, and Mexico's accession in August 1986 to the General Agreement on Tariffs and Trade (GATT) moves in this direction.

The political problem of opening involves how to shift economic policy in a way that least damages the PRI-government's power bases. Trade liberalisation would seem to injure the industries and associated unions that grew up during 40 years of ISI and which tend to see themselves unable to compete effectively with larger-scale firms, either domestic or international. If patterns elsewhere are a guide, the negative effects of opening arrive to specific groups such as labour and small business before the benefits appear to the broader consuming public in the form of lower-priced, better quality products.[10] Perhaps that is why such policies elsewhere have been hammered into place by armies and technocrats rather than by political parties. The policy of opening thus would make the government vulnerable to charges of abandoning the national and welfare projects of the Revolution, especially in the eyes of the nationalist intelligentsia. Also, economic opening implies decentralising in a geographical sense and strengthening certain business elites, both of which trends would challenge government power. The preferred option would appear to be a gradual opening that provides the PRI-government the time and political space to accommodate itself by rearranging its constituent party and bureaucratic bases and recasting its ideological formulae.

The analysis developed in the following chapters points to the conclusion that the nationalist development project is the least likely option and that the path toward opening will be pursued with one or another degree of skill. Whether the opening is achieved with least cost to various groups depends upon the quality of statecraft.

2 The Nature of Mexican Statecraft

In analysing Mexican politics each student makes a series of choices, consciously or not, about ongoing debates. Those choices in turn may alert the reader to biases. The following observations are the more important assumptions that guide the analysis of institutions and policies in succeeding chapters. Statecraft in Mexico as elsewhere is the art of making choices within a context shaped by historical experience and the international setting. The present task is to distinguish the general from the distinctive as we try to comprehend the issues confronting Mexico's political leaders.

With respect to the capacity of the present government to effect significant change, one must make a judgement about the 'weight' of history. Here we need to remind ourselves about the 700 or so years of advanced indigenous civilisation that evolved before the Spanish conquest of the sixteenth century, and the roughly three centuries of imperial rule that preceded the wars of independence during 1810–21. As in many cases complex, advanced indigenous societies antedated and shaped the emergence of the modern nation–state. Despite the importance of the industrialisation of the last quarter of the nineteenth century and the revolutionary turmoil of the early twentieth, the salient fact is the comparative recency, some two generations of so, of the transition from an agrarian to an urbanised service society. This is not to resurrect some simplistic notion of the 'oriental' or Hispanic ethos of contemporary Mexican society, a form of reductionism that often tends to obstruct rather than facilitate clear thinking. But it is to suggest that on the palimpsest of Mexican historical experience there lies a base of indigenous and Iberian ways of doing things over which liberal, urban and industrial manners have been written. The result is a complex and dynamic mix of attitudes and behaviour in a society in which inequalities have accumulated over centuries.[1]

Mexico, like virtually all peripheral countries, is shaped by delayed dependent development. In contrast to England and the Netherlands, where the industrial, commercial and technological revolutions originated more than two centuries ago, most of the process of development in the world has been reactive, that is, to either imitate the early developers or to resist them. The concept of delayed dependent development stresses that industrialisation and commercialisation occur in later historical periods and are shaped in significant ways by the early developers.[2] Concretely, substantial amounts of technology and capital are imported by late developers, and foreign markets strongly influence the pace and direction of economic change internally. In typical patterns of delayed development the state plays a more active role in shaping economic activity, sometimes by assuming entrepreneurial functions, as in banking or such strategic industries as electricity and steel, or by creating and protecting a domestic entrepreneurial class.

Although industrialisation proceeds in irregular cycles virtually everywhere, in the peripheral countries the process is especially uneven. This is because modernising elites introduce industrial and commercial processes in a hurry-up fashion in countries marked by rudimentary market and production arrangements. An implication of the uneven spread of development is that in some areas of a country a form of modern exchange economy takes root, whereas other regions may be marked by more primitive market relations, with attendant social forms, including clan rule, war lords and forms of tribute and varieties of what we typically call 'traditional' society.

Delayed dependent development in Mexico has produced a country with pronounced regional differences. In the more capitalistic, industrialised and commercialised north, seen especially in the states of Baja California Norte, Sonora, Chihuahua and Nuevo León, government played an important role in protecting and fomenting development. Still, in this region one finds the beginnings of an entrepreneurial stratum and something of a more democratic ethos. In the centre of this highly centralised country, government more completely dominates economic and social life. In the southern states of Oaxaca and Chiapas, social life more nearly approximates the traditional societies of the Central American countries.

Given the complexity of the Mexican political economy, one confronts the problem of how to depict the system for purposes of guiding description and grounding assumptions. The image of Mexico in transition to Western pluralist democracy proved misleading and was rather quickly superseded by an image of authoritarianism.[3] The concept of authoritarianism, while not completely adequate to the Mexican reality, was enriched theoretically by Juan Linz and applied suggestively to analyse policy-making in Mexico by Susan Kaufman Purcell and others.[4] Linz's core idea, discussed more fully in Chapter

6, is that authoritarianism should not be viewed as an imperfect mutant of liberal democracy or totalitarianism but rather as a distinctive regime type. This analytic approach has taken root in Mexican political science, especially after 1968.[5] Probably the more influential image of authoritarianism among Mexican scholars, however, is that of 'bonapartism', adapted from Marx's attempt in 1851–52 to characterise the coup d'etat of Louis Bonaparte.[6]

My working conception of the Mexican political system is one of a centralised, statist, inclusive system with corporatist features, in which the presidency confronts a number of contending forces, which it can manipulate to varying degrees. The system belongs to the family of populist movements in Latin America spawned by the Depression. As such, it is based on a multi-class coalition of groups, emphasises a nationalist and anti-imperialist ideology and endorses a reformist policy agenda. It is authoritarian in the sense that opposition elites are not allowed to contend for real power, and their resources – whether violence or votes – are carefully controlled. Within the broad genus, the species 'inclusionary authoritarian regime' has been suggested to denote the political spaces created by government for labour and peasant groups, so long as these adhere to the rules laid down by the PRI–government.[7] But the regime also proclaims democratic liberalism, which intensifies internal contradictions and poses a constant problem of regime legitimation. With respect to the regional and global setting, Mexico has been strongly influenced by external forces. This has been especially the case since the arrival of the multi-national firms in the 1960s, and subsequently even more so with the petrolisation of the economy and assumption of unsustainable debts in the 1970s and the early 1980s.

Useful though models may be to clarify thinking, one must guard against tautology. That is, one should not recast reality in terms of the model but must be alert to the distinctiveness and dynamism of the system. This is especially so when the job at hand is to analyse change in institutions and policies. As William Glade reminds us 'one of the hallmarks of the Mexican system – perhaps ever since the aboriginals took on Spanish ways and the Spanish missionaries provided a new saint for each of the ancient deities – has been its capacity for improvisation and pragmatic adaptation, notwithstanding the thematic continuity that runs through the liturgical language of revolutionary political discourse'.[8]

For the present perspective, the question is whether the Mexican system has retained its capacity for pragmatic adaptation, whether the overall development pattern followed since the late 1940s will permit reforms sufficient to spark a renewed cycle of growth. To approach this broader question we need to review briefly some aspects of socio-political change since the Revolution to grasp how the very modernisation that the regime has fostered has in turn complicated its political institutions and practices. Like most, this sketch views the Revolution of 1910–29 as the significant watershed and then chronicles subsequent events in six-year chapters.

FROM REVOLUTION TO NEO-POPULISM, 1910–1976

In basic respects Mexico experienced a classic 'Western' revolution, with preconditions of government resistance to increasing demands for participation, in this case from a growing generation of middle sector liberals and a traditional peasantry displaced by the commercialisation of agriculture. It also follows something of a classic progression, with the collapse of the old order in 1911, the rule of the moderate Francisco I. Madero 1911–13, an attempt to restore the old regime by General Victoriano Huerta in 1914, and a reign of terror in the civil war among contending factions during 1914–1919, before a coalition could be constructed to co-opt or destroy opposition forces.[9]

Impressive in its ferocity, the destructive phase of the Revolution left more than a million killed (or nearly 10 per cent of the population) and devastated whole regions of the countryside. In the sense of eliminating previous power contenders, the Revolution weakened actors that still hold considerable power in other Latin American countries, or that were not affected until much later: Catholic Church, standing army, landed class. It also weakened other groups that had grown powerful during the Porfiriato, such as commercial and banking elites and foreign investors.[10] The Revolution cleared the way as well for new groups. Among these were the Northerners, principally from Sonora and Coahuila, including the first Revolutionary presidents: Venustiano Carranza (1917–20), Alvaro Obregón (1920–24) and Plutarco Elías Calles (1924–28). New forces appeared with such nascent labour unions as the Casa del Obrero Mundial, peasant leagues, and new business–commercial groups, often from the ranks of the victorious soldier–entrepreneurs.

In completing the classic revolutionary cycle, new institutions were created. The ideological and legal basis of the new order was established in the Constitution of 1917, which added nationalist and social welfare dimensions to the liberal foundations of the 1857 constitution. Power quickly was concentrated in the office of the president, and the embryonic system returned to a centralised and personalist style. Over time presidential power became more institutionalised in the sense of self-imposed limits and predictability. Along with the presidency, the other cornerstone of the new political order was laid with the formation of an official party by Calles as *jefe máximo* in 1929. Established to integrate the numerous bands, parties, and factions into a national movement, the new party represented a remarkable act of political skill and statecraft. The assassination of President-Elect Obregón provided the opportunity for Calles to discipline the many ambitious politicians. The National Revolutionary Party (PNR) became the first step toward a polity based more on institutions than personalities. The *callista* tradition of discipline and institutions remains as a minor current in Mexican politics.[11]

The presidency of Lázaro Cárdenas (1934–40) marks a major step in forging the new order. A master of statecraft, Cárdenas was able to play off the international crisis of the Depression and approaching war with internal dynamics in order to transform the official party and launch Mexico along a more populist, reformist path. Created in 1938 as the successor to the PNR, the Party of the Mexican Revolution (PRM) was structured corporatively with its bases in mass organisations of peasants, labour unions, military forces and a residual popular sector. Cárdenas was able to use the dynamic of populist reforms such as land distribution, state protection for labour and nationalisation of petroleum to provide the foundation for a stronger and more active central government, one firmly committed to national sovereignty and social welfare. More than the *callista* tradition, *cardenismo* remains a strong current in contemporary Mexican politics, signifying a pronounced nationalist–welfare orientation.[12]

While Calles and Cárdenas are significant in initiating political institutions and in creating precedents for policy, the impact of World War II and the postwar industrialisation propelled the massive transformation of Mexican society from a rural and agricultural to an urban and service–industrial base. Manuel Avila Camacho's presidency (1940–46) might be considered transitional in the sense of shifting from the populist and socialist rhetoric of Cárdenas to a more pragmatic language, though still within the liturgy of the Revolution. As the last of the revolutionary generals, though not of first rank, he was able to smooth the way toward civilian rule; and as a practicing

Catholic, he could resolve the 25-year conflict with the Church, which had cost the nation some 200 000 lives. The official party was brought under closer presidential control, with the sectors headed up by the president's loyalists and the party newspaper, *El Nacional*, passing to the Interior Secretariat. The labour sector was weakened and independent farmers were allowed to join the peasant sector, while the popular sector was strengthened with the creation of the National Confederation of Popular Organisations (CNOP) in 1942. The rhetoric of wartime unity against fascism replaced that of class struggle.[13] Like Cárdenas, Avila Camacho retired into the background after 1946, thus helping create the essential role of the 'ex-president' and reinforcing the sexennial rhythm.

Miguel Alemán's presidency (1946–52) launched Mexico full force on the path of industrialisation. Alemán also oversaw the transition to a new generation of better educated professionals, lawyers for the most part, and the continued easing out of the old-style revolutionary figures. He created power bases among the newer industrial elites and agricultural exporters. His emphasis on industrialisation centred in Mexico City reinforced the process of hyper-centralisation in the Central Valley. He also introduced important legal–institutional changes. In the agrarian field, for example, farmers affected by land expropriation could turn to the *amparo* as a legal protection.[14] This effectively halted the expropriation of farmland under production and created a degree of stability that in turn promoted investor confidence. The transition to a new generation of labour leaders was continued, with the emergence of Fidel Velázquez of the CTM as the *primus inter pares*. Unions were brought under control by the government's combined use of co-option, anti-communist rhetoric and violence. Emergency wartime measures, the anti-sedition law and the Federal Security Directorate of the Interior Secretariat, were employed to control political opposition. Significantly, the official party was transformed at the outset of the Alemán *sexenio* as the PRI and utilised as an instrument of control and of ideological justification for the new orientation.

If Cárdenas bequeathed the nationalist revolutionary tradition in Mexican politics, Alemán might be considered the moderniser within the *callista* style of discipline. To many *cardenistas* the Alemán presidency is seen as the betrayal of the Revolution; yet to *alemanistas* and others, the 1946–52 *sexenio* was historically logical and necessary in order to move Mexico from centuries of backwardness into the modern world. They might even argue that Alemán was building on *cardenista* foundations in trying to foment a national bourgeoisie, but that the postwar order called for a different approach and ideological line. The Alemán family preserves a power base in business, especially in the Televisa communications conglomerate.

In terms of political institutions and practice, the presidencies of Adolfo Ruiz Cortines (1952–58) and Adolfo López Mateos (1958–64) reinforced the centralisation and bureaucratisation begun by Cárdenas and continued the rhythm of consolidation and innovation in policy-making. Ruiz Cortines is undergoing something of an historical re-evaluation as one who understood well the forces at play and, putting the system above the president's short-term perspective, worked to reduce the excesses of corruption bequeathed by the Alemán *sexenio*. He showed remarkably astute judgement about balancing central with local interests and in promoting competent young talent. López Mateos, the last president to both begin and end his term with broad popularity, demonstrated prudent statecraft even while confronting difficult challenges at the outset of his term. Distance puts something of a golden cast on the 1952–64 period, which many politicians recall simplistically as a lesson that the system works well in the hands of competent leaders. But basic policies introduced during that time created some of the underlying conditions that led to increasing tensions in the latter 1960s.

Mexico is distinctive in the Latin American region in the timing of sequences of development. Political institutions and a widely supported state ideology were established before the pressures of the latter stages of ISI were felt. In the cases of Argentina and Brazil, in contrast, volatile personalist or party arrangements in conflictive ideological settings could not manage the demands from organised labour and other dissident groups in the latter 1950s and 1960s, prompting military intervention and authoritarian rule. The Mexican experience, labelled 'stabilising development', stressed orthodox fiscal arrangements and promotion of the private sector.[15]

In 1954 the Mexican government devalued its currency from Ps 8.65 to Ps 12.50 with respect to the US dollar, and pledged to guarantee convertibility at that rate over the long term. The decision represented a change from Alemán's policy of growth with inflation, which in turn reflected the widespread view that bottlenecks and imbalances inevitably lead to inflation as a by-product of economic growth. In contrast, it was thought that a stable currency would attract savings through the banking system and promote domestic and foreign investment by removing concern about devaluation and non-convertibility.

The decision to guarantee stable exchange with the dollar meant that Mexican policy-makers had to observe as a basic parameter the rate of inflation in the United States, its principal trading partner and the issuer of the dominant world currency. Should Mexican inflation exceed that of the United States by significant margins and over sufficient time, pressures would emerge in the balances of trade and payments. That is, a slight over-valuation of the peso would – when joined with a system of import licences – subsidise capital and intermediate goods imports and promote industrialisation. At some point, however, over-valuation would penalise Mexican exports and tourism. And if the over-valuation became sustained and chronic, individuals might become sceptical about the government's ability to sustain exchange stability and convert from liquid to fixed assets or to dollars either to protect themselves against devaluation or to speculate for profits. Given other negative circumstances, such a context might create a self-fulfilling prophecy, in which doubt leads to speculation, which in turn lights the fuse for devaluation. This unhappy cycle appeared in the mid-1970s and continued to bedevil Mexico's leaders thereafter.

Committed to rapid growth, but also to exchange stability and therefore to low inflation, the Mexican government in the mid-1950s had to devise a mix of policies that would promote private sector investment along certain lines, complemented with public sector investment that could be financed primarily through domestic savings. In the virtual absence of capital markets, the banking system, both public and private, became the main promoter of the emerging arrangement. Banks could attract savings by paying positive interest in a stable currency and could promote investment along government-preferred lines by offering varied interest rates to borrowers. Government could borrow to finance investment through the *encaje legal*, the legal reserve requirement set by the Bank of Mexico. Such borrowing in turn lessened pressure on taxation as a source of revenue and further encouraged investment. Government development banks could raise funds both domestically and in international capital markets to finance large-scale projects either public or private. Many other instruments were added and blended in stabilising development, which was pursued from the mid-1950s to 1971. But the keys to the system were confidence, growth and profit.[16]

Individual savers would trust the banks as long as their savings paid real gains with complete security; this in turn rested on a stable currency, which derived from non-inflationary government policies. Such policies were implemented by individuals seen as prudent, operating in a system that was seen as predictable. Out of these basic conditions emerged a set of pacts and practices. The Treasury Secretariat concentrated power and ruled on development policy. Investments were undertaken with an eye to their direct productive value or profitability, in order to raise money in international capital markets. Labour unions consented to biennial wage adjustments that remained roughly in line with growth and productivity increases, though with enough flexibility to account for changing political conditions. The PRI and Interior Secretariat, backed when necessary by the army, were charged with managing conflict. And the president oversaw and harmonised the whole arrangement, which produced the 'Mexican miracle' of low inflation and real growth in excess of 6 per cent annually during 1955–71.

This development strategy came under pressure from accumulating tensions due both to changing internal as well as international conditions. Within Mexico, the policy promoted industrialisation, rapid urbanisation and the formation of middle sectors. Export agriculture was promoted, but the traditional rain-fed sector, which employs the great majority of the rural poor, was relatively neglected. Taken together, these trends meant little progress was being made towards reducing the grotesque maldistribution of wealth and income. Improvements in health and nutrition set off a population explosion that reached its peak annual growth rate of 3.5 per cent in the early 1970s. A generational change, urbanisation and the growth of a large university population reinforced expectations for progress on the Revolutionary projects.

Two assumptions of stabilising development proved increasingly troublesome. First, the strategy was based on internal savings, investment and taxation. As these proved inadequate to sustain the necessary pace of both directly productive and social overhead investment, the Mexican government turned increasingly to external borrowing, though on a scale vastly inferior to that of the mid-1970s and early 1980s. This was sustainable given Mexico's solid international credit rating, but it signalled a structural imbalance. The second problem was more serious. Stabilising development granted generous protection and high profits to nurture a national entrepreneurial class capable to generating sustained development. The goal was to create a risk-taking, visionary, dynamic business elite that would build the motor of growth and assume its responsibility to earn reasonable profits on efficient operations and to begin to pay taxes. The emerging reality was quite different. Though with some exceptions, Mexican producers, as well as the multinational firms that arrived increasingly in the 1960s, rapidly came to see protection, guaranteed markets, high subsidies, profits and low taxes as their due. With the discipline of international competition absent, insufficient attention was paid to efficiency, quality and service. When government moved in the late 1960s and early 1970s to introduce tax reforms to shore up its finances and reduce the need for international borrowing, business resisted tenaciously. The business argument that increased taxes reduced investment incentives was too often a device to preserve high profits.[17]

During this same period international conditions were rapidly changing. The relative calm of the mid-1950s and early 1960s gave way to the tumult of the latter 1960s. The United States, caught up in an unpopular war and domestic civil strife, saw a wave of inflation unleashed in its 1967 federal budget deficit and its President virtually forced from office in 1968. Left movements gained strength in various parts of Latin America. Youth revolts broke out in the United States and Western Europe.

The combination of internal stresses and international changes help explain what has become termed 'the events of 1968' in Mexico, a collective trauma which marks the watershed from the old order to the onset of crisis. The personality of President Gustavo Díaz Ordaz is significant as well.

In simplest terms, a series of secondary school student protests in July 1968 was exacerbated by police repression and spread quickly to the National Autonomous University of Mexico (UNAM), the National Politechnic Institute (IPN) and to provincial universities. The growing student movement served as a catalyst to attract wider anti-government protest, mainly from other middle sector groups, such as doctors and teachers. Student demands escalated to include the firing of the Mexico City police chief, the freeing of political prisoners and the disbanding of the riot police, all unacceptable to government authorities. As the student-led protest continued, the additional pressure of the Olympic Games, scheduled to begin on 12 October, complicated matters. President Díaz Ordaz, by nature a stern defender of the institutional order, refused to accede to student demands, and the demonstrations intensified. On 2 October, some five to ten thousand mostly young people converged on Tlatelolco Square in Mexico City to continue the demonstrations. In developments still not well understood, firing broke out, and the subsequent police and army fusillade killed several hundred persons.[18]

Tlatelolco produced a national convulsion, whose significance can be gauged in the enduring preoccupation with the event. Clearly, much more was involved than student protest. The Mexican government tended to blame external meddling, either by US or Soviet-bloc intelligence agencies. The left saw the massacre as proof that the system could not tolerate dissent, and some leftists moved into anti-system, sometimes violent, opposition. The right tended to view it as a student protest like many others that had been used by a variety of interests for different purposes, such as influencing the presidential succession. To the present, scholarly papers and newspaper commentaries continue to seek the meanings of Tlatelelco.

Two implications, however stand out: first, the massacre tipped the scale of elite opinion away from optimism or agnosticism about the liberal and egalitarian projects of the Revolution and reinforced doubt or cynicism; second, the event bolstered the position of Interior Secretary Echeverría, who carried out President Díaz Ordaz' orders with complete and unquestioning loyalty.[19] The first began the trend to undermine regime legitimacy, and the second led to the succession of a president who was to shift the logic and functioning of Mexican politics onto a quite different course.

This introductory note on the Echeverría presidency must perforce be brief and dry. But it should be stressed that Echeverría is viewed by many in the Mexican political class with great emotion, either as a maniacal aberration in the Mexican presidency, who put the system on a track of destruction, or as one who was well intentioned but victimised by mistakes and bad luck. We should try to recall the context of 1968–71 in Mexico. Guerrilla bands were operating in several cities and rural areas; university conflicts had broken out in at least seven cities; and the economy foundered in recession. As a shorthand characterisation, we might label the Echeverría presidency an attempt to open the system by reviving a 1930s-style populism, but an effort set in a very different context, and without Cárdenas' skill or luck.

With respect to policies and institutions, Echeverría increased emphasis on the central government as the promoter of growth, largely by relying on the bureaucracy and on deficit financing. He adopted this course in 1971 because he accepted advisors' arguments that stabilising development was basically flawed, but also due in good part to the drop in growth rate experienced in that year.[20] The overall logic of his statecraft retained some aspects of stabilising development but added new features to compensate for structural deficiencies, especially income maldistribution and the performance of the business sector. Important calculations such as tax reform failed to materialise, and over the *sexenio* the President came to rely more on labour and left support, reinforcing the alienation of business interests. Furthermore, Echeverría's personal style – harsh rhetoric, constant swirl of public hearings, meddling in technical matters, and reviving corruption – offended many in the established political class.[21]

Mexican fiscal policy had for several years subsidised a variety of interests to promote industrialisation. Among these were industrialists, who – through many mechanisms – enjoyed the benefits of protection and promotion but without paying much in return.[22] Urban groups generally had been subsidised through light taxation and public investments in urban infrastructure, such as health care, education and transportation. Echeverría continued these basic policies, adding substantial new benefits to higher education in the form of new facilities and financial support. The President also rapidly expanded subsidies to organised labour, as well as to rural and marginalised groups. Such programmes as housing, expansion of social security, nutrition and rural development benefited diverse groups in the lower income strata. When efforts failed in 1972 to reform taxation to pay for these initiatives, the government turned increasingly towards deficit financing, including foreign borrowing.

A rapid increase in the size of the central government bureaucracy accompanied the new policy direction.[23] Growth responded to several imperatives. The new agencies were to compensate in part for weak private sector performance in generating new investment and employment creation, as well as to attend to the needs of the poorer strata. Also, the expanded bureaucracy would increase the weight of the state in Echeverría's revival of populism. Recruitment of new employees gave the President the opportunity to co-opt many of the university dissidents alienated by the events of 1968. This influx of employees also created a personal base for Echeverría, separate from – and in many cases antagonistic to – the traditional political class. This in turn exacerbated tensions between *técnicos* and the old-style *políticos*, a theme considered in Chapter 3.

Mexican federal bureaucracy had largely served political maintenance roles, such as patronage, services to selected groups and control over specific populations. The new orientation required in addition greater efficiency. But without a professional civil service, mechanisms of effective policy coordination or capable field services, the expanded government bureaucracy proved quite inefficient.

Although Echeverría started his presidency on positive terms with the private sector, setting up the National Tripartite Commission in 1971 as a consultative mechanism, his fiscal and commercial policies and growing alliance with organised labour and Third World projects created tensions. The assassination of industrial magnate Eugenio Garza Sada in Monterrey in September 1973 marked a downturn in government dealings with business. In response to Echeverría's increasingly harsh rhetoric, business leaders replied with charges of government corruption, inefficiency, and authoritarianism. The *sexenio* ended with large-scale land expropriations as Echeverría responded to private sector threats of disinvestment. Rumours of a *golpe de estado*, either self-inflicted by Echeverría or by the right, created great unease and the initial challenge for López Portillo.

THE NATURE OF MEXICAN STATECRAFT

Statecraft everywhere is the art of managing conflict, while moving a polity toward goals prescribed by ideology. In this sense, governance in Mexico is a variation on general themes. As tensions increased after 1968 Mexican leaders turned to conventional tools. Especially important are managing symbols, retaining control over groups and – when necessary – neutralising dissent. Put more simply, the struggle intensified for the money and confidence of the wealthy, the hearts and voices of the middle strata and the leadership of the organised lower classes. Over time, government may have lost the confidence of the monied groups and is hard-pressed to retain that of the middle strata; but it has kept surprisingly firm control over the organised poor.

Much of the struggle for hegemony in the sense of daily politics takes place at the level of controlling the public debate. This may involve only limited elite circles, but couching the issues and defining legitimacy mean the difference between less or more coercion. Government may employ direct socialisation, such as patriotic symbols and school texts, or indirect means, such as mass media. Managing the media involves less of the sort of heavy-handed control that one associates with authoritarian practice than it does the steady application of legitimating techniques. Government must constantly reiterate the symbols of the Revolution and the Constitution of 1917 as the goals towards which it strives.[24]

Echeverría introduced a more openly critical appraisal of the regime's record and invited scholarly and popular criticism as part of democratic opening. Thus the style of legitimation changed. Prior to 1970 there was greater consensus on development strategy, and simpler, more docile communications media served as a reliable instrument to help government legitimate its projects. After 1970, dissent over goals and practices increased, a larger and more critical middle-strata audience proved more resistant to official messages and more openly critical newspapers and magazines appeared. The great expectations created and dashed by López Portillo bequeathed to the De la Madrid government a still more difficult situation of critical press and sceptical, now more cynical public.

After 1970 the government could still tout its development accomplishments, labelled 'triumphalism' (*triunfalismo*) by critics, while maintaining apparent candour about obvious shortfalls yet to be overcome. Similarly, political democracy continued as a legitimating goal, and government could speak in terms of progress toward 'perfecting democracy', as the formula is frequently put. Nationalism, and especially the threat of US meddling, remained a reliable symbol, as is that of creating and maintaining stability. To bolster the themes, government uses a gallery of heroes and villains. Among the former are the Liberal and Revolutionary forefathers, especially Juárez, Madero, Carranza, Obregón and Cárdenas; the latter include the French-imposed Emperor Maximillian, US Ambassador to Mexico (1910–15) Henry Lane Wilson, and the usurper, General Victoriano Huerta.

In addition to legitimating the regime, the government works to vilify (*desprestigiar*) opponents. It does this by casting them as anti-revolutionary or anti-national and manipulated by foreign interests. After the failure of the growth project under López Portillo, the Mexican government has turned increasingly for support to nationalism and stability, and in a more negativistic tone. This is understandable when one considers that López Portillo's bold undertakings in economic and foreign policy ended in a mammoth, unsustainable debt, renewed International Monetary Fund (IMF) supervision of development policies, and more difficult relations with the United States.

At present, government influence over the print and electronic media is extensive but far from complete. Again, this is neither fine tuned nor heavy handed, although the government's pressure against the conservative weekly, *Impacto*, in June 1986 showed iron under the velvet. In fact, the Mexican government has generously subsidised and promoted the media, as if they were another sector of industry to be developed.[25] In the broadly accepted rules of the game the media assist in reinforcing the legitimating symbols and in criticising opponents. Articles about specific agencies, persons or events can be arranged through bought columns or through *gacetilla*, which are easily identifiable public relations pieces printed as news stories. Underpaid journalists are prepared to cooperate with politicians and government agencies.[26] By and large, the provincial press is even more accommodating than that of Mexico City.

Elite discussion is also shaped by relatively independent periodicals and writers. Important among these are the capital city dailies *Unomásuno* and *La Jornada*, and the weekly magazines, *Proceso* and *Siempre*. Columnists such as León García Soler in *Excélsior* and Francisco Cárdenas Cruz in *El Universal* follow independent courses. Some provincial papers, such as *El Norte* (Monterrey) and *Zeta* (Tijuana), can be quite free-wheeling as well. Government gains access to these publications to some extent through orthodox means such as subsidies and *gacetilla*, but the more prevalent way is by getting pro-government writers into the print debate. Cultural magazines such as *Nexos* and *Vuelta*, and the scores of scholarly periodicals and publications, operate with a criterion of rigour and are open to critics and supporters of government alike. Opposition publications, for example PAN's *La Nación*, operate without censorship.

Print media reach relatively few readers. *Excélsior*, the leading daily, averages runs of about 120 000 (in a nation of some 81 million), and some wags refer to *La Jornada* (about 20 000 copies per day) as 'that letter among friends'.

Because they reach both elite and mass audiences, radio and television are more important, but at the same time less problematic to government. The Televisa conglomerate monopolises the private television networks, and its management is pro-government. The programming, aimed at the middle strata for the most part, is uncontroversial and generally pro-United States. Radio programming stresses music, cultural programmes and bland news reports with relatively little political commentary. Controls such as tax subsidies and licences are available to government. Though seldom invoked, their presence reminds all parties of potential sanctions. Also, government itself is more active in the electronic media, with three television networks of its own and considerable involvement in radio. Government and electronic media cooperate to reinforce regime legitimacy, bolstering in the process the pro-business and pro-US groups. Only quite recently, however, has government been able to compete with the private media in attracting viewers and listeners. Bearing careful watch, foreign programming via cable or satellite transmission has opened new sources of news and commentary to elite audiences and acts as a sort of conscience to the national media.

Even though support from the middle and upper strata began to erode somewhat after 1970, the government has enjoyed impressive success in maintaining political control over organisations. Individual dissent is freely tolerated, although comment on the President and his family and the military is still a sensitive area. But when organised opposition appears, the PRI–government must act quickly to identify and control it. Thus the requisites are preserving discipline in the party–government and monitoring oppositions.

It is worth recalling that the present system emerged from civil war and military organisations. Loyalty was enforced at gunpoint. Subsequently, discipline in the party and government has been maintained in good part by the constant circulation of people through posts in the party and federal bureaucracies and to electoral offices. Both the actual enjoyment of the impressive perquisites of office as well as the expectations of mobility serve to reward conformity.[27]

Those who remain loyal to the system, even after severe career setbacks, may be 'rescued' and rehabilitated. For example, Alfonso Martínez Domínguez, fired from his job as *Regente* (mayor) of the Federal District in 1971, was recalled in 1979 to become governor of Nuevo León as a piece of López Portillo's strategy to consolidate power. Hope, however remote, of rescue, plus the costs of dissent, operate to reinforce discipline. Rare is the prominent *priísta* who defects to the opposition.[28]

This requisite of loyalty and discipline also explains to some extent why the PRI–government feels compelled to control elections. Ideology is not a binding force. If the system is unable to monopolise rewards its constituent groups might grow restive. Capable young politicians might be tempted to defect to opposition parties. Among the scenarios for trouble in Mexican politics, the most serious posits a breakdown of discipline in the party–government, a point considered in the conclusions.

The importance of controlling organisations also explains part of the centralised bias of the system. Party and government officials prefer to leave control to leaders of the groups themselves, but group leaders need resources, government support and a benign public opinion. These intermediaries are expected to apply incentives flexibly and intelligently, with official sanctions brought to bear only when necessary. It is little wonder that the oppositions' main demand is the real democratisation of organisations, especially labour unions; and it is less wonder that the government cannot loosen its grip.

Oppositions do emerge, however, and government typically applies a political calculus in response. Where negotiation is possible, government can concede something of value to the opposition group's leadership in exchange for that group's alliance with the official party. This sort of co-optation gives the dissidents less than they sought, but grants some limited access and reward. A usual step at some point in co-optation is the government's splitting the opposition group's leadership, then negotiating with one faction while delegitimating the other.[29] If co-optation appears too costly, another response is to attack an opposition group and use the attack as a means of strengthening the PRI–government. Such frequently is the case with business opposition and the Catholic Church.

If co-optation seems unlikely and if a government attack is insufficient, the official response may be to destroy the opposition leadership politically, or – less frequently – physically. Government has at its disposal an inventory of legal or quasi-legal resources, from tax audits and criminal investigations to selective application of labour legislation.[30] Usually the hint of such sanctions suffices to neutralise an opponent. With executive control over the press and courts and with no effective counterweights in the system, the target of such pressure simply has no option but to desist.

Government has enough resources at its disposal to manage opposition leaders without resorting to negative sanctions or violence, which are costly in terms of legitimacy. It may be necessary occasionally to employ violence against opposition groups as a whole, either to send a message about rules of the game or to respond to threats. Nevertheless, Mexican politicians operate in an environment of sufficient danger and disorder that the 'low blow' (*golpe bajo*) cannot be discarded.[31]

Beyond this there exists as well a whole netherworld of politics in which violence is the standard currency. This is especially the case outside Mexico City, and a certain notoriety attaches to Veracruz,

Oaxaca, Guerrero and Sinaloa. It is seldom clear to what extent the federal government is applying the violence, or whether it might be semi-official violence such as that which leaders might employ to maintain control over their followings. Also, the multi-billion dollar illicit drug industry has increasingly penetrated normal politics, from local and state government to the national security police and the army. Drugs and violence are inseparable.[32]

I would reiterate that there is nothing unique or particularly exotic about Mexican statecraft. Governments everywhere engage in a daily struggle to legitimate their projects and to manage oppositions. They operate under generally understood, though not universally accepted, rules of the game, and draw upon a fairly standard inventory of resources of persuasion and coercion. Poverty, population pressures, and dependency further complicate the setting, but these are familiar problems throughout much of the world. What is distinctive about Mexico is its resilient authoritarian system, with a stronger government and more coherent and complex structures of centralised control that channel and absorb pressures, but that also act to postpone change. Also distinctive is the decline of confidence in what was once an impressively capable political class. Unique to Mexico is a 2000-mile border with world's pre-eminent superpower. The US economy and society operate spontaneously to affect Mexican politics, and the US government actively pursues its own agenda to influence its southern neighbor.

WHAT KINDS OF INSTITUTIONAL CHANGE?

Some broad options for change have been suggested in the general notions of muddling through, economic opening, or revival of the nationalist project. What might changes look like at the level of specific institutions and practices? My analysis of the presidency, bureaucracy, and PRI considers incentives as might be perceived by the actors themselves. What incentives might the President perceive to cede real power? Are there precedents for this? What incentives exist, or might be created, for better coordination, decentralisation, and efficiency in the federal bureaucracy? What specifically might motivate the PRI leadership to nominate candidates popular in specific districts, and to allow them some independence from presidential discipline? What incentives might induce sectorial leaders in the party to permit greater internal democracy in their followings?

Beyond the incentives, we should search for opportunities for change given the international context, the internal sexennial rhythm of politics, and luck – both good and bad. With respect to the external environment, the key considerations are debt, oil prices, export opportunities and the Central American crisis. Any of these, or more likely, some combination of them can create circumstances for change. Within Mexico, critical periods are the elections of 1985–86, and the presidential succession struggle that is decided in 1986–87.

3 Presidential Politics: López Portillo and De la Madrid

'Presidentialism' (*presidencialismo*) as a code word in contemporary Mexican political discourse divides two basic camps. To supporters of the *status quo*, the term signifies arrangements appropriate to Mexico's reality: a strong, centralising institution, personified in a figure who can preserve order amid conflict and underdevelopment while advancing the Revolutionary projects. The PRI leadership point with pride to former presidents such as Lázaro Cárdenas and Adolfo López Mateos, who set high standards of statecraft. Within the party, the debate about presidentialism pits Tlaxcala governor Tulio Hernández and others who call for limiting power against the CTM leadership and other supporters of continued centralisation.[1] Outside the party, critics on both the right and left view presidentialism as the core institutional flaw of a system that permits no checks on the personal power of the incumbent and which must by its logic oppose democratising forces. Critics rest their case by conjuring up the still vivid memories of Luís Echeverría and José López Portillo.

This chapter begins the examination of institutions and decision-making. It reiterates the importance of the larger structural setting, because the global order imposes constraints on Mexican domestic politics. At the institutional level, Mexico is a thoroughly presidential system, one based on extensive party–bureaucracy arrangements within the context of a series of pacts between social classes and groups. The structural perspective suggests that even with enlightened presidential leadership, increasing tensions and conflicts emerged in the late 1950s as the strategy of stabilising development encountered limits to continued rapid growth. This was the case not only within Mexico, but in other countries in the region as well, notably Argentina and Brazil.

Several factors converged to produce the overall failure of the López Portillo *sexenio*. The worsening combination of such international economic forces as declining oil prices, high interest rates and continued recession struck midway in 1981 at the most delicate point of the *sexenio*. However, that experience also teaches that when there is weakness at the institutional core, both in the incumbent and the presidency itself, the consequences are exaggerated throughout the whole system. López Portillo damaged perhaps for the long term the legitimacy of presidential governance.

Miguel de la Madrid inherited a debilitated system in the midst of Mexico's worst crisis since 1929. Perhaps the De la Madrid government should be judged less for dramatic results than for its effort to sustain difficult austerity programmes and to prepare the ground for the succeeding government. Nevertheless, the perceived failure of the President's anti-corruption campaign and his image of indecisiveness have undermined further the credibility of the system.

LOGIC OF MEXICO'S PRESIDENTIAL SYSTEM

Mexican political leaders after 1929 constructed a highly centralised polity with the presidency at the epicentre. It can be argued, especially by those disenchanted with the Revolution, that the present system is a reconstructed version of previous orders, be it the Porfiriato, the Spanish colony, or even the Aztec empire.[2] Clearly one finds a reiterated preference for hierarchical, authoritarian arrangements. Yet, to explain current institutions and policy-making, significant qualifications must be drawn.

The Revolution removed or weakened such important actors as the Catholic church and large landowners, and created a new order led by new elites and based on a state ideology of nationalism, liberalism and development. From the time of its installation in the late 1930s to its routinisation by the early 1950s, the Mexican system acted to centralise and bureaucratise power, both in the government and the official party. Distinguishing elements of the system have been presidential dominance and the strict observance of the no-reelection principle. These traits lend Mexican politics a predictable rhythm, permitting the circulation of elites and the continuous expectation for improvement that provide escape valves for elite and popular frustration.

Nine consecutive presidential *sexenios* since 1934 have reinforced patterns. Though every President brings a distinctive style to the office, each must resolve common challenges. As the PRI's nominee he must mount a credible campaign; once in office, he must consolidate power and break from his predecessor; then he has only a brief period to implement policies; and, finally, he must manage a stable succession. Alvaro Obregón, President during 1920–24, advocated the six-year term, observing only partly in irony that a four-year term forced the President to spend the first two years in office managing the discontented losers and the last biennium fighting off would-be successors. Plutarco Elias Calles, Obregón's successor, introduced the six-year term in 1928 as part of the constitutional reforms of the *maximato*.[3]

Within the *sexenio*, the period of consolidation, when the President installs his team, removes potential opponents and begins to implement programmes might occupy some eighteen months. The phase of programme implementation, during which the President reaches the apex of his power, lasts some two to three years, and the succession process occupies the last two years in office. Obviously, the phases overlap and might more accurately be considered as matters of sequential emphasis. Some Presidents, Echeverría for example, consolidated more quickly, ruled longer and managed the succession more completely than others. The President's primary responsibility is to preserve the institutions and manage these cycles.

Jorge Carpizo summarises the diverse strands of presidential power in Mexico:

1. The President heads the dominant party, which in turn includes the major labour, peasant and professional organisations;
2. Legislators, themselves members of the dominant party, offer no resistance because they know that such is pointless and that their political careers will suffer;
3. Members of the supreme court are themselves astute politicians who will not oppose presidential interests;
4. The central bank and state enterprises exercise marked influence in the economy, and the presidency wields ample powers in economic policy;
5. The army officer corps is professional, with disciplined leaders;
6. The presidency exercises dominant influence over public opinion by means of its control over mass media;
7. Economic resources are concentrated in the federal government, especially in the executive branch;
8. The President enjoys ample legal and extra-legal powers, such as the ability to designate state governors and his own successor;

9. The President has a virtually free hand in international politics, without senatorial constraint;
10. The executive directly controls the most important area of the country, the Federal District; and
11. In the public mind, the majority accept presidential domination.[4]

The presidency dominates 'high politics', both in interpreting the state ideology in concrete settings and in negotiating working pacts among key actors: labour organisations, national and foreign investors, the Church, foreign interests and the government bureaucracy. Depending on the incumbent's style and intent, presidency also controls daily politics by setting out the policy agenda, manipulating the communications media, and deciding personnel appointments in government and party from high to low levels. Nevertheless, this does not mean an omniscient, omnipotent President.

Carpizo stresses that the presidency encounters no effective restraint *within* government. Worth mentioning as a potential exception is the Mexican army, which influences decisions about foreign policy and internal order.[5] There are in addition significant 'irritating' restraints, such as the inadequate or filtered information that reaches the President, and the complex and sluggish federal bureaucracy.

In the wider political system the presidency confronts limitations from several quarters. Both national and foreign business elites limit presidential behaviour, because of the constant – and real – threat of capital flight. Organised labour may be loyal to the PRI–government system, but labour consistently exercises a negotiating power. The mass media enjoy increasing freedom, although the custom of avoiding direct criticism of the incumbent President and his family still holds.[6] More constraining perhaps is the increased penetration of foreign media, as through cable television or the proliferating satellite antennae that serve the middle and upper social strata. The international setting imposes limits in areas such as tourism, trade and even the vague 'world opinion'. Finally, the deterioration of the image of the presidency due to the turmoil of the last two *sexenios* probably constrains the present incumbent. The elimination of significant political groups over time and the accompanying concentration of the presidency on the government bureaucracy itself have strengthened the presidency in a narrow sense, but such tendencies have weakened the consensus that undergirds presidentialism.

In the sense of a complex of organisations, the presidency controls the PRI and the extensive federal bureaucracy and employs both organisations as subordinate instruments. Thus the party lacks identity and purpose separate from the presidency and the bureaucracy, giving real basis to the common label, PRI–government. Much of daily politics consists of the circulation of numerous teams within and between both pillars, vying for presidential support. The President's general and specific control over career advancement in party and government constitutes the real motor of centralisation. The emphasis on technical competence since the mid-1960s, consistent with the rise of the bureaucracy after 1971, had reduced substantially the career opportunities of those who stressed the political skills of building extensive alliances in the party, negotiating directly with constituent groups and cultivating a rhetoric rich in revolutionary slogans. The resulting tension between *técnicos* and *políticos* in turn has weakened the political class as a whole.

Following Peter Smith, the defining characteristic of *técnicos*

> pertains to the nature of their credential for recognition and employment: it is a certificate of expertise, usually a university degree (often a foreign one at that). Whereas intellectuals tend to present opinions and viewpoints on public matters of general interest, technocrats claim to be in command of special skills for the resolution of particular policy issues. Imbued with the prestige and authority of 'scientific' knowledge, they appear in various fields: agronomy, engineering, and, most recently and emphatically, economics. They differ in outlook and opinion among themselves, they take different sides of arguments, but they have one thing in common: a standard ticket for admission into decision-making circles.[7]

The emergence of the technocrat is a universal phenomenon resulting from the growth of educational institutions and proliferation of professions at the same time that governments have become more extensively involved in guiding the economy and society. Diverse systems harness technical expertise according to their particular institutional arrangements. In Mexico, the process of accommodating the *técnicos* took a peculiar turn when Echeverría passed over many qualified system regulars to promote a younger generation. Though more committed to older administrators, López Portillo was seen to rely heavily on *técnicos* as well, especially in the latter, turbulent days of his term. Thus, several unhappy connotations attach to the status of *técnico*:

1. Politically inept (promoted prematurely by failed presidents);
2. Foreign trained, or inspired, and thus the agents of inappropriate knowledge;
3. Urban, upper-strata backgrounds, thus out of touch with common people; and in several cases
4. Children of previous generations of successful politicians, thus using family advantages to impede upward mobility for those presumably more deserving due to humble origins and lengthy apprenticeships in the party.[8]

The widespread criticism of the inept government response to the September 1985 earthquake focused in part on the *técnicos*' inability to respond effectively. For example, the decision to expropriate scores of properties in downtown Mexico City was improvised on faulty information.[9]

One should avoid a static interpretation of the *técnico–político* tension. Power passed in a roughly similar way from military leaders to civilians with Alemán. After more than a decade of struggle, a new hybrid administrator–politician has emerged, as seen, for example, in the cases of Adolfo Lugo, Alejandro Carrillo and Alfredo del Mazo.[10] Quite apart from the stereotypes, the *técnico–político* debate feeds a troublesome delusion: if only the old-style politicians would return to power, the present crisis would melt before their presumed skills.

Mexican presidentialism demands discipline, and this depends ultimately on a monopoly of rewards, party and government offices and all the implied perquisites of power, being distributed from above on a basis of loyalty to intermediate leaders who are, in turn, loyal to the President. This logic substantially changes the significance of votes as a currency of power, either within the PRI's constituent groups or in general electoral competition. Of course, a genuinely popular and steadfastly loyal leader is to be welcomed. But votes count for less than control over those below and loyalty to those above. Similarly, satellite parties are rewarded in exchange for system support.[11] For example, electoral rules have been stretched to permit continued registration for the Authentic Party of the Mexican Revolution (PARM).

The logic of presidential control also reduces the importance of ideology as a basis of party cohesion. The PRI's 'revolutionary nationalism', discussed in Chapter 6, is a loosely drawn social democratic ideology that reconciles state rectorship of a mixed economy, promotion of the rights of the poor and respect for individual liberties. Presidential control also undercuts individual militancy at the party base as a route to the top. Connections and luck, not work, too often make the difference.

On the other hand, presidentialism elevates the importance of friendships, patron–client ties and corruption, the latter taken to mean the strictly illegal or broadly unethical use of party or government posts for personal enrichment. Friends are essential in a game in which laws may be stretched and which offers no unemployment compensation. Cultivating protection and support from those favourably placed is the key to upward mobility.

Corruption, which increasingly dismays Mexicans and fascinates foreigners, is a bit more complex. Keeping in mind Mexico's highly unequal income distribution and politics as a mobility channel, abuse of public office has provided a mechanism of opportunity. In the absence of a militant ideology or generalised attachment to governmental and party institutions, a limited degree of corruption can provide incentives for discipline. That is, one feeds at the trough with the understanding that loyalty to the system is expected. A young politician needs resources to promote his career; and an old one needs to set aside something towards retirement. This is not to suggest, I would stress, that all *priístas* are somehow corrupt by virtue of party affiliation. The point, rather, is that the logic of the presidential system foments corruption.[12] Further, those benefitting from one-party dominance of presidentialism can hardly be expected to cede power gracefully in democratic elections.

Some undefineable level of corruption contributed to the success of presidentialism up to the early 1970s. But the practice was exaggerated with the expansion of government activity under Echeverría, and with López Portillo the oil bonanza gave rise to abuses that have threatened presidentialism itself. So flagrant were the offences, especially the conspicuous mansions built for López Portillo and other officials, that confidence in presidentialism has been deeply shaken.

Figure 3.1 suggests how incentives to the actors in this system reinforce centralisation, as a background to understanding presidential power. The President controls the PRI largely by placing his own loyalists in pivotal positions in the National Executive Committee (CEN).[13] He dominates the administrative apparatus by appointing and then manipulating the top several levels of policy-makers. He also uses the CEN–Interior Secretariat linkage as the filter to nominate those loyal to himself and the system to state governorships and

Figure 3.1 The nature of Mexican presidentialism

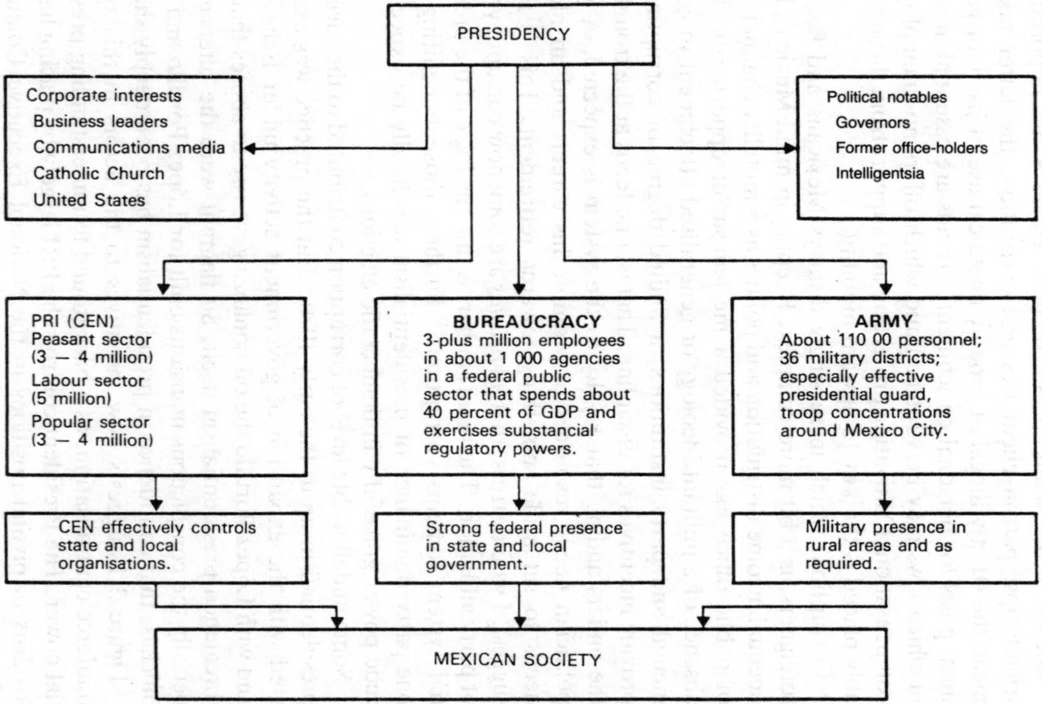

PRESIDENCY

Corporate interests
Business leaders
Communications media
Catholic Church
United States

Political notables
Governors
Former office-holders
Intelligentsia

PRI (CEN)
Peasant sector
(3 – 4 million)
Labour sector
(5 million)
Popular sector
(3 – 4 million)

BUREAUCRACY
3-plus million employees in about 1 000 agencies in a federal public sector that spends about 40 percent of GDP and exercises substancial regulatory powers.

ARMY
About 110 00 personnel; 36 military districts; especially effective presidential guard, troop concentrations around Mexico City.

CEN effectively controls state and local organisations.

Strong federal presence in state and local government.

Military presence in rural areas and as required.

MEXICAN SOCIETY

the national legislature.[14] Political 'notables', a diverse collection of cabinet members, governors, interest group leaders and influential former office-holders lobby the presidency–CEN–Interior triangle to influence appointments. Most seek merely to protect their own power bases and to advance their loyalists. A few are positioning themselves to 'play the big one', the presidential succession. The labour, popular and peasant sector leaders endeavour to protect or enlarge their historical shares of offices and to advance their own clients. Party activists and government bureaucrats manoeuvre to establish friendships with notables higher up in the party and government. They hope for that bit of luck known as the *dedazo* (literally, the 'big finger'), the signal from above to assume a higher post. The President also manages negotiations with political actors outside the party–government, most notably the Church, business, communications media and the United States.

Beyond law and patronage, what explains presidential power in Mexico? Some factors of course are universal: periodic crises, increased role of government in the economy, decline of legislatures and the tendency of modern communications media to personalise power. The strong executive, be it President, Prime Minister or party chairman is the norm in contemporary government. Important as well in Mexico are cultural traditions of an inclusive, unanimous, centrally managed system. Opinion surveys have shown the popular idealisation of the President, and a distinction was drawn in the popular mind, at least prior to Echeverría, between the corrupt party and bureaucracy as opposed to the President, seen as a benign father figure.[15] Rafael Segovia's study of Mexican schoolchildren underlines their attention to power:

> And this capacity to command, to keep all power in his hands is what most attracts the attention of infantile minds – and the more so the less infantile they are – and it will become the most valued trait. He is not the benevolent leader; he is above all the authoritarian leader, as capable of governing as of creating a material world – subways, dams, highways, stadia – by his mere will.[16]

The historical experience of chaos in the absence of a strong leader validates popular preference, as seen in the several constitutions and many extra-legal changes of office during 1821–76 and also during the Revolution. With characteristic pungency, Cosío Villegas notes the 'Wizard of Oz' quality of presidential power: the President is powerful because everyone believes he is.[17] His insight is echoed by the working politicians who recite with conviction the following creed: 'Not a leaf on that tree moves unless the president wills it.'

Contradictory trends during the 1960s and 1970s strengthened presidential power while debilitating the system as a whole. The rapid growth of the size and influence of the federal bureaucracy reinforced centralisation and presidentialism. These trends enhanced career mobility for younger generations of technical elites forging their careers in the bureaucracy, to the relative disadvantage of politicians rising within the party and elected posts as well as the bureaucracy. Such centralisation challenged the postwar pact with domestic businessmen, but failed to construct an alternative basis of growth. At the same time the overall Mexican political economy has become more closely integrated with the world economy, undermining in the process the presidency's base of power in the national economy. Confidence in presidentialism, already strained due to secular forces of economic growth, urbanisation and expanded education, was deeply shaken by the perceived capriciousness of the Echeverría administration and – as we shall see – by that of José López Portillo.

LÓPEZ PORTILLO: FROM BUST TO BOOM AND BACK

In characterising the López Portillo presidency I shall focus on the succession and general strategy of governance, the consolidation of power and attempts to implement a development programme and finally the succession to Miguel de la Madrid in 1981–82.[18] López Portillo began with important weaknesses but succeeded in consolidating power and launching an ambitious development strategy before a series of unfortunate events converged to complicate the succession and devastate the economy in the process.

It is generally agreed that the outgoing President chooses his own successor, although the factors that shape the decision remain obscure.[19] The pertinent question becomes why did Echeverría choose López Portillo? A plausible answer suggests that Echeverría sought a personal confidante who was a competent administrator and a weak politician. Echeverría's likely project was to extend his influence into the successor's term, to create a *minimato*.[20]

The preference for a weak successor is evident when one considers who lost out in the succession. All of the main contenders were

Echeverría's creations, rather than experienced politicians who had risen through the ranks, which reflected the trend towards concentration and personalisation of power. Porfirio Muñoz Ledo, the young Secretary of Labour, had cultivated support in the labour movement. Hugo Cervantes del Río, Secretary of the Presidency, had something of a political career, with prior service as governor of Baja California Sur. And Augusto Gómez Villanueva had developed a base as leader of the National Peasant Confederation (CNC) and later as Secretary of Agrarian Reform. But the most likely of the group was Mario Moya Palencia who – as Secretary of Interior – had assembled a team in the federal bureaucracy and in several of the states. Four of the five Presidents since 1946 had served as Interior Secretary, and the team-building had the effect of stabilising the succession. Moya's political strength and skill were not his only liabilities; he also was connected with the *alemanista* faction of the party, whose influence Echeverría was probably not eager to reinforce. Echeverría's choice of López Portillo, Secretary of Treasury, was both unorthodox and harmful to the political class. It also had the effect of politicising the Treasury Secretariat, which had remained on the margin of the succession struggles.[21]

Furthermore, in keeping with the project of extending his influence, Echeverría shunted aside Jesús Reyes Heroles as PRI President, and installed his own loyalists, Muñoz Ledo and Gómez Villanueva, to head up the party and manage the 1975–76 presidential campaign. López Portillo proved to be a vigorous and effective candidate, though one who chose not to question the incumbent's authority. He concentrated his own team in the party's Institute for Economic, Social, and Political Studies (IEPES), under the direction of Julio R. Moctezuma.

José López Portillo y Pacheco was born on 16 June 1920 and was raised in the Mexico City neighbourhood of Colonia del Valle. His grandfather, José López Portillo y Rojas, had been governor of Jalisco during 1911–13 and secretary of foreign relations under General Victoriano Huerta. The future President attended public schools throughout his formal education, receiving his law degree from the UNAM in 1946. He was a close friend from early childhood of Luís Echeverría, and the two travelled together on scholarships to study in Chile in 1942, where López Portillo took a law degree at the University of Santiago in 1945.[22]

Of pronounced intellectual and literary interests, López Portillo taught at the UNAM and pursued private legal practice until 1960.

His scholarly research focused on the theory of the State, and he specialised in the emerging subfield of public administration, founding a doctoral programme in the subject at the IPN. He also dabbled in fiction, writing a short novel on the myth of the Aztec god Quetzalcoatl.[23] He was regarded as energetic, creative, intelligent and a talented teacher and speaker.

In his geographical and class origins, López Portillo fit the evolving pattern of recruitment to higher offices in Mexico. Also typical of general patterns was his career emphasis on the bureaucracy and his relative inexperience in party matters.[24] His career progression put him in close touch with the public works and state enterprise aspects of administration and with the increasing emphasis on planning and coordination: 1959, technical adviser, Secretariat of National Patrimony (SEPANAL); 1960–65, Federal Board of Material Improvements of SEPANAL; 1965, Head of Juridical Office, Secretariat of the Presidency, involving work on Public Administration Commission and on the Commission for National Development Planning; 1968, Subsecretary of Presidency; 1970, Subsecretary of SEPANAL; 1972, Director, Federal Electricity Commission (CFE); and 1973–75, Secretary of Treasury.

Though a lifelong friend of Echeverría, López Portillo's apparent mentor was Emilio Martínez Manatou, who – as Secretary of the Presidency during 1964–70 – had vied with Echeverría for the succession. Martínez Manatou had assembled a group of UNAM intellectuals to support him in the succession. In the view of some, the 1968 student movement invloved a whiff of succession politics, and Martínez Manatou and the UNAM group appeared to suffer a setback. López Portillo, however, emerged unscathed, and in 1970 Echeverría granted his friend a respectable post as subsecretary of SEPANAL.

The *minimato* explanation fits the facts rather well. Echeverría may have influenced Díaz Ordaz to appoint López Portillo as a subsecretary at Presidency. Later, it was useful to lend apparent support to Moya while protecting López Portillo at the subsecretary level. When Treasury Secretary Hugo Margain resisted deficitary fiscal policies, Echeverría had a ready candidate for the job. The intriguing mystery is the extent of Echeverría's influence after 1976.[25]

The notes on López Portillo's career progression are significant in understanding the appointments to the governing team. Table 3.1 sets out the original cabinet appointments as well as several significant subcabinet posts.

Emilio Martínez Manatou (Health and Welfare) was recalled from

Table 3.1 The López Portillo Cabinet, December 1976

Interior: Jesús Reyes Heroles
(Javier García Paniagua, Federal Security Director)
(Margarita López Portillo, Communications)
Foreign Relations: Santiago Roel
Defence: General Félix Galván López
Navy: Adm. Ricardo Cházaro Lara
Treasury: Julio R. Moctezuma
Programming and Budget: Carlos Tello
(Rosa Luz Alegría, Evaluation)
Patrimony and Industrial Development: José Andrés de Oteyza
Commerce: Fernando Solana
Agriculture and Water Resources: Francisco Merino Rábago
Human Settlements and Public Works: Pedro Ramírez Vázquez
Communications and Transport: Emilio Mújica Montoya
Education: Porfirio Muñoz Ledo
Health and Welfare: Emilio Martínez Manatou
Agrarian Reform: Jorge Rojo Lugo
Labour and Social Welfare: Pedro Ojeda Paullada
Tourism: Guillermo Rosell de la Lama
Federal District: Carlos Hank González
Attorney General: Oscar Flores Sánchez
Attorney for the Federal District: Agustín Alanis Fuentes
Rural Credit Bank: Everardo Espino de la O
Social Security Institute: Arsenio Farell Cubillas
National Finance Bank: David Ibarra Muñoz
ASA: Enrique Loaeza Tovar
Roads and Bridges: Hector M. Calderón
Institute for Foreign Commerce: Adrián Lajous Martínez
PEMEX: Jorge Díaz Serrano
Public Works Bank: Enrique Olivares Santana
Fertilizers: David Gustavo Gutiérrez
Military Industry: Javier Jiménez Segura
CONASUPO: Manuel González Cosío
COPLAMAR: Francisco Guel Jiménez
Presidential Private Secretary: Enrique Velasco Ibarra
National Lottery: Roberto de Lamadrid
ISSSTE: Carlos Jonguitud Barrios
COVE: Juan Pérez Abreu
National Railroads: Luís Gómez Z.
IMPI e IMAN: Marco V. Martínez G.
Nacional Monte de Piedad: Luís Barrera González

Source: *Excélsior*, 1 December 1976. Agency titles conform to 1977 Law of Public Administration.

retirement in part to counter *echeverrista* influence. Pedro Ojeda Paullada (Labour) and Guillermo Rosell de la Lama (Tourism) were colleagues from SEPANAL (1960–65). Julio R. Moctezuma (Treasury), Emilio Mújica Montoya (Communications and Transport), Fernando Solana (Commerce) and Carlos Tello (Programming and Budget) had worked with López Portillo under Martínez Manatou in Presidency during 1964–70. The friendship with José Andrés de Oteyza (SEPAFIN) dates from SEPANAL (1970–72), and Arsenio Farell (IMSS) succeeded López Portillo at the CFE (1972–73). Others, including Miguel de la Madrid and Mario Ramón Beteta, had their roots in the Treasury–Bank of Mexico group, and were befriended during López Portillo's tenure as Treasury Secretary (1973–75). Jorge Díaz Serrano (PEMEX), Santiago Roel (Foreign Relations) and Roberto De Lamadrid (National Lottery and subsequently Governor of Baja California Norte), were long-time personal friends, as was Roberto Casillas (Private Secretary). Rosa Luz Alegría (Subsecretary, SPP) joined the inner circle during the presidential campaign. The President's long involvement in administrative reform issues provided another source of loyal expertise, including Luís García Cárdenas (Coordinator at Commerce) and Alejandro Carrillo Castro (presidential adviser). Family members rounded out the core team: José Ramón López Portillo (son, subdirector in SPP); Margarita López Portillo (sister, director in Interior); José Antonio Ugarte (nephew, adviser in presidency); Guillermo López Portillo (cousin, director in education).[26]

López Portillo's explicit strategy of governance was ambitious and conceptually well integrated. He called for an 'Alliance for Production', an administrative reform, and a political reform. The first was to re-establish a pact among labour, business and government in order to stimulate investment and growth. The second, of long-standing personal interest, was to bring order to the chaotic public bureaucracy. And the third was to open new spaces for political participation. Taken together, the logic was to restore confidence in and reinvigorate the PRI–government system. The reforms fit into a sexennial schedule: two years for recovery, two more to establish the basis for sustained growth, and the last biennium for attaining high growth.

Central to the project was petroleum development. In the wake of the 1973 oil shock, the unanticipated discovery of enormous oil reserves in south-eastern Mexico would attract foreign investment and credit, and could finance as well a stronger government effort to resolve long-standing problems.

The tacit strategy was to re-equilibrate political forces internally, which implied reducing Echeverría's influence either apparently or in reality. With respect to macroeconomic policy, the IMF had negotiated an Extended Fund Facility (EFF) agreement in 1976 with the outgoing Echeverría administration that constrained policy with respect to debt, inflation and employment, as well as promoting commercial policies intended to open the Mexican economy more to international influences. The agreement had the effect of re-establishing a degree of credibility for the Mexican government in the eyes of lenders and businessmen both in Mexico and abroad. But it also proved to be a source of division within the new government. In foreign policy the strategy was to continue the broad lines of the *echeverrista* activism in Third World issues, but in a less abrasive style. A new element was to thaw out the icy relations Echeverría had established with the United States. Some went so far as to see a 'package' arrangement with the northern neighbour, involving some combination of assured access to petroleum in exchange for acceptable trade, investment, and immigration policies.[27]

However, as so common with statecraft, the *sexenio* diverged from the plan. During 1977–78, the President emphasised restoring confidence in the economy and consolidating power. The downturn in relations with the United States in 1979 appeared to close off a major option. But the vast new petroleum wealth seemed to open others. Consolidation was largely achieved by mid-1979, and from that point until mid-1981 the government focused on programme implementation, shifting to full growth and a more assertive foreign policy. Spring 1981, with the first crack in oil prices, until December 1982 was a period that began with critical mistakes and culminated in financial panic and government arbitrariness. Figure 3.2 illustrates the normal sexennial rhythm and important events under López Portillo and De la Madrid.

Considering his weak personal group, López Portillo's consolidation of power was skillfully accomplished. In customary fashion, he blended into his cabinet individuals identified with both the Díaz Ordaz and Echeverría camps, and others considered as independents. Much success was due to his personal skills, from his brilliant inaugural address, in which he seemed to pierce the tensions accumulated from the previous *sexenio*, to his adroit manoeuvring among antagonistic forces. Some success was due as well to his heeding the advice of Interior Secretary Jesús Reyes Heroles, who managed the political reform and functioned with the President's blessing as head of cabinet.

Figure 3.2 The sexennial rhythm and recent experience

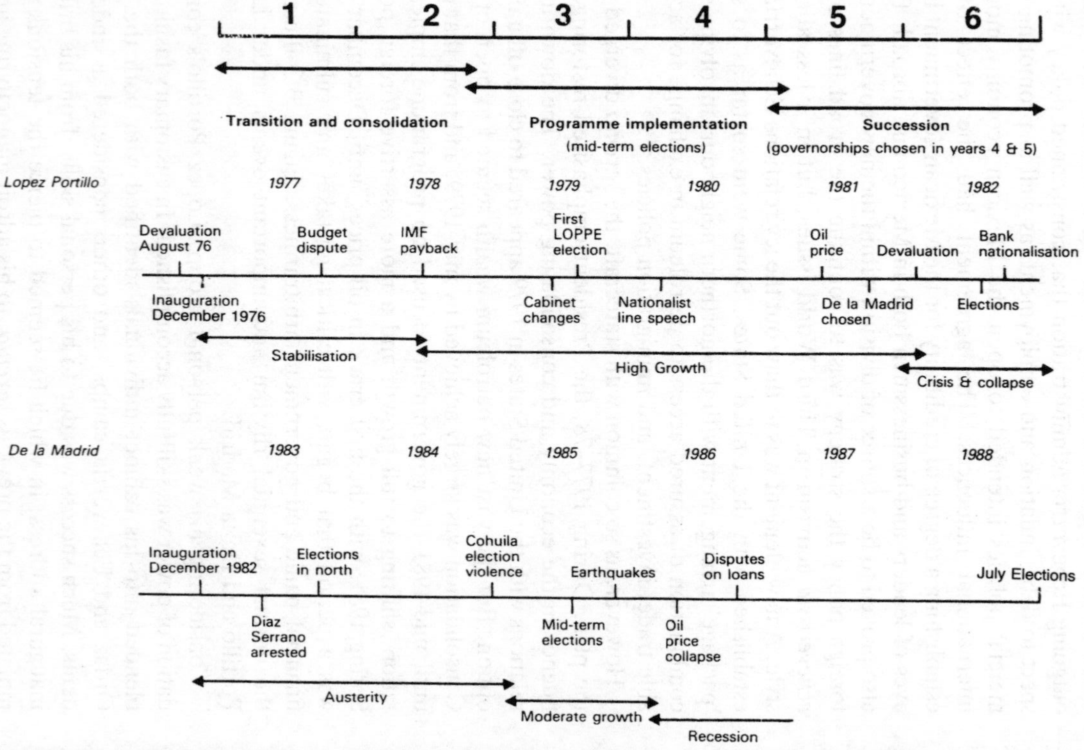

1 2 3 4 5 6

Transition and consolidation

Programme implementation
(mid-term elections)

Succession
(governorships chosen in years 4 & 5)

Lopez Portillo

1977 *1978* *1979* *1980* *1981* *1982*

Devaluation August 76
Budget dispute
IMF payback
First LOPPE election
Oil price
Devaluation
Bank nationalisation

Inauguration December 1976
Cabinet changes
Nationalist line speech
De la Madrid chosen
Elections

Stabilisation
High Growth
Crisis & collapse

De la Madrid

1983 *1984* *1985* *1986* *1987* *1988*

Inauguration December 1982
Elections in north
Cohuila election violence
Earthquakes
Disputes on loans
July Elections

Diaz Serrano arrested
Mid-term elections
Oil price collapse

Austerity
Moderate growth
Recession

Continuity with the Echeverría government was seen in the appointments of Muñoz Ledo to Education, Cervantes del Río to the CFE and Gómez Villanueva to head the Chamber of Deputies. To contain Echeverría's ambitions, *diazordacistas* were placed in critical political posts: Javier García Paniagua, the son of Díaz Ordaz' defence secretary, as head of the political police; and Oscar Flores Sánchez, former governor of Chihuahua, as the attorney general.

Careful balance characterised policy-making during 1977–78, in this case balance between adherents to the IMF guidelines and those who called for more active government intervention to address the problems of recession and unemployment. Balance was shown, for example, in resolving the first important disagreement in the new government. In formulating the 1978 budget, Treasury Secretary Julio R. Moctezuma called for a fiscal deficit in line with the IMF guidelines; SPP Secretary Carlos Tello advocated a larger deficit to reactivate a flaccid economy. Compromise proved impossible, and López Portillo split the difference between spending proposals. He replaced Tello and Moctezuma with a new team, also balanced: Ricardo García Sainz at SPP, viewed as close to business interests, and David Ibarra at Treasury, an academic economist with experience in NAFINSA, the major public development bank.[28]

The presidential strategy evolved sensibly and skillfully: cultivate support from various factions to avoid dependence on any single one. Though the specifics varied by issue, the underlying style involved creating an equilibrium between business and labour, conservatives and progressives.

To reassure business, López Portillo opened a dialogue with the principal business associations. Furthermore, he repudiated Echeverría's distributive agricultural policy and stressed the need to raise productivity. And in a symbolic gesture, he appointed ex-President Díaz Ordaz as Mexico's ambassador to Spain. To placate labour, the President backed the CTM's effort to strengthen its hold on housing subsidies distributed through the public housing agency. He also granted a long-standing labour demand by creating the Workers Bank in October 1977, appointing Afredo del Mazo, who served subsequently as governor of Mexico and cabinet secretary under De la Madrid. To balance the Díaz Ordaz appointment, ex-president Echeverría was sent to represent Mexico in UNESCO. Further, in August 1978, the PRI formally redefined itself as a workers' party with a social democratic ideology, although the leadership stretched 'worker' to include everyone who works, including industrialists. (And at the same time, Gustavo Carvajal was moved from the labour Secretariat, where he had administered fairly harsh medicine to the unions, to become the party's general secretary.)[29]

Also, consolidation involved timely warnings to those who might push too hard to influence the new government. In this case, corruption charges were brought in September 1977 against Félix Barra García, who as Agrarian Reform secretary in the preceding administration was alleged to have extorted large sums from a landowner. The action against Barra García, the first secretary-level official to be charged with corruption, was widely interpreted as a signal to Gómez Villanueva to tread lightly. As if to reinforce the message, charges were brought as well against Alberto Ríos Camarena, who had served as Gómez Villanueva's private secretary. Gómez Villanueva resigned his post as head of the Chamber of Deputies to assume the ambassadorship to Italy. In early 1978, corruption charges were levelled against Eugenio Méndez Docurro, Subsecretary of Education, who had served as Secretary of Communications and Transport under Echeverría.[30]

Further shuffles strengthened the new President's hand. In November 1977, López Portillo removed Munõz Ledo from his post at Education. Munõz Ledo reportedly was unhappy, in part due to the hard line the new government adopted against political activity in the universities. Related as well was the allegation brought by Ríos Camarena that at least part of the money embezzled by the Agrarian Reform Secretariat went to pay for electoral fraud in the 1975 elections in the state of Nayarit. Munõz Ledo had been involved in the complicated negotiations following the election.[31] The President shifted Fernando Solana from Commerce to Education, and Jorge de la Vega – of a more independent stripe – was called from the governorship of Chiapas to take up the Commerce post. Finally, Echeverría himself resigned his post at UNESCO in late 1978 to accept the ambassadorship to Australia. Paradoxically, moving Echeverría farther away probably had the effect of increasing the manoeuvrability and influence of *echeverristas* in Mexico.

By early 1979 consolidation appeared to be progressing well, even though commentators continued to see Echeverría's hand in government policy. Then, abruptly, López Portillo moved to assert his own power. In January 1979 he removed Carlos Sansores Pérez as head of the PRI and replaced him with Gustavo Carvajal. Four months later, on 19 May, the President flew to Cancún to consult with Costa Rican President Rodrigo Carazo Odio about the situation in Nicaragua.

Eighteen days later, he dismissed three key cabinet figures: Jesús Reyes Heroles (Interior), Santiago Roel (Foreign Relations) and Ricardo García Sainz (SPP). Their respective replacements signalled shifts in both policy and style. Enrique Olivares Santana implied a retreat from the political reform and the assertion of the President in political matters; Jorge Castañeda, a career diplomat, implied greater attention to foreign policy with perhaps a shift away from special attention to the United States; and Miguel de la Madrid reflected the continuing search for someone to make the new planning–budgeting apparatus work. What had happened?

López Portillo's style of governance stressed administrative rationality and comprehensive planning. SPP, the centrepiece of his ambitious administrative reform, was charged with creating a Global Development Plan which in turn would guide the drafting of sectorial plans. His substantive priorities stressed agricultural self-sufficiency and rapid development of petroleum exploitation. In theory, the Plan would address the key issues of the proper pace of petroleum development and the appropriate balance between industry, agriculture and services. The good to be sought was balanced development that would generate rapid employment and correct distortions in the economy: inadequate income taxation, negative balance of payments, deficient food production and inefficient industry. The evil to be avoided was the petrolisation of the economy, whereby dependence on petroleum exports would shape key aspects of economic behaviour. In practice, the Global Development Plan did not appear until April 1980, by which time important decisions had already been set by petroleum development policy and the sectorial plans elaborated by the Secretariat of Patrimony and Industry (SEPAFIN) and the Secretariat of Human Settlements and Public Works (SAHOP).

Several factors converged to push López Portillo onto a different course. Most important was oil. PEMEX director Jorge Díaz Serrano had set the goal in 1977 to increase petroleum production from 900 000 barrels per day (bpd) to 2.25 million bpd by 1982. By 1979 it was apparent that Mexico could indeed exceed this timetable. At the same time, OPEC had anticipated a gradual increase in oil prices for 1979, from $13.35 to $14.54 per barrel *before* the Iranian crisis pushed the basic price for that year to $18.00 and the maximum to $23.50 per barrel.[32] The decisions to invest heavily in PEMEX proved timely. These developments in the oil market in turn strengthened Mexico's hand to confront a new foreign policy situation. First, the opening towards the United States was thwarted in late 1977 when the United States rejected linking the purchase price of Mexican gas to the BTU equivalent of number 2 fuel oil and showed little interest in moving towards greater accommodation on migration and trade. The resulting irritation was recorded during President Carter's visit to Mexico City in February 1979, when López Portillo stated: 'Between friends there can be no room for deception.' Second, the fall of Anastasio Somoza of Nicaragua in mid-July 1979 forced a series of decisions. Mexico openly and enthusiastically endorsed the Sandinista Front for National Liberation, a policy that soon came to irritate the US.

Within Mexico other trends contributed to the policy shift. In the political realm, the President's decision to assert his own power grew out of his impatience with Reyes Heroles' independent style in the political reform process. The Interior Secretary's reservations about Pope John Paul II's visit to Mexico in January 1979 might have irritated as well. In the economy, pressures were accumulating to resume rapid growth to bolster wages and to create new jobs for the growing population. The anticipated oil bonanza provided the basis for confidence in the economy while moving towards faster growth. Mexico prepaid the IMF in June 1978, thus terminating its obligations, and by late 1979 complaints were heard that control of budget expenditures was slipping.[33]

While the decisions in early 1979 pointed to rapid growth and a more independent foreign policy, it was not until early 1980 that an operational strategy appeared. On 18 March, the day Mexico celebrates the 1938 nationalisation of the petroleum industry, President López Portillo announced three significant decisions with respect to oil, trade and agriculture. First, oil policy would be guided by an upper limit of 2.5 million bpd, of which approximately 1.25 million bpd would be available for export. An additional margin of 10 per cent would be allowed to cope with market fluctuations. The upper limit would presumably avoid both petrolisation and a too rapid depleting of national reserves. The country would seek to diversify its export markets so that in principle no more than half the exports would be directed to a single nation, a measure aimed at the United States. Second, Mexico would postpone its entry into GATT, putting to rest a debate that the President had allowed to boil during the preceding year. The General Agreement on Tariffs and Trade, while not a binding treaty, establishes rules that guide participants with respect to their economic and commercial policies. Entering the GATT would reduce the freedom of choice of the Mexican government, which those on the nationalist left especially saw as undesirable. Third, the Mexican Food System (SAM) would be the principal strategy to achieve food self-sufficiency.[34]

In April Miguel de la Madrid announced the long-awaited Global Development Plan. By and large, the Plan reinforced the President's policy decisions, setting out the assumptions and details for rapid growth.[35]

Taken together the decisions indicated a renewed inward-looking development policy in which petroleum income would finance a deepening of ISI and an attack on agricultural stagnation. Postponing GATT entry freed Mexican trade policy for bilateral negotiations. An aspect of oil policy, for example, was to exchange petroleum for technology and capital. The agricultural policy clearly was designed to achieve self-sufficiency rather than to seek market complementarities with the United States. Self-sufficiency was even more attractive politically in the wake of President Carter's partial embargo of grain exports to the Soviet Union due to its invasion of Afghanistan.[36]

The political implications of these decisions were fundamental. The primary beneficiary was the government bureaucracy, which would set the basic lines of economic growth, undertake directly a broader range of activities and enjoy greater independent financing through oil income. The government now had the resources to avoid confronting tax reform, economic liberalisation and the modernisation of the *ejido* system. Business interests were dazzled by growth possibilities. In reality the decisions not only postponed necessary adjustments, they seriously aggravated structural distortions.[37]

In essence, the policy decisions taken in 1979 and announced in 1980 rested on two critical judgments: oil prices would continue to rise; and borrowing interest rates would stabilise, and then fall in real terms. Both proved disastrously wrong.

Oil prices seemed different from other commodity prices in 1979 due to oil's special role in transportation, heating and industry, thus the greater difficulty in product substitution and the lower price elasticity of demand. The art of oil price forecasting is highly subjective due to the complexity of the known variables and the significance of the unknowable, as appeared in the turmoil in Iran in November 1978. In 1979 respected experts predicted robust price increases into the 1980s.[38] Jean-Jacques Servan-Schreiber merely reinforced the widely believed when he wrote:

> We know that the price of petroleum will not stop climbing. Having jumped in 10 years from 2 to 32 dollars a barrel, it is seen officially – and OPEC has thus announced it – that [the price] will be doubled from here to 1985. Or even before if, as is probable, another 'accident' of the Iranian type happens. This is something known.[39]

López Portillo is said to have sent copies of the book to his cabinet.

The interest rate decision was equally serious. Petroleum development proved a net cost to the Mexican government due to the heavy investment required for exploration and production development. Oil did not begin to contribute significant earnings until 1981, precisely when the price softened.[40] In the meantime, financing was based on borrowing both within Mexico and abroad, especially in the Eurodollar market that was rapidly expanding due to the heavy flow of earnings from other oil exporting countries. Furthermore, Mexican businessmen were encouraged to borrow abroad to finance expansion. There they encountered bankers eager to place loans. The implications of this heavy indebtedness require a simplified glimpse at international finance.

The first oil shock of 1973 had been accommodated in the international economy in good part through inflation. The roots of this in turn take us back to the 1967 decision by Lyndon Johnson to finance the Vietnam war and domestic social programmes through inflation. This, along with other forces, led to the 1971 decision by Richard Nixon to abandon the dollar–gold link, which permitted freer – thus more inflationary – monetary policies in various countries. During Jimmy Carter's term annual inflation reached 11.3 per cent. Rational economic actors in such circumstances borrow heavily with full expectation of paying back in cheaper dollars. Monetary authorities seemed obliging, and thus there was some basis to expect a continued accommodation through inflation. In September 1979, however, Federal Reserve Chairman Paul Volcker turned away from open market transactions to more potent monetary instruments to control inflation: increasing the rediscount rate charged member banks; more careful tracking of money supply. The prime rate charged by US banks rose from 12.7 in 1979 to 18.9 per cent in 1981.[41]

The election of Ronald Reagan in November 1980 seemed to promise relief from high interest rates. This politician spoke of fiscal austerity, getting government off peoples' backs and letting market magic work. Reagan's package of tax and spending cuts, along with a defence build-up, what Vice President George Bush had earlier labelled 'voodoo economics', might take pressure off monetary policy. In the event, the tax cuts sailed through Congress in 1981 while the spending cuts stalled. This, along with the defence build-up, resulted in rapidly rising federal borrowing requirements. At the same time, the anti-inflationary monetary policy intensified pressures on interest rates, leading to contradiction: expansionary fiscal policy and restrictive monetary policy. These trends coincided with the international recession due to the 1979 oil shock and reinforced by the high prevailing US interest rate, which attracted savings from abroad, reinforcing capital flight in the process.

The mistake, then, was in misjudging Volcker's determination and in misreading Reagan. Or, to paraphrase one Mexican policy-maker on Reagan: We thought someone who preached from the Bible had at least read it! With the policy strategy in place by mid-1980, López Portillo led his nation on an economic boom into the face of rising interest rates and a deepening international recession.

The Mexican economy recorded extraordinary growth during 1979–81, as shown in Table 3.2. The most impressive accomplishments were recorded in industry, construction, mining (essentially petroleum development), and – briefly – agriculture. Also significant was the pace of job creation. The government had set a target of lowering open unemployment to 5.5 per cent by 1982, but López Portillo claimed in September 1981 that the goal had been surpassed in 1980, when the average unemployment rate dropped to 3.5 per cent. Some 3.25 million new jobs were created during 1978–81.[42] Worrisome trends appeared in fairly predictable areas: inflation, balance of payments, and fiscal deficit. Still, optimism about oil prices overrode the worries.

The first tremor in the oil market appeared in May 1981, and the Mexican government's response set the course to disaster. Mexicans ruefully recall Alvaro Obregón's lesson in statecraft: 'In politics you don't make mistakes. You make one mistake, and all the rest are consequences.' Unfortunately, the consequences converged at the middle of the fifth year of the *sexenio*, precisely when the succession was being determined.

Jorge Díaz Serrano returned from Europe in early May concerned about signs of market softness. He huddled with his advisers over a weekend and concluded that Mexico needed to reduce oil prices quickly to avoid losing market shares. With López Portillo's approval, on 3 June 1981 he announced a price cut for the standard

Table 3.2 Mexico's gross domestic product by major sectors, 1976–83 (in billions of 1970 pesos and annual percentage change)

	1976	*1977*	*1978*	*1979*
Total	635.8 (4.2)	657.7 (3.4)	712.0 (8.2)	777.2 (9.2)
Agriculture, forestry, fishing	63.4 (1.0)	68.1 (7.5)	72.2 (6.0)	75.7 (−2.1)
Mining	15.8 (6.1)	17.1 (7.6)	19.5 (14.3)	22.4 (14.7)
Manufacturing industry	155.5 (5.0)	161.0 (3.5)	176.8 (9.8)	195.6 (10.6)
Construction	34.4 (4.6)	32.5 (−5.3)	36.5 (12.4)	41.3 (13.0)
Electricity	9.2 (12.2)	9.9 (7.6)	10.7 (7.9)	11.8 (10.3)
Commerce, restaurants and hotels	163.1 (3.2)	165.9 (1.8)	179.0 (7.9)	200.0 (11.7)
Transport, storage and communications	39.8 (5.1)	42.5 (6.6)	47.8 (12.5)	55.2 (15.5)
Insurance, real estate and financial services	68.9 (4.0)	71.5 (3.7)	74.6 (4.4)	78.6 (5.3)
Social, community and personal services	93.2 (5.7)	96.8 (3.8)	103.3 (6.7)	134.6 (7.9)
Imputed banking services	−7.5	−7.6	−8.5	−9.8

barrel of Mexico's marker crude from $34.60 to $30.60, effectively undercutting the prices established at an OPEC meeting held on 26 May. Shortly thereafter, however, López Portillo changed his mind about the price reduction. Using as an excuse that Díaz Serrano had failed to consult with the Economic Cabinet, several members – led principally by José Andrés de Oteyza – objected that Mexico's unilateral decision would undercut efforts by OPEC to preserve the market.[43]

In a subsequent meeting Oteyza argued firmly that the price softening was transitory and that Mexico should stand by its OPEC allies to prevent the sort of indiscipline that was bound to worsen situation. Clients demanding price reductions would suffer when the oil price recovered. Other members of the group seemed not to engage the issue, with the exception of Commerce Secretary De la Vega. He observed that Mexico had committed itself to a petroleum

Table 3.2 (continued) Mexico's gross domestic product by major sectors, 1976–83 (in billions of 1970 pesos and annual percentage change)

	1980	*1981*	*1982*	*1983*
Total	841.9 (8.3)	908.8 (7.9)	903.8 (–0.5)	861.8 (–4.7)
Agriculture, forestry, fishing	75.7 (7.1)	80.3 (6.1)	79.8 (−0.6)	82.6 (3.4)
Mining	27.4 (22.3)	31.6 (15.3)	34.5 (9.2)	33.7 (−2.2)
Manufacturing industry	209.7 (7.2)	224.3 (7.0)	217.9 (−2.9)	201.9 (−7.3)
Construction	46.4 (12.3)	51.9 (11.8)	49.3 (−5.0)	42.2 (−14.3)
Electricity	12.6 (6.5)	13.6 (8.4)	14.6 (6.6)	14.7 (1.3)
Commerce, restaurants and hotels	216.1 (8.1)	234.5 (8.5)	230.0 (−1.5)	210.3 (−8.6)
Transport, storage and communications	63.0 (14.1)	69.7 (10.7)	67.1 (−3.8)	64.4 (−4.0)
Insurance, real estate and financial services	82.2 (4.6)	86.1 (4.8)	88.6 (2.9)	90.6 (2.2)
Social, community and personal services	119.8 (7.5)	128.9 (7.7)	134.6 (4.4)	134.5 (−0.1)
Imputed banking services	–11.0	–12.2	–12.5	–13.2

Source: Miguel de la Madrid, *Segundo informe de gobierno; Anexo Sector política financiera* (México: 1985), pp. 629, 33.

policy that required a given level of revenues to finance state sector activity. It made sense to switch from oil quantities to dollar income levels. López Portillo concluded that De la Vega's proposal would tie Mexico too strongly to oil as the motor of development. Instead, the government would cut current spending and would cover income shortfalls with borrowing.[44] Díaz Serrano resigned on 6 June and the marker price was increased by $2, which immediately dampened sales.

In a mid-June address to Congress, Oteyza warned customers that a 'barrel lost by them today, may be lost forever'.[45] Mexicans later marvelled at his prophetic judgement, as PEMEX watched exports virtually halved before finally cutting prices to restore competitiveness.

Thus, the price for a mixture of Maya and Isthmus ended up at $30.70 per barrel, just 10 cents above the price that had ushered in the chaos. Meanwhile, the Mexican government estimated that the lost exports had cost it $1 billion in an episode facetiously called the 'billion dollar dime'.[46]

Six trends converged in the second half of 1981 and the first months of 1982 to produce veritable economic panic:

1. The billion dollar oil price mistake;
2. The government in 1980–81 assumed $15.3 billion in short-term loans, which went almost in its entirety to fund capital flight[47]
3. Government expenditures remained high, and inflation grew to 98.8 per cent by yearend 1982;
4. The crawling-peg adjustment of the exchange rate was inadequate and the peso became overvalued;
5. Dollarisation increased as many became concerned about the government's apparent inability to confront the crisis;
6. Capital flight of unprecedented dimensions appeared. Bankers who had been so eager to loan to Mexico arrived by the planeload to queue up at Treasury for assessments.

In purely contrafactual speculation, the government might have made a stand. In February 1982, recognising the inadequacy of the pesos depreciation, the peso was devalued from 26.5 to 46 (or some 67 per cent) with respect to the dollar. The measure might have restored some confidence if stiff wage and price controls had accompanied it. Instead, in April the government announced wage increases to compensate for the inflationary effects of the devaluation. Observers could rightly conclude that political imperatives now controlled economic policy.

Throughout the summer of 1982 a virtual run on the peso appeared as individuals either sought protection in dollars or actively speculated against the peso. In June Mexico's difficulty in placing a $2.5 billion 'jumbo' loan at acceptable commercial rates signalled the shaken confidence of capital markets. On Thursday 12 August Treasury Secretary Jesús Silva Herzog notified US financial authorities that reserves were virtually depleted. During what came to be called the 'Mexican weekend', a rescue package was negotiated. The shock of the rescue was followed by two successive blows.

To prevent a continued flight from the peso, the Mexican government abandoned free convertibility on 19 August and adopted a complicated system of currency controls. One aspect of this was the freezing of about US$ 11 billion in so-called Mexdollars, or dollar-denominated accounts in Mexican banks. And in his 1 September report on the state of the nation, López Portillo announced the nationalisation of the banks and generalised exchange controls. Though the nationalisation shocked the owners and elements of the business class, the measure met with widespread public support. The currency controls, however, came as a blow to the many thousands who had confided in the long- standing commitment to free convertibility. Alongside the wealthy, workers and small businessmen watched their savings cut in half; and foreign consular officials could offer only sympathy to distraught retirees whose savings had been decimated.

Much of the crisis described here was due to national and international economic and financial trends. But a concluding note on López Portillo as presidential politician is required. The point was best captured by a foreign student of Mexican politics who observed that while Echeverría may have done some pretty wild things, no one ever doubted who was in control. With López Portillo it wasn't clear that anyone was in charge.

The President appeared to concentrate increasingly on foreign policy after 1980.[48] In part, this reflected the worsening problems in Central America and the growing importance of Mexico's involvement in the international economy. But it may also have reflected a diminishing interest and involvement in the details of domestic political management. The crisis that unfolded in 1981–82 seemed to find him increasingly harried and distraught. The apparent loss of personal control in his otherwise masterful 1 September 1982 speech – when he seemed to weep with anger and frustration – contributed further to the deterioration of the image of the presidency, and to a general crisis of confidence.

In the view of many, López Portillo had behaved inappropriately as President. Most Mexicans are generally tolerant of their Presidents, but they expect certain forms to be observed. At times López Portillo appeared too emotional. 'Frivolous' was an adjective frequently heard, though 'cynical' and 'pompous' were occasionally used as well.[49] One transgression should make the point. Nepotism was not unknown before López Portillo, but the President's appointment of his son, 'the pride of my nepotism', as a subsecretary set the example for state governors and other officials. The state of the presidency was painfully reflected when restaurant patrons reportedly barked at López Portillo, mocking his February 1982 pledge to defend the peso 'like a dog'.

In fairness, López Portillo became the scapegoat for much bitterness and frustration. But important lessons were drawn immediately. Some in the political class concluded that López Portillo demonstrated the worst consequences of Echeverría's folly of attempting to preserve power by choosing an inexperienced and untested *técnico*. Some businessmen concluded that the long-standing agreement to leave politics to the PRI no longer worked.

DE LA MADRID: THE POLITICS OF AUSTERITY

Miguel de la Madrid inherited an even worse economic crisis and a more debilitated political system than did López Portillo. The bank nationalisation and currency controls sent shockwaves throughout the middle and upper classes. The old rules of the game had been shattered. As with López Portillo, we might consider first the succession and consolidation and then turn to the strategies of governance. Aspects of programme implementation are considered in the chapters that follow, and the 1987–88 succession is discussed in the conclusion.

Three factors characterised López Portillo's management of the succession. First, he returned to a more orthodox style of guarding his choice, as opposed to Echeverría's theatre of lists. Second, he was regarded as weaker politically than his predecessor, which prompted a premature futurism (*futurismo*) among cabinet members. So evident did the problem become that Interior Secretary Reyes Heroles felt obliged to chide his colleagues in 1977 as did PRI President Gustavo Carvajal in 1979. Third, in contrast to Echeverría's cabinet, where several secretaries appeared qualified, López Portillo's choices seemed scantier. 'The herd looks very skinny', ('La caballada está muy flaca') was the judgement frequently heard.

Among the contenders the *político* Carlos Hank González was constitutionally ineligible for the presidency due to his father's German birth. Another *político*, PRI President Javier García Paniagua, was considered too close to the military due to his father's service as Defence Secretary with Díaz Ordaz. PEMEX director Jorge Díaz Serrano was seen as a private sector candidate with close ties to the US. System loyalist Pedro Ojeda Paullada (Labour) had committed himself to López Portillo early in the Echeverría *sexenio*. Jorge de la Vega (Commerce) was another system loyalist with ties to *echeverristas* and *diazordacistas*. The remaining 'finalists' were *técnicos*: Miguel de la Madrid (SPP) and David Ibarra (Treasury).[50]

Why De la Madrid? A plausible explanation is that the SPP secretary enjoyed the support of those closest to López Portillo, including Rosa Luz Alegría, Ramón López Portillo and José Andrés de Oteyza. It is probable that this group had worked for the ouster of Jorge Díaz Serrano, who appeared in strong contention as late as February 1981. Also, De la Madrid had succeeded in assembling a planning apparatus in SPP, a priority in López Portillo's eyes. Finally, De la Madrid projected an image of competence and moderation, which might reassure business and foreign interests made uneasy by the turbulence unfolding in 1981.

So profound was the discontent with López Portillo that De la Madrid entered office in December 1982 in a virtual power vacuum. No *lopezportillista* or *echeverrista* contingent had to be accommodated. De la Madrid had a free hand in forming his governing team, and – as shown in Table 3.2 – he emphasised personal friends from the finance bureaucracies, Treasury, Bank of Mexico and SPP. This was clearly the most *técnico*-dominated group ever. Two hypotheses, complementary in nature, might account for this emphasis. The new President sought competent personal confidantes, and he felt no obligation to involve politicians from a discredited past order. Also, the finance group might help reassure the business community, much battered by the wave of populism in 1981–82.

Miguel de la Madrid was born on 12 December 1934 in the capital of the west coast state of Colima, where his father, Miguel de la Madrid Castro worked as a lawyer and public notary. The De la Madrid family had been prominent in the region since the 1700s. After the father's death in 1936 the family moved to Mexico City, where the future President attended Cristobal Colón preparatory school and later the UNAM. De la Madrid received his law degree in 1957, with a thesis entitled 'Economic Thought of the 1857 Constitution'. Throughout his youth and career, De la Madrid benefitted from the sponsorship of his maternal uncle, Ernesto Fernández Hurtado, who rose within the Bank of Mexico to become director during the Echeverría government.

As to his explicit statecraft, De la Madrid's complicated 'seven theses' of government might be reduced to two imperatives: economic recovery ('economic realism') and combatting corruption

Table 3.3 The De la Madrid cabinet, December 1982

Interior: Manuel Bartlett Díaz
Foreign Relations: Bernardo Sepúlveda Amor
Defence: Gen. Juan Arévalo Gardoqui
Navy: Adm. Miguel Angel Gómez Ortega
Treasury: Jesús Silva Herzog
Programming and Budget: Carlos Salinas de Gortari
Controller: Francisco José Rojas Gutiérrez
Energy, Mines and Parastatal Industry: Francisco Labastida Ochoa
Commerce and Industrial Development: Hector Hernández Cervantes
Agriculture and Water Resources: Horacio García Aguilar
Communications and Transport: Rodolfo Félix Valdés
Urban Development and Ecology: Marcelo Javelly Girard
Public Education: Jesús Reyes Heroles
Health and Welfare: Guillermo Soberón Aceveda
Agrarian Reform: Luís Martínez Villicana
Tourism: Antonio Enríquez Savignac
Fisheries: Pedro Ojeda Paullada
Federal District: Ramón Aguirre Velázquez
Federal Attorney General: Sergio García Ramírez
Federal District Attorney: Victoria Adato de Ibarra
President's Private Secretary: Emilio Gamboa Patrón
Bank of Mexico: Miguel Mancera Aguayo
CONASUPO: Jose Ernesto Costemalle
NAFINSA: Gustavo Petricioli
PEMEX: Mario Ramón Beteta
SIDERMEX: Miguel Alessio Robles Fernández
National Railroads: Eduardo A. Cota
IMSS: Ricardo García Sainz
CFE: Fernando Hiriart Balderrama

Source: *Excélsior*, 1 December 1982.

('moral renovation of society'). Economic realism required a short-term policy to reduce inflation and correct balance of payments deficits (the Programa Inmediato de Recuperación Económica, or PIRE) and a longer-term effort to restructure the economy to eliminate distortions and prepare for closer integration with the international economy. The tacit programme involved moving away from confrontation with the United States over Central America, and maintaining the party base while controlling organised labour. There was no elaborate calendar for this. The changes would require the whole term, and the government might be considered successful if it set the direction and managed a smooth succession in 1987–88.

The crucial challenge to De la Madrid's statecraft was that both moral renovation and economic realism undermine the existing party–government system. Moral renovation of society implied eradicating the forms of corruption essential to preserve discipline. Greater efficiency requires changes in the public sector, including elimination of some agencies and substantial job lay-offs. The government must cut or eliminate subsidies to the middle and lower classes, such as housing, public education and nutrition programmes. Also, trade and investment liberalisation threatens many of the less efficient industries and associated labour unions that prospered during the long period of import-substitution industrialisation. To the extent liberalisation strengthens the private sector, it promotes centres of power outside the government and beyond Mexico City. Such new centres might in turn be attracted to the opposition PAN. Foreign investment and 'economic realism' antagonise the nationalist left, which excercises influence less through numbers than through its ability to legitimate the present order.

As subsequently implemented, economic realism has fared somewhat better than moral renovation. Though with many delays and detours, the government entered the GATT in August 1986. Even so, the campaign to win back the confidence of investors has fallen short, and capital flight has remained a serious problem. The effort to reduce corruption in the public administration may have produced some improvements at the top and middle levels, but it has failed to impress a sceptical public.

The following chapters analyse trends in institutions and policies, beginning with the federal bureaucracy. Not much can be established about the record of the De la Madrid government until some time after it has passed from office. This President has appeared different in style from his two predecessors. His statecraft by and large has been a defensive coping with a difficult situation, preparing the ground for something still unclear.

4 Federal Bureaucracy and the Administrative Reform Project

Mexicans frequently use the term 'political bureaucracy' (*burocracia política*) to refer to the federal government administration and party bureaucracy that constitute an organic part of the regime that emerged from the Revolution and took form during the late 1930s. The term stands in useful contrast to 'public' or 'civil' because it stresses the close integration of the bureaucracy with the dominant PRI and the myriad activities designed to keep current elites in power. In a highly centralised presidential system marked by the weakness of the national congress and judiciary, the political bureaucracy is arguably the most significant arena of decision-making taken in the sense of both formulating and implementing programmes.

At the institutional level, the presidency dominates Mexican politics. The federal bureaucracy has increased in importance in relation to the PRI as a basic support pillar for the presidency. Symptoms appear, for example, in the gradual 'infiltration' of the PRI apparatus by *técnicos* and in the appointments to President Miguel de la Madrid's cabinet, in which the Treasury–SPP fraternity dominates and only three of his secretaries have held an elective office.[1] More significant is the proliferation of federal programmes and agencies that link groups directly to government, thus bypassing the party. With these trends underway since the 1970s, it would seem that the ascendency of the bureaucracy is fairly well consolidated, although party militants still chafe.

In the broader structural context, this shift in the relative power of the bureaucracy and party stems from the exhaustion of a traditional populist style of politics that emphasised economic and social reforms to benefit the labour and peasant base of the PRI. President Echeverría attempted to revive the populist tradition through increased public sector activity and a variety of initiatives in domestic and foreign policy. Under López Portillo came the effort to create a new form of populism based on state largesse financed by petroleum revenues, managed by *técnicos* and distributed through public agencies.[2] The resulting size and activity of the bureaucracy in turn upset the postwar government–business pact and alienated many businessmen.

With the economic collapse of 1981–82 followed by massive debt and austerity programmes, there is no longer the petroleum option to finance the 'new populism'. Rather De la Madrid apparently sought a path to open the economy towards greater foreign trade and investment. Such an opening requires a new set of agreements with new or different coalitions of domestic and international investors, who will be more involved in the international economy than were the 'nationalist' businessmen of the ISI era. Trade and investment liberalisation also threatens both the traditional PRI constituencies and the recently expanded central government bureaucracy. The latter faces the challenge of reorienting its style from emphasising political support behaviour such as spoils and favouritism to one stressing a more efficient support role for private sector activity.

Simply put, to succeed in its new challenges the federal bureaucracy must become more effective in carrying out complex tasks. Three areas stand out: central coherence in policy development, especially through planning and budgeting processes; decentralisation to break the log-jam in Mexico City and strengthen regional and local governments; and efficiency in directly productive activities. This is especially the case for public enterprises in essential products and services, as for example SIDERMEX (iron and steel), FERTIMEX (fertilisers), PEMEX (petroleum exploration, processing and distribution) and CONASUPO (food purchasing, processing and distribution).

This chapter analyses the recent evolution of the central government bureaucracy in its political setting and assesses the progress of administrative reform with respect to policy coordination, decentralisation and efficiency. As noted in Chapter 3, administrative reform was one of three components in López Portillo's statecraft; it remained important in the De la Madrid presidency, although without the high profile of the previous *sexenio*. Beginning with a brief note on the terminology of Mexican administration, the chapter describes the recent evolution of federal agencies and reviews generalisations about administrative politics and policy-making. Considerable progress has been achieved since 1977 to create the machinery for better policy coordination, but decentralisation and efficiency have proven more difficult to achieve.

MEXICAN BUREAUCRACY: TERMS AND CONCEPTS

As of 1983, the Mexican federal public sector (excluding state and local) consisted of some 1075 agencies employing approximately 3.34 million persons (about 17 per cent of the total workforce) and operating with a budget of some 7662 billion pesos (or about 44 per cent of the GDP).[3] Before analysing the recent evolution of the central bureaucracy and discussing political dynamics, some basic terminology should be introduced.

The large, complex central line agencies are called secretariats (*secretarías*), perhaps to underline the point that they operate as executive instruments of the President; that is, the principals are secretaries not ministers, and while they may be called to testify before congress they serve at the sole pleasure of the President.[4] The most salient political fact is that since 1934 the presidential candidate has been selected from among the secretaries. These individuals hold constitutional status and their required co-signature on presidential decrees constitutes one of the few formal restrictions on presidential power. Secretariats act as delegated instruments of the presidency and as such lack independent legal status and are financed directly from the annual budget process.[5] A contribution of the 1977 reform was to standardise the internal organisation of the secretariats, which hitherto had followed an informal but fairly uniform internal structuring. Figure 4.1 depicts the typical internal structure of a secretariat.

Internal organisation follows common practice, with the major line divisions as subsecretariats. The secretary's staff is usually divided between an office which attends to personal and political duties (the *privado*) and one which acts as the secretary's eyes and ears within the secretariat (the *particular*). General staff activities, such as correspondence, legal counsel and acquisitions, are vested in the subsecretariat for administration (the *oficial mayor*), an office of considerable importance. A secretariat may have separate committees or commissions to oversee specific activities, as for example Interior's Federal Electoral Commission. The coordinator of regional delegations oversees the secretariat's field offices in the 31 states and the Federal District. These field offices, in turn, include the major line divisions. The emphases of the field offices obviously vary according to region. For example, the agriculture secretariat's forestry agency has quite a lot more interest in tropical Chiapas than in arid Sonora, while the irrigation branch's priorities are reversed.

Figure 4.1 Central and field structures of a Federal Secretariat

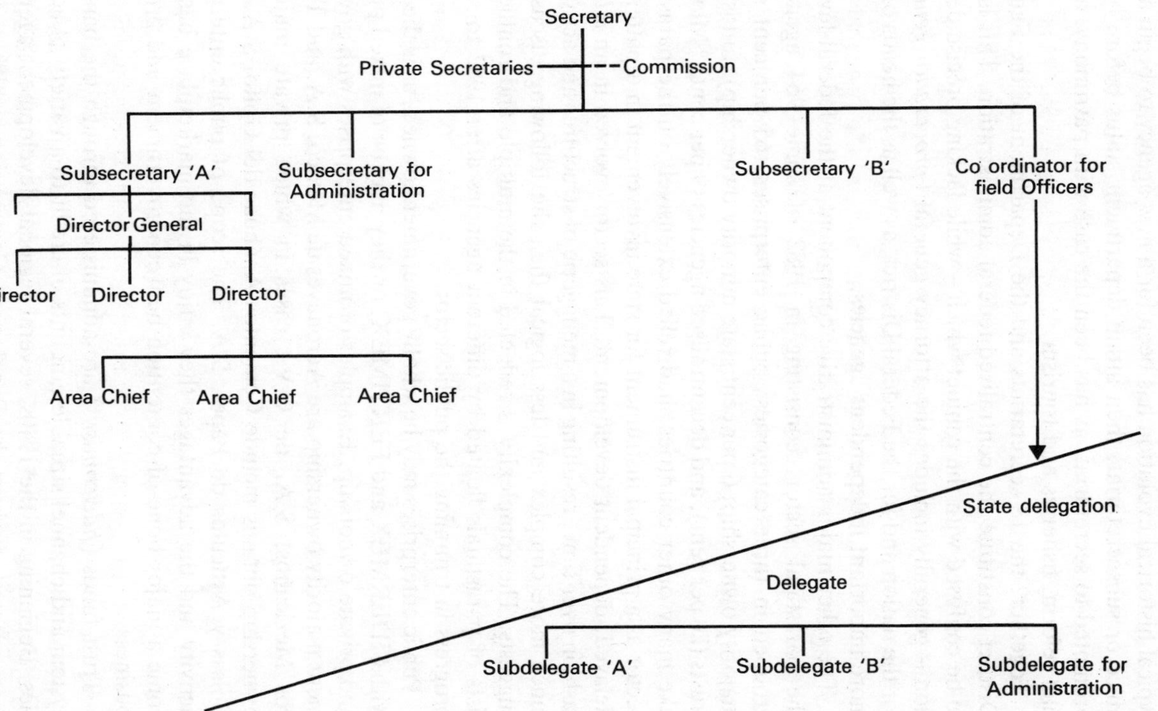

Of slightly lesser administrative status is the department, the only one currently being the Department of the Federal District. The typical historical evolution has been for a new agency to begin as an office or subsecretariat, then attain department status before being promoted to secretariat, as has been the case with patrimony, agrarian reform, fisheries and tourism.

Together, the 18 secretariats and the Department of the Federal District constitute the centralised federal administration. This is not to be confused with the cabinet which – while lacking precise definition – generally includes the attorney general (*procurador general*) for the nation and for the Federal District, as well as the heads of the more important independent agencies.

The other major administrative component at the federal level is the parastatal sector, consisting in 1982 of some 964 agencies, grouped in three categories: public enterprises (65 per cent state majority ownership; 6 per cent state minority ownership), funds and trusts (20 per cent), and decentralised agencies (9 per cent).[6] Mexico, like many other countries, had relied extensively on the parastatal sector as a principal instrument for state involvement in a pattern of delayed, dependent development. This sector evolved in an *ad hoc* fashion over time, resulting in a menagerie of structures and activities much more complex and less logical than the following discussion suggests. The complexity is reflected in the multiple and conflicting lists of parastatals floated by different agencies after 1982 to show progress in trimming the public sector.

Public enterprises may be wholly government owned, as is the case with SIDERMEX and FERTIMEX, or they may be of mixed public and private ownership. Examples of mixed enterprises with government majority ownership are Aeronaves de México, S.A. and Tabacos Mexicanos, S.A. de C.V.; cases in which private majority ownership obtains include Cementos Anáhuac del Golfo, S.A. and Bolsas y Artículos de Papel, S.A. The scope of public enterprise activity and the advantages they enjoy in the marketplace has become a major bone of contention between government and private business.

Trust funds (*fideicomisos*) are administered through the banking system and channel sizeable amounts of credit to a variety of activities. Beginning in the 1940s, several regional development agencies were created, such as the Papaloapan Commission, which evolved into the Bolsas Project in 1960.

Decentralised agencies are not usually engaged in directly productive activity, as are the public enterprises, but rather are created to allow a greater degree of administrative autonomy. Examples include a variety of news and cultural agencies, such as INMEVISION and NOTIMEX.[7] Some agencies enjoy greater real autonomy than others, with the national universities – especially the UNAM – least controlled.[8]

Public enterprises, trust funds and decentralised agencies offer the convenience of organisational forms which can operate somewhat apart from cumbersome central government controls. This sector is enormously complex, with agencies varying in size and importance from small theatres to the vast petroleum development agency. Practice since 1965 has been to concentrate central budgetary control over the most important agencies (28 as of 1984), which together account for about 85 per cent of the parastatal sector's budget, and to employ sectorialisation (described below) to coordinate the sector as a whole.

Federal expenditures and programmes dwarf those of the states and municipalities. Both secretariats and many parastatals maintain field offices, headquartered in the Federal District and the state capitals. As one might imagine, the coordination of the federal field offices among themselves, then with their superiors in Mexico City and finally with state and local agencies is quite complex. There appears to be no designated coordinator of the federal agencies in the field, and much depends on the talents and energies of the various governors and delegates. Coordination and cooperation are obviously crucial to successful decentralisation, and I return to this topic in a later section.

RECENT EVOLUTION OF THE FEDERAL BUREAUCRACY

Rapid expansion of the central bureaucracy is a phenomenon common to populist governments, and was experienced in earlier time periods by Argentina and Brazil. The bureaucracy strengthens government elites in carrying out reform agendas and rewarding chosen clienteles. Mexico is distinctive in the delayed appearance of this phenomenon. Table 4.1 shows the proliferation of units during 1974–84, especially in subsecretariats and general directorates. De la Madrid announced in September 1985 that some 187 administrative units had been cut in comparison with the 1982 level. He also reported the fusion, liquidation or transfer of 482 parastatals from

Table 4.1 Proliferation of Federal Administrative Units, 1974–1984

Unit type	*1974*	*1975*	*1976*	*1977*	*1978*	*1979*	*1980*	*1981*	*1982*	*1983*	*1984*
Secretariats	14	14	16	16	16	16	16	16	17	18	18
Departments	3	3	1	2	2	2	2	2	1	1	1
Attorneys general	2	2	2	2	2	2	2	2	2	2	2
Presidential general coordinators	–	–	–	3	3	5	6	7	7	–	–
Subsecretariats	42	42	42	45	48	48	47	49	51	55	61
Subsecretariats for administration	22	22	22	20	20	20	20	20	20	21	21
General Directorates	381	381	381	485	477	464	447	440	514	457	494
Commissions, councils and others	68	68	68	48	77	79	97	97	101	102	73
Parastatal agencies	–	–	–	898	892	893	903	873	980	952	916

Source: Miguel de la Madrid, *Segundo informe de gobierno; anexo sector política económica* (México: 1985), pp. 849, 53.

the 1155 recorded as of 1982.[9] Critics wonder privately if personnel are really leaving the payroll. The President must have wondered about the political costs of firing thousands of redundant employees in the midst of economic recession.

While one might use formal-legal or technical categories to classify public agencies for purposes of description, I find it useful to analyse the bureaucracy in an eclectic sense as agencies belonging to five functional clusters. As will be obvious, some agencies tend to overlap more than one cluster, and more or fewer clusters might be defined.[10]

The most important clusters from the point of view of system survival are 'central guidance' and 'political control'. The central guidance cluster works out operational strategies for the administrative apparatus as a whole and monitors its progress toward goals that have been chosen through political processes. The key agencies here are Presidency (SP), SPP, and Treasury (SHCP, including the Bank of Mexico). The political control cluster monitors the population at large or specific groups. We might subdivide this cluster into *general* control agencies comprised of Interior (Gobernación), the General Prosecutor's Office (Procuraduría), Defence (SDN), and *specific* control agencies. Three such specific control agencies are Agrarian Reform (SRA, to supervise the *ejidos* and the rural poor), Labour (STPS, to control, or at least to negotiate with, organised labour), and the Controller (SCGF, created in 1982 to monitor the bureaucracy itself).

In addition to central guidance and political control are 'economic development' and 'social welfare'. The development cluster includes such bureaucratic empires as Commerce and Industrial Development (SECOFIN, which oversees, among many other parastatals, CONASUPO, the agency that provides basic staples at subsidised prices to lower income groups) and Energy, Mines and Parastatal Industry (SEMIP, which putatively oversees PEMEX, among others). Also large and significant is the Secretariat of Agriculture and Water Resources (SARH, which is oriented more toward commercial agriculture as opposed to the *ejidos*). It also includes smaller-scale secretariats, such as Fisheries (SEPESCA) and Tourism (SECTUR). Social welfare includes Public Health (SSA), Education (SEP), the two main social security institutes (IMSS and ISSSTE) and agencies such as COPLAMAR, which is oriented towards rural problems.

The final cluster is 'foreign relations'. The Secretariat of Foreign Relations (SRE) should be paramount, but with the financial crisis and trade difficulties superceding interest in Central America, Treasury and

Table 4.2 Evolution of bureaucratic clusters, 1958–84

Central Guidance	*Control*	*Economic development*
I. Basic Configuration, 1958–77		
*Presidency	Interior	Industry & Commerce
Treasury	Defence	Agriculture & Livestock
(Bank of Mexico)	Prosecutor	Water Resources
	Labour	*National Patrimony
	*Agrarian	*Public Works
	Reform	Communications & Transport
		*Tourism (1974)
II. *López Portillo: Administrative Reform, 1977–82*		
Presidency	Interior	*Patrimony & Industrial Dev.
Treasury	Defence	*Agric. & Water Resources
*Programming &	Prosecutor	*Human Settlements & Public Works
Budget	Labour	*Commerce
	Agrarian	Communications & Transport
	Reform	Tourism
		*Fisheries (Department)
III. *De la Madrid: Administrative Reform, 1983–85*		
Presidency	Interior	*Commerce & Industrial Dev.
Treasury	Defence	*Ecology & Urban Dev.
Programming &	Prosecutor	*Energy, Mines & Parastatal Industry
Budget	Labour	Communications & Transport
	Agrarian	Tourism
	Reform	Agric. & Water Resources
	*Controller	*Fisheries (Secretariat)

* Indicates new or substantially altered agency

SECOFIN have assumed greater importance. Other agencies belong as well. The Navy Secretariat (Secretaría de la Marina) is charged with coastal and riparian defence, which implies a number of international duties. To some extent SDN fits here, as does Interior, with its jurisdiction over media, immigration and political refugees, as well as a few specialised financial and commercial agencies. As the policy of economic opening advances, one would expect agencies such as SECOFIN, SEMIP and SARH to adapt themselves by adding units and/or adjusting existing ones.

The last comprehensive reorganisation of the federal secretariats before 1977 came with the administrative reform of 1958, formulated by the Ruiz Cortines government but implemented at the outset of the administration of Adolfo López Mateos (1958–64). Noteworthy changes were introduced in the intervening years in piecemeal fashion. For example, Agrarian Reform was promoted from depart-

Table 4.2 (continued) Evolution of bureaucratic clusters, 1958–85

Social Welfare		*Foreign Relations*
I. *Basic Configuration, 1958–77*		
Health & Social Assistance	IMSS	Foreign Relations
	ISSSTE	Navy
Public Education	*PIDER	IMCE
	*INFONAVIT	
	CONASUPO	
	*COPLAMAR	
II. *López Portillo: Administrative Reform, 1977–82*		
Health & Social Assistance	IMSS	Foreign Relations
	ISSSTE	Navy
Public Education	PIDER	IMCE
	INFONAVIT	
	CONASUPO	
	COPLAMAR	
	*SAM	
III. *De la Madrid: Administrative Reform, 1982–85*		
Health & Social Assistance	IMSS	Foreign Relations
	ISSSTE	Navy
Public Education	PIDER	
	INFONAVIT	
	CONASUPO	

* Indicates new or substantially altered agency

ment to secretariat status, a large number of parastatals were created and administrative study units were introduced at the subsecretary level. But the basic configuration remained intact until 1977, when President López Portillo introduced the comprehensive administrative reform. According to Moreno Rodríguez the reform meant the transfer of 59 administrative units, the relocation of 79 000 positions, the *regularización* (tenuring) of 3169 workers, and the reassignment of 29 billion pesos, or a bit more than ten per cent of current expenditures.[11] I shall only sketch here the most significant changes in the secretariats and the principal parastatals.[12] Table 4.2 summarises the trends.

Beginning with the guidance cluster, the 1958 reforms introduced SP and raised the Department of National Patrimony (SEPANAL) to secretariat level. SP was essentially the logical next step in institutionalising the modern presidency, a process underway since the 1930s.[13] Besides housing the routine sorts of staff activities necessary for a complex office, for example, legal counsel, scheduling and correspondence, the new agency was to introduce central planning. This did not succeed, however, due to opposition from the private sector and from other secretariats. Given López Mateos' progressive rhetoric of the day, the private sector feared too much extensive and direct government involvement in the economy, which might result in public enterprises competing with private companies as well as in too much government regulation. The other secretaries feared the creation of a superagency which might intervene in their jurisdictions, and whose principal might enjoy a head start in the succession race.

SP also took the lead in carrying out administrative studies which laid the foundations for the comprehensive administrative reform of 1977. Although there was an attempt to reduce its policy involvement with the creation of SPP, Presidency retained the legal basis to carry out studies and to coordinate programmes in priority areas. In fact, renewed involvement of Presidency in policy-making activity emerged during the López Portillo administration. This direct involvement appeared to subside a bit under De la Madrid, who introduced a system of technical cabinets.

After Presidency, the most significant guidance agency was Treasury, which over the years had consolidated control over fiscal and monetary policy, as well as aspects of commercial policy. Treasury also had developed the most impressive of the career services based in the Bank of Mexico.[14] Though powerful, Treasury appeared not to threaten private sector interests, because of its pro-business leadership. Also, since the Treasury secretary in the 1952–70 period enjoyed the complete confidence of the presidents, the other secretaries had to tolerate a concentration of power in that agency.

SEPANAL was promoted in status in order to better carry out its duties of overseeing national properties, especially as this concerned supervising the growing parastatal sector. In theory, SEPANAL, Presidency and Treasury were to form what López Portillo and others liked to call a 'triangle of efficiency'.[15] Presidency was to formulate plans, Treasury was to stress the financial aspects of implementation and SEPANAL was to oversee implementation and evaluate the results. The agencies were to cooperate closely at all points in the cycle. Presidency's problem with introducing planning and the competition among the agencies to out-do each other in controlling other agencies prevented the successful realisation of the 'triangle' concept.[16] Nevertheless, important progress in coordination was achieved at the working level. That is, by the early 1970s general directors from the three agencies came to constitute an effective working group (*subcomisión*, which included De la Madrid from Treasury) on public expenditure. Thus, as the Echeverría administration was projecting government much more extensively into the economy, a coordination mechanism was taking shape.

The most significant change in the central guidance cluster came with the creation of the SPP as the centrepiece of the 1977 administrative reform. The principal components of the reform were reorganisation of the line secretariats, the 'sectorialisation' of more than 900 parastatals under the tutelage of 17 line secretariats designated as sector heads, and the introduction of programme budgeting throughout the federal government.[17] SPP was to replace the triangle of efficiency with a straight-line concept. The functions of planning, budgeting and evaluation were to be constituted as subsecretariats within SPP. Organisationally, the planning unit was drawn primarily from Presidency (with some personnel from SEPANAL), budgeting was transferred virtually intact from Treasury and evaluation was newly created, but with a statistics unit from Commerce. The straight-line logic called for programming to take the lead in formulating a five-year plan; budget and evaluation would cooperate in deriving a one-year operational programme from the five-year plan; programme and budget would oversee implementation, and evaluation would then assess results. The process would be continuous and self- adjusting.

SPP did not work out as intended during the López Portillo period. Quite apart from the enormous technical difficulties in implementing programme budgeting on a government-wide basis (one need only recall the failure of a less ambitious version of programme budgeting in the United States during 1965–68, or even the short-lived 'zero base' episode of 1977–80), conflict between SPP and Treasury prevented the formation of a plan at the outset. Not until April 1980 was the third secretary of SPP, Miguel de la Madrid, able to produce the Global Plan for 1980–82. Then, with the budget cuts necessitated by the oil price collapse of mid-1981, the SPP apparatus was diverted from medium-term programming to short-term coping. When De la Madrid won the presidential nomination, he left as SPP secretary Ramón Aguirre, formerly undersecretary of budgeting. Aguirre, in turn, restructured SPP to magnify the importance of budgeting, as opposed to planning, as the primary coordinating mechanism. Four general directorates were created in the budget subsecretariat, each to integrate several sectors along major programme lines, for example, agriculture and fishing, energy and industry.[18] This new arrangement continued after 1982. The likely implication is that budgeting, with some aspects of its traditional Treasury orientation, has displaced planning as the primary function of SPP, and that policy coordination has improved as a result.[19] The profound financial crisis has shifted SPP's role from development planner to budget cutter.

The political control cluster evolved in fairly stable fashion during 1958–86. Noteworthy exceptions are the promotion of the Department of Agrarian Reform to secretariat status in 1974 and the creation of the Secretariat of the Controller in 1982. Also, problems of various types culminated in a significant reorganisation of Interior in 1985–86. Most serious of these was the apparent involvement of elements of the Federal Security Directorate in drug trafficking. In response the Federal Security Police was purged in mid-1985 and integrated with the more professional Political Studies Directorate. Pedro Vásquez Colmenares was called from his post as governor of Oaxaca to assume control of the new subsecretariat.

The 'agrarian problem', to use shorthand, has grown in importance since the late 1960s. To give only a simplistic notion, the rural sector contributes the core voting support for the PRI, and an agency is required to manage the *ejidos* in the sense of providing assistance and advice, to process literally thousands of land claims, to grant titles of immunity to certain farmers and ranchers and to decide the hundreds of disputes that grow up among *ejidatarios* and between them and independent farmers. It is, in short, a complicated and constant set of problems, and SRA depends on its delegates in the several states to prevent problems from reaching national attention.

Revitalising agriculture was a priority of the Echeverría government. SRA was to contribute to this effort by organising the *ejidos* on a cooperative basis, as opposed to individual plots, and in carrying out title certification programmes. These programmes could be implemented more effectively by a line secretariat. Although it enjoyed a brief renaissance of status under Echeverría, SRA is widely regarded as one of the least efficient agencies in the Mexican public sector. (One study found that some 33 steps were required to deliver land with title to peasants, a process requiring on average some 15 years.)[20] But the complications and delays help to subordinate the peasantry, and inefficient programme administration is really more effective in political manipulation. Control gained in this way, however, carries a high cost in production lost by heightened uncertainty.

Thus, the De la Madrid government has made land title certification its priority in the agrarian reform field. Here we see the contradiction in which a reform useful for economic production undercuts traditional forms of PRI–government strength.[21]

SGCF was created by President De la Madrid in 1982 as a weapon in his campaign of moral renovation and the battle against corruption, which had reached extraordinary proportions under López Portillo. With the passage of tougher legislation against administrative malfeasance, the new government wanted an independent agency to oversee the activities of public employees. In this respect, for example, SGCF required detailed financial statements from higher-level appointees. The creation of the Controller suggests that the Procuraduría had failed to control administrative malfeasance and that SPP had not succeeded in its task of coordinating the central audit and preparing the annual budget account. Nor had the Controller's Office of the Federation, established in the Congress in 1977 as part of the political reform, proven effective in preventing corruption.[22] The real meaning of the new agency is that the presidential system seeks additional bureaucratic mechanisms to solve problems, rather than allowing more effective checks as in a stronger Congress, more independent PRI, real electoral competition or greater freedom of criticism.

Based solely on impression, my sense is that SGCF succeeded in striking fear in the hearts of middle-level functionaries but without reaching the bottom levels. In some respects SGCF has hampered efficiency and effectiveness by complicating routine decision-making, for example about acquisitions, or those operations that require speed and flexibility.[23] On the other hand, the new agency paid temporary dividends in creating the image of action against corruption.

While the political control cluster evolved incrementally, there was considerably more organisational shuffling in the development cluster. Here two subsets are noteworthy: Patrimony, Commerce and Industry on the one hand, and Agriculture and Water Resources on the other.

In the 1958 configuration SEPANAL was charged with overseeing the uses of national resources, as set out in Article 27 of the Constitution. It did this somewhat indirectly by setting policy and overseeing activities of the parastatal enterprises. SEPANAL also made important advances in sectorial planning, especially during the tenure of Horacio Flores de la Peña in the early 1970s. Industry and Commerce was charged with promoting industrial development and collecting data for use for commercial activities. In the 1977 reform Patrimony was fused with Industrial Development to form SEPAFIN, and Commerce was split off and given substantially more authority over the promotion and regulation of commerce, such as authority to set price controls on a broad range of items and to issue import licences. The fusion of Patrimony with Industrial Development implied that the more statist and nationalist orientation of SEPANAL would shape industrial development, and such was the case under José Andrés de Oteyza during 1977–82. The restructuring of patrimony in 1982 in the new Secretariat of Energy, Mines, and Parastatal Industry (SEMIP) may indicate that the nationalist and statist orientation has been somewhat narrowed to the energy and basic industries sector. At the same time, the rejoining of Industry with Commerce in SECOFIN, but now with industry getting 'second billing', may imply that industrial development will be more closely coordinated with commerce and thus the US and global economies.

Agriculture has been an area of growing concern since at least 1970, when for the first time in many years Mexico imported food in significant volume. Food self-sufficiency was a top priority of the López Portillo government, as it remained in a less comprehensive way for that of De la Madrid. As a step towards self-sufficiency, the 1977 administrative reform sought to rejoin water use with agricultural production; thus, the secretariats of Agriculture and Livestock and Water Resources were combined in SARH, as they had been during the early 1940s. The remarriage was neither particularly happy nor successful, in part because Water Resources was a well integrated agency in which the engineering profession dominated and which served a powerful clientele – agri-business in the irrigated zones, especially in the north and northwest – while agriculture was a heterogeneous agency in which diverse professions carved out fiefdoms serving specific clienteles: cattle, crops, forestry. The turf struggles and assorted start-up delays so hampered López Portillo's efforts to launch an integrated food programme that Presidency assumed oversight of agricultural policy in 1980. The fact that Agriculture Secretary Horacio García Aguilar was the first to leave the De la Madrid cabinet in July 1984 suggested continuing problems. His successor, Eduardo Pesqueira, had belonged to De la Madrid's inner circle in SPP, which indicated stronger leadership at SARH.

Of perhaps less consequence in the development cluster was the separation of Public Works from Communications and Transportation in 1958. Subsequently, Human Settlements was joined with Public Works to recognise the importance of urban infrastructure development in the range of public works activities. The subsequent mutation to Ecology and Urban Development (SEDUE) in 1982 is yet another indication of the emphasis on urban development as well as greater attention to the ecological crisis. The earthquakes of September 1985 put SEDUE to the test, which many concluded it failed. The second secretary to head the agency under De la Madrid was forced from office in February 1986.

The welfare cluster evolved largely intact after 1958, and remained relatively untouched by the 1977 reform. INFONAVIT was created to provide housing for unionised workers. PIDER and COPLAMAR were established to direct resources to the poorest rural areas. The Mexican Food System (SAM) extended the scope of these programmes under López Portillo. Changes also came with the enormous expansion of operations in both health and education, beginning with Echeverría and continuing with López Portillo. SEP absorbed some aspects of primary and secondary teaching, which previously had been under state and local jurisdiction. Similarly, health care was expanded throughout the 1970s to keep pace with population growth, and extensive new sectors of the population were brought under social security coverage. Under De la Madrid, efforts to decentralise have focused largely on these two programme areas. De la Madrid also cut back in the welfare cluster, axing SAM and merging COPLAMAR's programmes with SPP.

With this introduction to the scope and complexity of the federal bureaucracy, we can turn to a brief consideration of some informal dynamics.

ADMINISTRATIVE POLITICS AND POLICY-MAKING

The highly centralised presidential system implies that careers are made and values allocated in Mexico City by bureaucrats. Further, the absence of a general career service should be emphasised, although I have noted islands of professionalism in Treasury, the armed forces, and SRE. Mexico is hardly remarkable in this sense, in that to my knowledge there is no *general* career service in any Latin American country. But its absence has important consequences for structural and procedural aspects of decision-making.[24] The De la Madrid government undertook studies to prepare for some kind of general service, but the reform apparently languished. Given the significance of patronage in holding the PRI–government system together, a truly inclusive civil service would transform present arrangements. Once again, greater efficiency would erode presidentialism.

Lacking a career service, with guarantees of job tenure, promotion according to merit and stable hierarchies, the importance of personal loyalties and patron–client ties within the political bureaucracy increases, as does overall presidential control. In administrative policy-making, we therefore begin with the significance of personal loyalties and the interaction of teams. Grindle has shown how informal exchange networks develop among Mexican administrators because they provide support, career mobility and improved communications. Such networks unite individuals within one agency against encroachments by another. They also provide linkages among federal agencies, across different levels of government and between bureaucratic and political chiefs.

The environmental conditions that structure career mobility are important to understanding administrative politics and policy-making. Among these conditions, Grindle stresses personal confidence, the formation of administrative teams that span different backgrounds and skills, and the cycle of the *sexenio*.[25]

Administrative–political teams (*equipos* or *camarillas*) are therefore central to policy-making.[26] The first commitment of team members is loyalty to the leader, someone often at the level of secretary, subsecretary or general director, though not necessarily in the same agency. Teams cross government branches to include legislatures and courts, and link secretariats with parastatal agencies, state, and local governments and extend beyond government. Networks of teams enhance agency responsiveness to presidential leadership, since the President controls career mobility during his *sexenio* as well as after, by designating his own successor. Depending on presidential cues, teams and loyalty may weaken agency responsiveness to clienteles, although this varies from one agency to another and also according to the level of office within the agency. With the rise of the *técnicos*, team-building stresses career training and bureaucratic experience. Significant teams in the De la Madrid government included those of Carlos Salinas de Gortari (SPP), Ramón Aguirre (D.F.), Alejandro Carrillo (ISSSTE), Guillermo Soberón (SSA), and Alfredo del Mazo (SEMIP).[27] But regardless of team strength, these men wielded only the power the President permitted.

Networks of teams perform various linkage and integrative functions and can enhance administrative responsiveness to presidential control. But they incur important costs as well. As a practical matter, prominent administrators and politicians are forced to 'warehouse' considerable talent to ensure that capable and loyal personnel can accompany them from one post to another. Thus, in situations where skills may be scarce generally, talent may be misallocated through a kind of 'team redundancy' phenomenon. Furthermore, loyalty typically is valued over skill. Also, the fluidity, and thus insecurity, of team circulation implies that considerable time must be invested in information gathering and turf-guarding.[28] And insecurity clearly contributes to corruption. Finally, the personnel movement implicit in these arrangements aggravates policy discontinuity. Too often individuals lack the time needed to *learn* their jobs, much less make useful contributions. This might be tolerable if government's direct role in society were marginal and most administrative skills rudimentary, as was more the case in Mexico prior to the 1970s. But the rise of active government and the adoption of sophisticated planning procedures require a broader merit system.

During the 1950s and 1960s, the apex of Mexican bureaucratic elite, the cabinet secretaries, was marked by relative stability in the Latin American context. This has continued into the 1970s and 1980s. Of the major Latin American countries, Colombia and Argentina are found at the high end of turnover rates, with Brazil and Mexico near the bottom.[29] This is not the place to discuss at length what constitutes optimum turnover rates, but clearly at some point high turnover impedes effective policy-making. With regard to Mexico, Godau has shown that changes at the top of the agency reverberate quite far downward; that is, when the secretary leaves, most of the team follow.[30]

Table 4.3 provides data on agencies from four clusters for the period 1977–83: guidance (Presidency, SPP), political control (Interior and Defence), development (SARH) and foreign relations (SRE). The figures reflect the levels of turnover of personnel in several senses. Basically, the higher the number, the higher the turnover rates.[31] Column 1 reports the number of secretaries during 1977–81; Column 2 shows the turnover rate for all significant positions in the agency, that is, secretary, subsecretary, division heads, directors general and – in some cases – directors; Column 3 reflects the turnover only for those above the director general level; Column 4 reports personnel change during 1979, when the secretaries of

Table 4.3 Personnel turnover rates in selected Mexican Federal Agencies, 1977–81, 1983

Cluster/Agency	1 *Secretaries 1977–81*	2 *Turnover all positions*	3 *Turnover top positions*	4 *Turnover during 1979*	5 *Turnover into new government*
Guidance					
Presidency		6(8/126)		19(4/21)	95(18/19)
Budget (SPP)	3	21(26/124)	26(9/35)	58(14/24)	93(37/40)
Control					
Interior	2	28(28/100)	33(8/24)	50(10/20)	90(26/29)
Defence	1	25(33/133)	20(3/15)	24(6/25)	64(18/28)
Development					
Agriculture (SARH)	1	10(23/226)	14(6/44)	15(6/41)	86(49/57)
Foreign Relations					
Foreign Relations	2	16(18/115)	10(3/29)	45(9/20)	79(27/34)

Source: México, Presidencia, Coordinación General de Estudios Administrativos, *Directorio de la Administración Pública Centralizada y Paraestatal, 1977–81, 1983*

Interior, SRE and SPP were replaced. Finally, Column 5 shows the rates of carryover of personnel into the De la Madrid government.

The findings (Column 2) indicate that during the first five years of the López Portillo government, Presidency was the most stable agency (6) and Interior the least stable (28). SARH shows relative stability (10), which we might expect of a technical agency, as does Foreign Relations (16), one of the few career services. Two cases that require some explanation are SPP (21) and Defence (25). With regard to the former, the high turnover rate reflects the difficult start-up challenges of generating a national plan and assembling a team to implement it. The rate for Defence is somewhat inflated in that a number of changes are the same individuals shifting among positions within the agency.

Patterns become clearer when we restrict the focus to top positions (Column 3). SPP and Interior show higher turnover rates (26 and 33 respectively), while the more professional agencies, Defence and SRE, show lower rates (20 and 10 respectively). The rate in agriculture (14) is only slightly higher than its five-year average.

As shown in Column 4, 1979 is an interesting year. With a change in secretary, SPP jumps 37 points over its average, while the comparative figures for Interior and Foreign Relations are 22 and 29 respectively. In short, a change in secretary carries with it high rates of turnover at lower levels. But 1979 was abnormal for Presidency and SARH as well, with the former some 13 points and the latter about 5 points over the five-year averages. Defence stays close to its normal pace. We cannot infer too much from limited data, but plausible hypotheses to account for the patterns in Presidency and SARH are personnel adjustments needed to prepare for the mid-term election of July 1979 and the normal degrees of personnel juggling. The data also suggest that Defence is largely isolated from the mid-term effect.

Having observed the high turnover rates in some cases, we should note key subsecretaries whose tenure provides a degree of continuity. With respect to Interior, such a figure was Fernando Gutiérrez Barrios, who entered the agency as a young army captain in 1950 and stayed until December 1982.[32] In SRE comparable personages were Alfonso de Rosenzweig Díaz, who served as subsecretary throughout the López Portillo period and carried over into the De la Madrid government, and Jorge Eduardo Navarrette, who began as subsecretary for economic affairs with Jorge Castañeda in 1979 and continued into the new government in 1982. There appears to be no comparable continuity in SPP.

With regard to policy-making and the cycle of the *sexenio*, a 'normal' pattern is for the last two years to be concerned with the succession, with bureaucratic teams preoccupied with their own career prospects and with completing projects already underway. Thus, there is considerable structural disjuncture in policy-making at the ends and beginnings of *sexenios*. Administrations since Díaz Ordaz have exaggerated this disjuncture. Echeverría encountered a recession in 1970–71 and left office in 1976 in the midst of serious economic disorder and political tension; López Portillo began with an IMF austerity programme in 1977–78 and left office in financial crisis and with another IMF programme.

Conventional wisdom is supported when we examine the degree of continuity into the De la Madrid government (Column 5). Turnover rates are high in the 'political' agencies (Presidency – 95; Interior – 90) and relatively lower in the career services (Defence – 64; SRE – 79). SPP remains unexpectedly high (93), reflecting perhaps a continuing flux in policy and operations; also, SPP was the source of several high-level appointments in the De la Madrid cabinet. SARH also shows high turnover (86) for an agency with complex technical missions.[33]

Table 4.4 Proliferation of policy-relevant positions in selected Mexican Federal Agencies, 1977–1981, 1983

Cluster/Agency	*1977*	*1978*	*1979*	*1980*	*1981*	*% change 1977,81*	*1983*
Guidance							
Presidency	23	31	36	36	50	+117	22
Budget (SPP)	30	30	31	31	36	+ 20	47
Finance (SHCP)	37	38	43	40	39	+ 5	42
Political control							
Interior	20	25	26	25	28	+40	38
Defence	28	29	29	29	33	+18	33
Agrarian Reform	54	70	105	113	92	+70	88
Labour	30	21	22	22	33	+10	33
Controller							20
Development							
Agriculture (SARH)	43	62	62	61	65	+51	64
Settlements & Public Works	48	48	48	49	50	+ 4	47*
Welfare							
Health & Welfare	34	51	50	50	49	+44	41
Education	64	53	55	55	59	− 8	64
Foreign Relations							
Foreign Relations	27	34	31	32	37	+37	40

* Changed to Ecology and Urban Development, December 1982

Source: As Table 4.3

Table 4.4, which shows the number of positions listed in the *Directorio de la administración pública federal* for 1977–81, reflects some aspects of bureaucratic evolution within the *sexenio*. Interesting here is the recentralisation of personnel and programmes in Presidency. Beginning in 1977 with the appointment of Julio R. Moctezuma as director of special development programmes, and continuing with the appointments of Casio Luiselli as head of SAM and Francisco Cano Escalante as coordinator for staple products, Presidency took charge of priority programmes. Looking at positions under President de la Madrid, it would appear that Presidency contracted to its 1977 level and that SPP assumed direction of the priority programmes. Most likely, the rapid growth of Presidency during the López Portillo *sexenio* reflects that President's impatience with the slow start-up of the reorganised administration.

In line with our expectations, growth characterises the other agencies shown in Table 4.4, with the exception of Education. The rapid jump in the number of positions in SRA in 1979 is due mostly to the inclusion of the state delegates in the *Directorio* for the first time. Though it might be coincidence, Treasury grew with De la Madrid as subsecretary (1977–79), while SPP began to prosper during his tenure there as secretary (1979–81). The pattern for Interior, SRA, SARH, SRE and SSA seems to be one of start-up delay in getting people into position and their names entered into the *Directorio*, which accounts for the jump in numbers between 1977–78. Defence and Public Works, and Treasury to a lesser degree, show more gradual growth.

With some attention to teams and the policy cycle, we can consider an aspect of administration and policy-making. The absence of a career service increases agency responsiveness to presidential leadership and may reduce or increase clientele influence depending upon presidential preference. Nevertheless, there are elements that argue for some degree of agency independence and clientele influence. At a global level, dependent capitalist development itself heightens state attention to business elites, especially in the post-1981 financial crisis. At the agency level, the image is more complicated. Spalding qualifies notions of state autonomy and presidential omnipotence and points up the existence of bureaucratic enclaves not fully penetrated by the presidency. Greenberg and Benveniste have emphasised the importance of professions in influencing policy-making.[34] In a similar vein, Purcell and Purcell found that they could characterise patterns of agency orientation to some extent, but they concluded that 'the most significant element to an observer of political decision making is not that so many ministries have consistent policy positions but rather that so few do'.[35] Perhaps patterns can be found if we reconsider presidential control, agency autonomy, and clientele influence in terms of functional clusters. Because responsiveness cannot be measured, I must speculate. Also, some factors influence all the clusters.

It is important to remember that the *sexenio* obeys a rhythm such that the first 18 months or so are usually taken up with staffing agencies and initiating routines. From the latter part of the second year until the beginning of the fifth attention shifts to programme implementation. During this time as well, presidential influence peaks and greatest control over agencies is exercised. In the last quarter of the fifth year the successor is chosen, and from this point until the inauguration the incumbent's influence wanes. This is not to imply a weak or docile President by any means, as both Echeverría and López Portillo showed. Rather it means that many bureaucrats begin to couch their behaviour in terms of their expectations about the succession.

Apart from cycles, bureaucratic complexity itself resists control in virtually any system. More layers of offices obviously reduce the effectiveness of overhead control. It follows that agencies with large field services, such as IMSS, SARH or CONASUPO enjoy greater autonomy. Similarly, the complexity of the task conditions control, with programmes of agrarian reform more comprehensible than, say, those of PEMEX or CONASUPO.

With cycle and complexity held constant the agencies most responsive to presidential control are probably those of central guidance, political control and foreign relations. My reasoning is that in comparative terms one finds a relatively high consensus on agency goals; the agencies are small; professional services count in SHCP, SDN and SRE, and – with the pronounced exception of STPS – clienteles are either weak, illegal or nonexistent. A caveat here is the problem of corruption that plagues many agencies, but especially the police. Their clients may be illegal, but they often have money. Still, without the professional commitment of a general career service, corruption forms a bond of loyalty to the presidential system.

More difficult to control are agencies of the development cluster. This is because there is greater internal conflict over agency goals, with ideological and programmatic differences within and among a greater number of groups and professions. Also, clienteles, especially the producer associations, are well organised and active. Finally, with the exceptions of SECTUR and SEPESCA, the agencies in this cluster are comparatively larger and more complex, and several – SARH and SEMIP, for example – operate large field services or wrestle with large parastatals.

Possibly least responsive to presidential control are the agencies of the welfare cluster. They are staffed by strong unions and professional guilds (teachers and medical doctors among them), and they are enormously complex with extensive field services. By and large, the clienteles they serve are only weakly organised.[36]

Presidentialism tells us much about the structure and behaviour of the federal bureaucracy. Those aspects of administrative reform consistent with presidentialism, for example, reorganisation, sectorialisation, improved policy coordination, have advanced. Other reforms, such as a professional civil service and independent Controller, have not. As we turn to decentralisation and parastatal efficiency, we see again how presidentialism shapes the reform efforts.

THE QUEST FOR DECENTRALISATION

At least from the time of La Reforma of the 1850s to the 1860s, decentralisation has stood for progress. It continues as a constant stated goal in the post-Revolutionary rhetoric. The dynamic since 1929, however, has been to concentrate power to create order and promote development. A perverse cycle has seen the central government distrustful of the loyalty and competence of state and local governments, and these have developed accordingly: underfunded and largely incompetent. In fairness, it should be stressed that central government often had good reason to doubt the probity and capacity of local officials; and it would be a grave error to expect civic virtues to flower if only the central government would decentralise. Nevertheless, some formula for decentralisation is needed to show progress toward ideological goals and to break the administrative log-jam of recent years.

Mexican administrators distinguish between decentralisation (*descentralización*) and deconcentration (*desconcentración*), with the former understood as the devolution of decision-making *and* implementation functions both to federal field offices as well as regional, state and local bodies, while the latter implies that decision power remains in Mexico City but lower bodies have greater independence in policy implementation. Much emphasis has been placed on both meanings since at least the latter 1950s, but with scant results.

López Portillo brought a renewed commitment to decentralisation in his administrative reform. The main instruments were multipurpose grants extended to state government: the single Coordination Agreement (Convenio Unico de Coordinación, or CUC); and the Integrated Rural Development Programme (Programa Integral de Desarrollo Rural, or PIDER). State and local governments and local groups were involved more fully in complex planning arrangements with the federal government. Also, a limited form of revenue sharing, introduced during the Echeverría administration, was continued. In addition, state governors were strengthened somewhat in their dealings with federal agencies in their states. Graham concluded that 'when examined in content and impact, however, these [instruments] are classic examples of the strategy of decentralizing to centralize more effectively'.[37]

> By 1979 there could be little doubt as to how intergovernmental relations operated. The central government had moved in the direction of promoting coordinated administrative action in development programs at the regional level and was working within existing political demarcations. But which programs were to be funded and how they were to be executed followed the preferences of central authorities. Since they were subject to the changing priorities of those in the capital, one year's program might well not be funded the next and no realistic projections could possibly be made beyond the current *sexenio*.
>
> All over Mexico municipalities are today more than ever administrative dependencies of state government. They are autonomous and self-governing entities only in a formalistic sense, in that their officials are elected on separate slates.[38]

President De la Madrid has continued the quest by emphasising regional programmes, the revitalisation of municipal government and the decentralisation of health and education. The regional programmes most prominently mentioned include the southeast (Chiapas, with its special problems along the border with Guatemala, and Tabasco), Colima and border development zones along the US.[39] With regard to the municipalities, the principal efforts appear to be a strengthening of their juridical status, as seen in constitutional reforms at federal and state levels designed to cede greater financial autonomy. But the recession and economic austerity programme limit new investments the government might make to encourage economic decentralisation.[40]

Two observers of the decentralisation effort suggest that in essence the De la Madrid administration has constructed two separate, and not necessarily parallel, systems of decentralisation. One is channeled through SPP to the state planning apparatus and would appear to involve the federal agencies in their normal administrative functions. The other operates through Interior and appears more politically oriented with the goal of providing state and municipalities with some independence from central financial control. Precisely how these processes operate they cannot determine. 'What is evident is that the structures for decentralization are complex and cumbersome.'[41]

With regard to federal programmes, decentralisation of education obeyed both political and administrative logics. On the political side, arguably the most powerful single organisation in the PRI's popular sector is the National Educational Workers Union (SNTE), which claims some 800 000 members nationwide. By splitting SNTE into 32 state unions, the government might better isolate and control local and regional disputes, thus reducing the disruptive effects of specific issues on national politics. Also, the centralised administration of the educational system was creating increasing dissatisfaction among the rank and file teachers. De la Madrid's appointment of Jesús Reyes Heroles as Secretary of Education pitted an astute decentraliser against an equally canny centraliser, SNTE boss Carlos Jonguitud Barrios. Reyes Heroles' death in February 1985 and the administration's drift into the second half of the *sexenio* apparently halted decentralisation in education.

In health care the administration has taken several steps to prepare the way for a general decentralisation of operations and has begun to implement some of these. Decentralisation is an aspect in creating a national health care system, in line with the constitutional reform of February 1983 which established health care as a basic right of citizenship. Much of the work has been to create the legal framework for a decentralisation that will delegate health care operations to the states while SSA retains power to coordinate and set standards. This involved a general law setting out a division of functions between central and state governments and executive decrees establishing the forms of general and specific agreements between the states and central government. The specific arrangements in health are negotiated through the mechanism of the CUD (Single Development Agreement, the successor to the CUC). The decentralisation aims to benefit those not covered by social security systems. Health care employees remain under federal law, thus preserving their federal pay and benefits and defusing a potentially important protest. As of mid-1985 all 31 states had concluded agreements in principle and 12 had negotiated specific arrangements through the CUD. More time is needed to assess how decentralisation has affected resource flows and the relative influence of local interests on health care.[42]

The devastating earthquakes of September 1985 offered a unique opportunity to accelerate decentralisation. However, the apparent response was a minimal relocation of offices to cities immediately adjacent to Mexico City: Cuernavaca, Toluca and Puebla.

STRUCTURAL LIMITATIONS ON PARASTATAL EFFICIENCY

President De la Madrid's announcement in February 1985 that some 237 parastatal agencies would be sold signalled a recognition that the state sector had grown too large. The sale constituted a significant item in the continuing tensions between government and the private sector. The more important issue, however, involves the actual and potential efficiency of public enterprise as production units in a mixed economy. This is because in whatever strategy Mexico pursues to revitalise the economy and political system, state enterprises will play important roles. As presently constituted, however, the presidential system impedes parastatal efficiency.

Parastatal inefficiency derives less from administrative details than from the extreme inequality which pervades Mexican society, which was reinforced by ISI pursued since the 1940s. Market arrangements, allowed full reign, would in the short run expose the majority of the population to additional hardships. Thus, over time, a complex system of state controls and activities has evolved to cushion market effects and to promote socially useful production. Also, state agencies promote private companies with subsidised goods and services. State expansion in turn strengthened the PRI–government elite. This logic, typical of populist regimes, has continually reinforced an expanding public sector. The mechanism adopted in many cases is the public enterprise. These agencies carry considerable ideological baggage, with President De la Madrid referring to them as 'the bulwark of our nationalism'.[43]

In the polemical exchanges about development strategies, free market proponents condemn public enterprises as hopelessly corrupt and inefficient. Defenders point correctly to flaws and vices in private firms and insist upon measures other than quality or profit to judge the social benefits of public enterprises. The exchange produces little. Concretely, proponents of state-led development need to confront the issue of how to organise production units that can create productive employment, adapt modern technology to meet national needs, and achieve efficiency and quality levels that can make selected Mexican products competitive in national and foreign markets.

Furthermore, an extensive public enterprise system must achieve acceptable levels of productivity across virtually all lines of activity, creating non-inflationary systems of financing and subsidisation that provide for continuing investment requirements.

It requires too lengthy a discussion to measure the degree of parastatal inefficiency. López Portillo continually stressed the need for improvements, and De la Madrid put 'economic realism' at the top of his priorities. A quick analysis shows that the current system of parastatals operates at high costs and that political factors operate to prevent administrative reforms to correct production deficiencies. The schematic model shown in Figure 4.2 overleaf suggests some sources of inefficiency in a typical public enterprise. When the agencies are joined in production chains, for example, steel, electricity, transportation, petrochemicals and paper products, the inefficiencies multiply to put end product costs beyond competitive levels.

The reforms indicated include privatisation in some cases, the implementation of career services and careful monitoring of productivity along with appropriate incentive schemes. Ironically, privatisation requires additional state spending in many cases in order to make enterprise attractive to investors. Unless economic opening is also pursued in order to create competitive pressures, privatisation would merely exchange inefficient private monopolies for public ones.

In all, the changes needed to modernise the political bureaucracy would transform the presidential system as it has evolved since the mid 1940s.

Figure 4.2 Sources of parastatal inefficiency

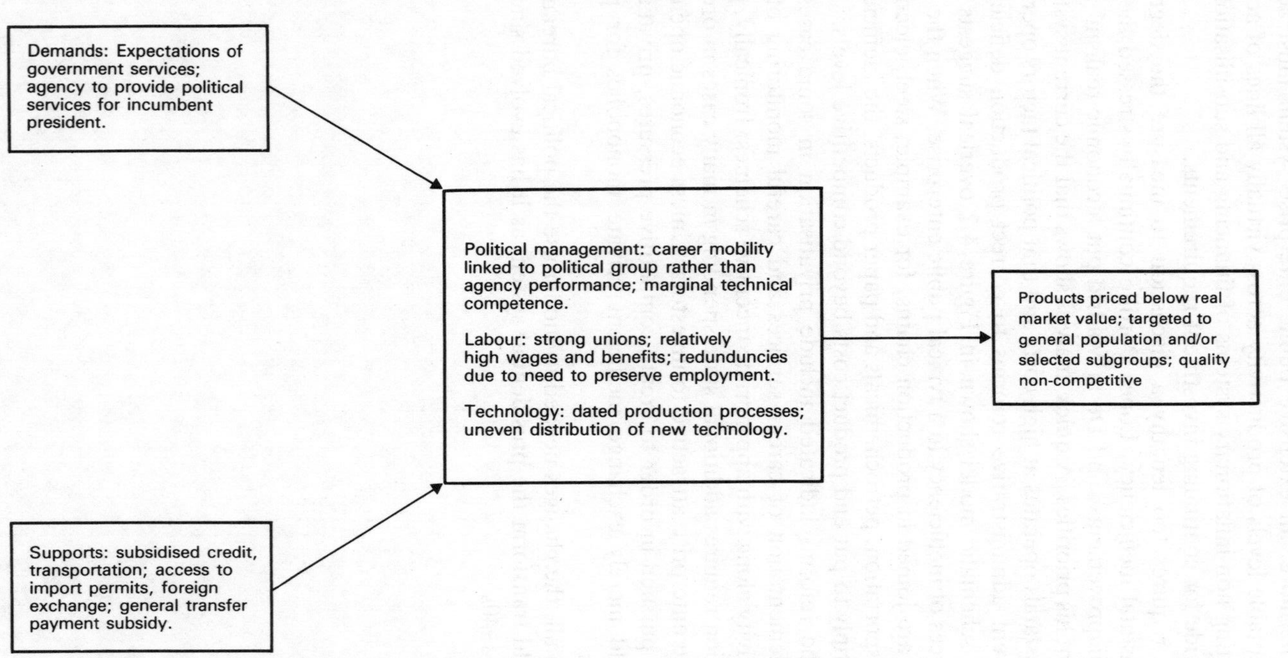

5 The PRI and the Political Reform Projects

Both supporters and opponents often use the term *instituto político* (political institute) to refer to the PRI. The term emphasises the close integration of the party with the presidency and bureaucracy. In February 1985, when President De la Madrid announced the sale of 237 public enterprises, opposition leaders joked about searching the lists carefully in hope of finding the PRI on the auction block.

Like Peru's APRA, the PRI is a genuinely indigenous party, one that has evolved over time in response to a series of specific historical challenges. The party was founded in 1929 by General Plutarco Elias Calles, in his effort to integrate the many disparate and competing revolutionary forces. The succession crisis caused by the assassination of President-Elect Alvaro Obregón provided the opportunity to act. The party was structurally transformed by President Lázaro Cárdenas in 1938 as part of a brilliant series of efforts to broaden its base and to radicalise domestic and foreign policies. It assumed its present name in 1946, during the presidential campaign of Miguel Alemán, as a symbol of the transition from an era of military *caudillos* to one of civilian institutions.[1]

Mexico might formally be classified as a multi-party system, with some nine parties registered for the 1985 elections. But the practical reality is the overwhelming dominance of the PRI, which garners an average of 70 per cent of the votes and has not lost a presidential or gubernatorial race in 57 years. In 1970 Samuel Huntington classified the PRI as an established one-party system. 'In a one-party system . . . other parties may exist – as indeed they do in Poland, China, and Mexico – but they have little effect on the course of events.'[2] But this condition no longer obtains. The PRI might most usefully be viewed as a semi-authoritarian, hegemonic party which – while voicing liberal aspirations – serves primarily as an instrument of government to maintain an elite in power and pursue goals that emanate from the Constitution of 1917.[3] As argued previously, the party stands as a basic pillar of a strong presidential system, along with the central government bureaucracy, with which it is thoroughly integrated.

Three points follow from the above. The PRI lacks an identity separate from the government in terms of structure or purpose. Also, tensions within the PRI reflect problems in the overall presidential system and appear in the functions that the party is called upon to perform. Finally, significant initiatives will not originate in the party; rather the party will reflect whatever is authorised by the presidency. Nonetheless, changes within the party might be significant for the broader system.

Two causes of the party's decline are that the Constitution itself posits conflicting projects, and the party is caught up in contradictory roles; also, the PRI was constructed in its essential form nearly 40 years ago, and the society and economy have changed enormously since that time. Both of these factors are exacerbated by the worst economic crisis since the Great Depression.

The Constitution serves as the basic legitimating document of the Revolution and sets out nationalism, social welfare and liberalism as the main projects. The PRI has claimed for itself the mantle of the party of the majorities with the historical mission of carrying out these projects. To the extent that the party could demonstrate continuous economic growth and progress towards a better life for the majority, there was less urgency in achieving liberal democracy. But as growth and opportunity foundered, the PRI–government attempted after 1977 to revive the liberal project of real electoral competition, honest elections and the like as a basis of legitimacy. Rather than plebiscites to reconfirm the government's rule, elections were to serve as opportunities for meaningful popular choice among competing elites. This is a difficult challenge, because as Juan Molinar has noted, liberal democracy – Madero's legacy – is the weakest of the Revolutionary projects.[4] Furthermore, the very meaning of democracy given in the Constitution's Article 3 and in PRI statutes and ideology subordinates votes and elections (or formal democracy) to the protection and advancement of society's weaker groups. When the PRI does lose elections the temptation grows to ignore formal democracy in favour of the populist version. This is especially the case when it loses to the PAN, which many *priístas* view as anti-national and anti-revolutionary.[5]

Structurally and procedurally, the PRI simply is not designed to compete as a party. Rather, it was constructed in its essential features during the late 1930s as a mechanism to integrate new elements, principally labour, farmers and emerging middle-sector groups into politics in a controlled fashion. The party became a kind of holding company of *groups*; thus, the politics of the PRI concerns more the control over groups than the waging of campaigns for the votes of individuals. In turn, the groups (party sectors and bureaucratic elites) that enjoy privileged status within the PRI would be jeopardised by reforms that might strengthen the party in electoral competition, for example, greater ideological rigour and increased local-level participation in candidate selection.[6]

Furthermore, the party was constructed at a time of relative societal simplicity. The country was largely rural, with only embryonic labour movements or entrepreneurial groups. Thus, a corporatist design, with labour, farm, military and popular sectors, might usefully categorise society for purposes of political organisation. Since World War Two, however, Mexico has undergone social change of monumental proportions, and the party is struggling to accommodate itself to the new social complexity.

This chapter discusses the functions of the PRI in the context of a strong presidential system, describes the party structure and leadership during the mid-1980s and reviews aspects of the political dynamics within and about the party. The last section assesses efforts to reform the PRI and the electoral system. The general argument is that some *priístas* have long accepted the necessity for change and have reasoned that electoral reform would reinforce efforts to change the PRI as well. In practice, initiatives prior to 1977 produced relatively little change in either the system or the dominant party. The political reforms introduced in 1977 reached their apogee in 1983 and subsequent elections witnessed a general retreat from the liberal project and put greater emphasis on stability and nationalism. The retreat from electoral reform, however, has revived efforts to decentralise candidate selection within the PRI, a long-standing goal of party reformers.

FUNCTIONS OF THE PRI IN A PRESIDENTIAL SYSTEM

Despite the line of analysis that emphasises the PRI's decline, the party still performs functions critical to Mexico's presidential system. As noted in Chapter 2, in comparative terms, the PRI figured importantly in Mexico's distinctive political evolution. With a claimed membership of 14 millions and with state and local organisations throughout the country, the PRI provides a channel of information to the presidency that complements those of the army and federal bureaucracy.[7] While less significant than the bureaucracy as a source of policy, it exercises important policy functions. For example, it organises support for presidential initiatives, be they 'moral renovation', 'economic realism' or 'revolutionary nationalism'. It offers a complex structure to absorb and broker conflicts, and it undergirds the presidency in the critical succession process, when a variety of interest demands are often heightened. In a broader system perspective, the party contributes to socialisation of both elite and popular strata, making easier the achievement of ideological hegemony for government. With control over thousands of elected and appointive jobs, it provides channels of recruitment for the politically motivated and the incentives to discipline an able political class. Finally, as an electoral machine, the PRI structures the vote in the electoral arena.[8]

Given the sexennial rhythm of the presidential system, the national party is least active during the first two years, which allows time for installing and testing new leadership and cadres and for trying out new ideas. Only one governorship, albeit in the important state of Baja California Norte, is up for election. (In the second year no governorship is chosen.) By the third year, the party is throttling up to speed, with the mid-term election of 400 national deputies, seven governors – including the important states of Nuevo León and Sonora – and hundreds of state and local officials. The fourth year begins the critical phase, with 14 governorships at stake and the presidential succession gathering steam. Blunders and miscues at this point cost more than at the outset of the *sexenio*. The party's presidential candidate is selected at some point in the last quarter of the fifth year, and from that time until the inauguration on 1 December of the sixth year the party assumes its greatest importance as the source of new programmes and personnel for the next administration.

PARTY STRUCTURE AND LEADERSHIP

The reader should recall that the President appoints and controls the party leadership, and that the national-level party acts in a top-down fashion to control its lower-level organisations. At the same time, the sectors enjoy considerable internal autonomy. Much of the party's success depends on the personal skills of negotiation and persuasion of its militants, and the role of the sectorial and general delegates (discussed below) is especially important. Thus the *políticos* maintain that *técnicos* should not meddle in political affairs without first serving an apprenticeship.

Figure 5.1 depicts effective – as opposed to statutory – lines of

Figure 5.1 National organisation of the PRI/CEN

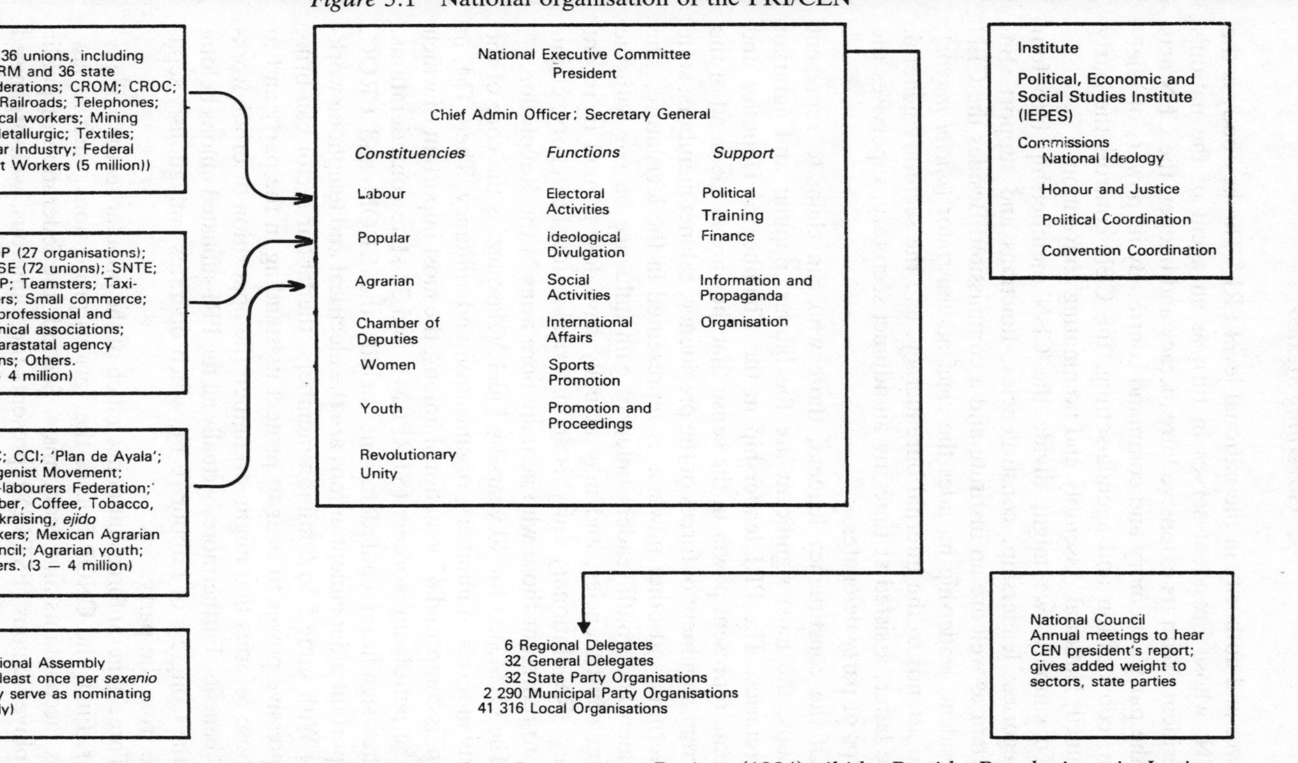

Source: PRI, Secretaria de Divulgacion Ideologica, *Documentos Basicos* (1984); *ibid.*, *Partido Revolucionario Institucional* (1985), p. 11; interview material.

power and authority in the national-level PRI.[9] The key body is the CEN, whose President serves in turn as an agent of the nation's President. With its extensive bureaucracy and budget, the CEN acts as the party's memory and command centre. By its powers of selection, convocation and agenda-setting, the CEN controls the party Council, National Assembly and nominating convention.

To simplify, we might divide the CEN membership into four categories: leadership, constituencies, functions and support. Important as well are an institute and a commission. Besides the CEN President, leadership includes the chief administrator (*oficial mayor*), who attends to the internal bureaucracy, and the secretary general. The latter, assisted at times by an adjunct secretary, supervises the corps of party delegates.

Of the constituency leaders, those who can claim to represent groups, the most significant are the labour, popular and agrarian secretaries. The PRI leadership in the Chamber of Deputies and Senate represent power in the sense that they are at the head of the current alignment of forces of the presidency, cabinet members, state governors and other powers, as represented in the legislature. The women and youth leaders failed to gain influence on par with the other constituencies, and may actually have lost ground in recent years. 'Revolutionary unity' is an historical residual category, claiming to represent those who actually bore arms in the Revolution.

The CTM, led for 40 years by Fidel Velásquez, is the core of the party in terms of numbers, organisation and militancy. The CTM, in turn, is comprised of 36 national unions, the most important of which is the petroleum workers (STRPRM), and 32 state confederations. Other significant confederations include the CROM and CROC. Important independent unions are the electrical and telephone workers. With some 5 to 6 million members, the labour sector can bring impressive power to bear to protect its standing in the party and to oppose reforms that might strengthen the opposition or erode workers' benefits. Furthermore, virtually all the PRI–affiliated unions belong to the Congress of Labour (CT), which operates ambiguously separate from the party.

Three general forces influence much of the popular sector's behaviour. First, the CNOP houses the various professions, such as lawyers, accountants and economists. Second, the federation of public employee unions (FSTSE) represents the numerous, well-organised and well-situated bureaucrats. Especially important are the 800 000 or so teachers organised in the SNTE. Other important unions here are the social security workers of ISSSTE and IMSS. FSTSE also participates in the Congress of Labour, acting at times as a counter-weight to the CTM. Third, the 'small farmers' (CNPP) can be significant as well, representing the more productive and wealthier farm groups. With some 3 to 4 million members, the popular sector has the numbers and talent to influence the party, and has won a growing percentage of elected positions. But the sector is riven by too many heterogeneous organisations and lacks the continuous and effective leadership that gives additional influence to the labour sector.

The agrarian sector rests largely on the *ejido* farmers of the National Peasant Confederation (CNC). Another farm organisation, the CCI, was created in the early 1960s in an effort to intensify farmers' demands for government support. Over time the CCI was co-opted into the party. A similar syndrome apparently occurred with the Plan de Ayala group, which emerged in the 1970s. By and large the significant functions of control and participation operate more fully in the complex agricultural bureaucracy of the *ejido* cooperatives, farm banks and assistance agencies. With some 3 to 4 million members, the agrarian sector has steadily lost ground to the other sectors in terms of influence.[10]

The constituency secretaries are appointed and removed by their groups. In contrast, the functions and support secretaries are appointed and removed by the CEN. Although there is no confirming study, I suspect the CEN leadership is sensitive to sectorial balance among the other secretaries. If a balance cannot be achieved among the secretaries themselves, such balance is likely sought at the subsecretarial levels. That is, if the secretary of political training, for example, is from the popular sector, very likely the subsecretaries include representatives from the labour and farm groups.

Attached to the CEN are several commissions and an institute. The Political, Economic and Social Studies Institute (IEPES) is the party's 'think tank', which can assume importance in three basic ways. It may be useful to the President for the party to adopt positions different from the government's, this to strengthen his negotiating hand. For example, with respect to Mexico's external debt, the party has formulated a more confrontational line. IEPES is the body that thinks through the arguments and assembles the data. Also, during the presidential campaign, much of the succeeding government's programme is put together in IEPES and several important individuals will be drawn from it as well. Furthermore, each state party organisation has a counterpart commission, called CEPES, and these comprise a national network led by IEPES. The CEPES-IEPES provide the natural entry point to the PRI for bright young *técnicos*. Among the commissions, that charged with convention coordination has assumed importance recently, due to the party's efforts to decentralise candidate selection.

The CEN controls the National Assembly and National Council by setting their agendas, membership and meeting dates. By statute, the National Assembly meets at least once every six years. It may also be convened as an assembly and then converted to a presidential nominating convention. The National Council meets by statute every September to hear the CEN President's annual report. The Council's composition gives added importance to the sectors and the state parties.

At the state level, the governor selects the state party President and typically controls appointments to the state party committee (CDE), which in turn oversees municipal party organs. Though much depends on skill and luck, the governors usually enjoy considerable independence in the political management of their states. The governors, in turn, are monitored by both CEN and Interior.

In addition to constant telephone communications and the special ceremonies and visits that keep local, state and national officials in close personal touch, the CEN employs several types of delegates to carry out party policy. A general delegate is assigned to each state on a continuing basis. In addition, the party sectors may assign delegates to oversee activities in their organisations. Finally, the CEN may assign special delegates to attend to specific problems on an *ad hoc* basis. Six multi-state, regional delegates act as coordinators between the CEN and the general delegates. Designation as a CEN delegate carries status, since it is the party's recognition of ability and prestige.

A primary assignment for the delegate involves consulting the party sectors and a variety of interests, sometimes including opposition parties, in recommending PRI candidates for elections. Called *auscultación*, roughly how the doctor listens with a stethoscope, this function is essential to the successful working of a centralised party. For many, the 'union card' as a *político* as opposed to a *técnico* is successful service as a delegate. The job offers many possibilities for failure, since the delegate is frequently subjected to conflicting pressures from the various 'pre-candidates' and their patrons. As state and national elections occur, the importance of the general and sectorial delegates increases. States such as Baja California Norte,

Chihuahua, Coahuila, Guerrero, Jalisco, Nuevo León, Sonora and Veracruz have become difficult in recent years, and others may present special problems on occasion. Over time, an elite group of party delegates has evolved for such challenges.

The President adjusts the party leadership in keeping with his own needs at various points in the *sexenio*. Thus, with López Portillo changes were made in 1979 to weaken the *echeverristas* and build a personal base in the party, and again in 1981 to set the stage for the succession. With De la Madrid the technocrats have pretty well integrated themselves into the CEN, as shown in Table 5.1, and we see a kind of logical division of labour, with the experienced *políticos* holding certain positions, while the younger political technocrats serve a sort of apprenticeship. Note also that a fairly broad cross-section of states is represented in the CEN and that there is some effort to balance appointments from the sectors to the other party offices such as organisation and IEPES.

POLITICAL DYNAMICS WITHIN AND ABOUT THE PRI

Two considerations help in understanding the tensions and dynamics within the PRI, between the party and government and party–government and society: the party serves as an instrument of the presidency, and the dynamics take on a particular form due to the party's centralised, sectorial organisation.

Beginning with internal dynamics, a structural tension holds between the national leadership and party militants at the grass roots. Sectorial leaders at the national level need prestige patronage positions, such as deputy or senator, with which to reward their followers and thus reinforce loyalty and discipline. Such patronage and loyalty are essential in turn to the system as a whole. The struggle takes place on a two-step basis: organisations within the sectors compete among themselves for shares of sectorial quotas of positions; and the sectors compete as well to protect or increase their shares of the total number of positions available. For example Fidel Velázquez, as head of the CTM, needs to be able to distribute prestige positions based on a calculus of loyalty and importance to the CTM and the labour sector and not to voter's preferences in some district. Gaining the positions pits him first against the other unions in the labour sector and then against other sectorial leaders, who in turn lobby for their own followings. Table 5.2 shows the continual ascendancy of the labour

Table 5.1 Membership of the CEN, July 1985

PRESIDENT: Senator Adolfo Lugo Verduzco (b. 1933, Hidalgo, law and master's/UNAM, graduate work in public administration/ENA/Paris, background in SHCP, IMSS, CONASUPO, Diconsa, SPP, father was governor of Hidalgo) (*Popular*)

SECRETARY GENERAL: Deputy Irma Cue Sarquis (b. 1938, Veracruz, law/UNAM, background in Treasury, CONACYT, and Presidency/ Administrative Studies) (*Popular*)

ADJUNCT SECRETARY GENERAL: Senator Manuel Garza González (about 50, Tamaulipas, long experience in party and electoral politics, expert on practical political questions) (*Popular*)

SECRETARY FOR ADMINISTRATION: Deputy Genaro Borrego Estrada (b. 1949, Zacatecas, industrial relations/UIA, background in SEPAFIN, SPP, and state government: Hidalgo) (*Popular*)

SECRETARY FOR LABOUR: Blas Chumacero Sánchez (b. 1908, Puebla, several-time deputy, CEN member in late 1940s, labour representative on CEN since 1964, deputy candidate in 1985, close to Fidel Velázquez) (*Labour*)

SECRETARY FOR FARMERS: Senator Mario Hernández Posada (b. 1929, Veracruz, agricultural engineer, active in PRI since 1952, deputy on two occasions, experience in CNC, background in SRA, and Ejidatario Bank) (*Farm*)

SECRETARY FOR POPULAR SECTOR: Deputy Enrique Fernández Martínez (b. 1938, Guanajuato, law/UNAM, general delegate of CEN on several occasions, from political family) (*Popular*)

SECRETARY FOR POLITICAL ACTION (DEPUTIES): Deputy Humberto Lugo Gil (b. 1934, Hidalgo, law/UNAM, former deputy, long experience in CEN, CNOP as general delegate, cousin of Adolfo Lugo Verduzgo) (*Popular*)

SECRETARY FOR POLITICAL ACTION (SENATE): Senator Antonio Riva Palacio (b. 1928, Morelos, active in PRI since early 1950s, general delegate of CEN and of CNC, former deputy from Morelos) (*Farm*)

SECRETARY FOR ORGANISATION: Deputy Héctor Hugo Olivares Ventura (b. 1944, Aguascalientes, secondary school teacher, political science/UNAM, active in PRI since early 1960s, significant offices since 1969, general delegate of CEN and CNC in several states, former senator from Aguascalientes) (*Farm*)

SECRETARY FOR POLITICAL TRAINING: Arturo Núñez (mid-30s, Tabasco, economist, background in administrative studies/Presidency, 1977–82) (*Popular*)

SECRETARY FOR ELECTORAL ACTION: Fausto Villagómez Cabrera (Guanajuato, former subsecretary for electoral action and official in National Voters Registry of SG) (*Popular*)

SECRETARY FOR IDEOLOGICAL DIVULGATION: José Natividad González Parás (mid-30s, Nuevo León, specialist in public administration/ France, background in administrative studies, Presidency, 1977–82) (*Popular*)

SECRETARY FOR INFORMATION AND PROPAGANDA: Deputy Juan Saldaña Rosell (D.F., formerly an adjunct secretary) (*Popular*)

SECRETARY FOR SOCIAL ACTION: Deputy Alberto Miranda Castro (b. 1932, Baja California Sur, primary school teacher, active in PRI and SNTE since early 1950s, most of professional work in Baja California Norte) (*Popular*)

SECRETARY FOR INTERNATIONAL AFFAIRS: Senator Humberto Hernández Haddad (b. 1951, Tabasco, former deputy on two occasions, specialist in international relations, law/UNAM, graduate work at Harvard, Johns Hopkins) (*Popular*)

SECRETARY FOR SPORTS PROMOTION: Deputy Antonio Murrieta Necochea (b. 1935, D.F., engineering/UNAM/UIA, Deputy for Veracruz, active in PRI since early 1950s, background in CONASUPO, SEPAFIN, SECOM) (*Popular*)

SECRETARY OF FINANCE: Jorge Thompson Aguilar (D.F., formerly of SPP) (*Popular*)

SECRETARY COORDINATOR FOR REVOLUTIONARY UNITY: Jesús Vidales Marroquín (*Popular*)

REPRESENTATIVE OF NATIONAL MOVEMENT OF REVOLUTIONARY YOUTH: José Encarnación Alfaro Cázares (Sonora, former general secretary of Popular Revolutionary University of PRI) (*Popular*)

REPRESENTATIVE OF NATIONAL REVOLUTIONARY WOMENS GROUP: Sen. Yolanda Sentiés de Ballesteros (b. 1940, State of Mexico, chemistry/UNAM, law/State of Mexico, public administration Oaxaca, active in PRI since early 1960s, former mayor of Toluca, deputy from State of México) (*Popular*)

DIRECTOR OF INSTITUTE FOR SOCIAL, ECONOMIC AND POLITICAL STUDIES (IEPES): Sen. Angel Aceves Saucedo (b. 1940, Puebla, economist/UNAM, graduate work at NYU, former deputy, close to CTM leadership) (*Labour*)

GENERAL DIRECTOR OF PROMOTION AND WORKS: Roberto Madrazo Pintado (b. 1940, D.F., former deputy from D.F., son of former PRI president Carlos A. Madrazo) (*Popular*)

Sources: Presidencia de la República, *Diccionario biográfico del gobierno mexicano* (México: 1984); interview material.

and popular sectors in the Chamber of Deputies since 1964, much of which comes at the expense of the farming sector.

Other interests enter as well at the national level. Cabinet secretaries and state governors manoeuvre to have their people selected. The army lobbies for its historical quota. Party leaders in turn factor in the need for technical expertise in the PRI's congressional delegation in areas such as economics and finance. Finally, the party often finds it useful to nominate a celebrity such as professional boxer Rubén Olivares. In sum, a variety of needs enter at the national level

Table 5.2 Estimated sectorial distribution of PRI deputies in National Chamber (single-member districts), 1940–88 *

Legislature	*Worker* %	*Farmer* %	*Popular* %	*Sector unknown* %	*Opposition* %	*Total* *N* =
1940–43	14.8	47.9	36.6	0	.6	169
1943–46	16.7	45.8	37.5	0	0	144
1946–49	9.2	52.1	31.0	2.1	5.6	142
1949–52	9.2	48.2	39.0	0	3.5	141
1952–55	13.8	48.8	31.9	0	5.6	160
1955–58	11.8	49.7	32.7	0	5.9	153
1958–61	13.1	52.3	29.4	0	5.2	153
1961–64	6.8	56.5	33.9	0	2.8	177
1964–67	15.3	46.3	37.3	1.1	0	177
1967–70	19.5	21.3	48.9	9.2	1.1	174
1970–73	16.0	27.3	48.0	8.7	0	150
1973–76	14.6	22.7	44.9	16.8	1.1	185
1976–79	25.0	33.7	40.8	0	.5	196
1979–82	22.3	27.3	48.0	0	1.3	300
1982–85	23.3	22.0	53.0	1.3	.3	300
1985–88	23.3	22.3	48.6	1.9	3.6	300

* These figures should be regarded as tentative, because they were estimated from sources that give conflicting and incomplete data

Sources: O. Rodríguez Araujo, 'Catálogo de senadores y diputados (1940–1973)', *Estudios políticos*, 1: 3–4 (Sept.–Dec. 1975), p. 160; K.J. Middlebrook, 'Political Change and Political Reform in an Authoritarian Regime: The Case of Mexico', (paper prepared for conference on 'Prospects for Democracy: Transitions from Authoritarian Rule', sponsored by the Latin American Program of the Woodrow Wilson International Center for Scholars, October 1980), p. 28; J. Patiño C., 'Elecciones de diputados: su significado político, jurídico y estadístico', in P. González C., (coord.) *Las elecciones en México: evolución y perspectivas*(México: Siglo XXI, 1985), pp. 217–18; *Directorio de la Cámara de Diputados, 1982–1985; ibid., 1985–1988.*

that do not necessarily take into account the electability of the candidate at the district level.

'Down home', and especially in the more developed and urbanised districts, party militants need attractive, electable candidates at a minimum and, even better, some assurance that militancy might some day earn prestige posts. The party can mitigate this national–local tension a bit by ceding greater local influence over the offices of municipal President and city council. As former President Adolfo Ruiz Cortines supposedly commented: 'The municipalities are for the people; the state legislatures are for the governors; and the national congress is for the President.' Problems may arise when governors intervene capriciously in municipal nominations in order to promote their own influence in the state. Such intervention may create tensions with local level leaders, who then seek assistance from national party organs. The CEN's general delegate in the state is expected to referee, but he might be neutralised by cross-cutting pressures. The worst scenario from the party's point of view posits an unpopular governor, selected by presidential whim, who then uses his personal friendship with the President to offset party resistance to his own project of personal aggrandisement. Since municipal elections often excite greatest emotion, a meddlesome and unpopular governor can create problems first for the party, then for Interior and ultimately for the President.

The national–local tension is neither uniform nor inevitable; that is, probably only a minority of PRI candidates serve national needs only and prove difficult to elect. Also, in many cases local elites might prefer a congressional or gubernatorial candidate with strong national connections. Occasionally, the local party may be badly divided, and a candidate from Mexico City can restore order. Also, a powerful governor may attempt to carve out a fiefdom, and Mexico City may have to intervene. All too often, however, unattractive candidates are simply assigned to states or districts. Gubernatorial races present less of a problem, because in most cases opposition parties lack the strength to run effective statewide races. But even so, several states bordering the US cannot be taken for granted. Congressional and municipal contests can be much more difficult, and unattractive *priístas* can lose. Some observers point to the labour sector as the most prevalent source of problems. The popular sector, on the other hand, has greater latitude in selecting effective candidates. The farm sector presents least difficulty due to the party's virtual lock on the rural vote.

Overall, the party's ability to generate resources and mobilise votes has tended in the past to overcome the tensions between national and local needs. But with the 1977 electoral reform and the economic crisis of the 1980s, tension grew as opposition parties, especially the PAN, began to mount more effective campaigns to benefit from voter unrest.

At the local level, the sectorial design may create additional problems. The tendency by and large is for sectors to lay historical claim to an electoral district in national elections and to state and municipal districts (sometimes an agreed share of city council seats) for local elections. The sectors repeated in 1982 and 1985 in 203 of the 279 chamber districts for which data are available.[11] To the extent that the district is predominantly rural (thus CNC), industrial (CT) or urban (CNOP), there may be congruence. For example, it is logical for the STRPRM to receive a candidacy in the Coaltzacoalcos area of Veracruz, where petroleum is the main industry and the union is engaged in a variety of service activities. But other districts are less clear-cut in their demographic characteristics. Assuming even that the candidate has local roots and some popularity, his designation by one sector may imply lack of knowledge about the other sectors and sometimes lack of real support by them in the campaign. (Reconsider the Veracruz example cited above from the perspective of the CNOP and CNC locals, who may be frozen out of a national deputy nomination and must settle for lesser prizes.) Also, the pace of social change itself can create friction with sectorial assignments and present opportunities to opposition parties.[12] The problems are usually manageable where there is cooperation and tolerance among the sectors and where a prudent governor and state party leader can preserve harmony. Conflict may also be reduced by promising some future consideration to a candidate or sector, or by awarding alternate (*suplente*) posts. But absent such conditions, and where the sectors may suffer a history of tension and the state-level leadership plays upon tensions for personal gain, there may be conflicts and occasional breakdown. Disappointed office-seekers may even bolt the PRI to run as candidates for opposition parties (which might apply to several recent cases in northern Mexico).[13] Thus, even if a sector's quota is maintained at the national level, the specific district may experience problems.

Internal tensions also arise among the party sectors as these jockey to preserve or increase their power within the party. Labour is the most cohesive and militant sector, and a reflection of this competition is labour's periodic campaign to have the PRI designated a 'workers party', thus pushing the party towards the populist militancy of the Cárdenas era. The CNOP and party bureaucracy typically press to retain the formula of the party as a 'permanent alliance of the fundamental forces of the Mexican people'.[14] The 'scorecard' in the sectorial competition is usually the tally of nominations for the senate and chamber of deputies at the national level, as well as the continuous tabulation of gubernatorial nominations as these occur over the *sexenio*. The balance among the sectors at the state and local levels tends to remain fairly stable and to reflect in general terms the local characteristics, as discussed above. I noted the tendency over the past years to strengthen the popular sector in response to the presidency's efforts to build a personal following as well as the party's effort to accommodate to a more complicated society. One also hears occasional complaints about 'Florsheim' or 'wingtip' farmers, as popular sector individuals infiltrate the farm sector, which is less able to protect its turf than is the labour sector.

Three currencies of influence operate in the party: friendships, numbers (thus votes) and strategic importance in the sense of capacity to create pressure. In an unstable and personalistic context, friendships can mean career survival, and *políticos* cultivate extensive networks of friends. The result, of course, is that friendships weight heavily in candidate selections and party appointments. This reinforces a centralised and personalist style of politics and works against projects of decentralisation and electoral competition. A prudent President balances friendship with qualities of ability and experience that also strengthen the party. Since Echeverría, critics claim that Presidents have placed their personal interests above the party's, and they invoke a special term, *amiguismo*, to denote the problem.

With regard to numbers and strategic importance, control over organisations is the key. Sectorial leaders strive to maintain control over their own groups, and sectors may compete for the right to organise new groups. Tension occurs at times between labour and the CNOP over which new organisations belong where. The nationalisation of the banks in 1982, for example, set off a brief scuffle over which of them would organise the bank employees, who previously had been legally barred from union membership. (CNOP 'won'.) Often the lines that separate the labour and popular sectors are drawn from custom and usage rather than elegant logic. Thus, at the national level, the FSTSE belongs to both the CT and PRI's popular sector. At the local level, to cite a mundane example, taxi drivers in different cities may belong to either labour or CNOP affiliates.

The sectors do agree, however, on limiting the influence of the party bureaucracy. That is, the three sectorial leaders – and especially labour – prefer a small CEN in which their votes and lobbying efforts might carry more weight. The increase in CEN positions, from eight in 1958 to 23 in 1985, both strengthens the hand of the party President and allows the party to respond to greater societal complexity without reinforcing the sectors. Had the youth and women, for example, been organised within the three sectors, they would likely have received even less attention and would have reinforced the sectorial leaders. In the 1984 party assembly, the CTM called for a reduction in the size of the CEN, and the youth leader criticised the CTM's undemocratic style.[15] Also interesting in internal politics is the responsiveness of the various party offices to sectors' orientations. For example, at different times IEPES has been more responsive to the technocrats and CNOP to labour.

Centralisation, among other factors, hinders militancy at the grass roots level, and the national leadership searches for ways to revitalise the base while at the same time preserving the sectorial and centralised logic of the party. In early 1983 party President Lugo Verduzco hit upon the idea, quickly discarded, of encouraging national-level officials to attend party meetings and to participate in party activities in their home towns. A related effort at about the same time was the revitalisation of the ideology commission to clarify party thinking and thus presumably to educate and motivate the base. Mostly, however, Senator Lugo gave speeches exhorting greater militancy, and occasionally hinting at sanctions against the passive.[16]

Apart from internal dynamics, a separate but related set of tensions involves relations between the party and the national government bureaucracy, even though the overall relationship is more one of support and cooperation. This dynamic in turn resonates within the party in either strengthening or weakening the contending forces. These tensions include the party's demand for partisan militancy *versus* the indifference or hostility of bureaucrats; the party's and sectors' lobbying for specific policies *versus* the bureaucracy's broader and longer, or at least different, view of issues; and the tensions that arise where the distinctive functions that the party and bureaucracy perform in Mexican politics come into conflict.

PRI militants complain about the decline of partisanship in the bureaucracy. A PRI survey of 3500 top-level administrators in February 1984 showed that 42 per cent indicated no party preference.[17] The response was for Senator Lugo and President De la Madrid to exhort greater partisan involvement from the bureaucrats. The campaign reflected the President's belief, expressed frequently by Lugo and other party spokesmen, that there is no place for ideological neutrality in the public administration. Related to this was the revival of soliciting party dues from middle to high-level bureaucrats, and the pressure on functionaries to participate in election campaigns.

The reaction to such pressures has been generally unfavourable. The campaign provided the PAN and the left opposition parties common ground to point out the contradiction between real democracy and the PRI hegemony, and the opposition advanced legal constitutional arguments about freedom of conscience and expression against the militancy campaign. As might be imagined, many bureaucrats themselves balked at paying party dues.[18]

A second area of party–government tension involves public policies, including general government orientation as well as specific programmes. At the general level, such broad goals as revolutionary nationalism and development provide threads of consensus between party and government. Typically, the party works as the government's evangelist, carrying the message forward as either an echo or amplifier of government statements.

In the economic growth period of 1946–71, the PRI gained strength in allying itself with progress and development, but in the period of crisis of the 1980s, the party found itself defending difficult and unpopular policies. The party tried to separate itself a bit from government to prevent the oppositions' monopolising criticism, but ultimately it reunited with the President. The party's *Manifiesto al Pueblo de México* in late 1983 expressed fairly strong criticism of government. By the Twelfth National Assembly in August 1984 the PRI was attempting to come to terms with the austerity programme. Finally, for the July 1985 congressional elections, the party had prepared for its candidates a sturdy question–answer defence of the government's economic policy.[19]

At the sectorial level, it is common for the CTM and CNC to pressure government on specific issues of concern to labour and farmers. The CNOP is too diverse to take positions as a sectorial entity on specific policy questions, except perhaps such symbolic concerns as nationalism. However, its constituent groups, such as the economists or accountants, commonly take pro-government positions on policy issues. Overall, the sectors operate in the difficult terrain of supporting government programmes and serving as a conduit to secure goods and services for their members, while at the same time criticising the relevant agencies and advocating greater attention to their clients' needs. The sectors need to maintain loyalty in the ranks, thus preventing defections and countering new groups that might emerge outside the sector to organise interest demands.

In terms of party and government functions, the prevailing relationship is close cooperation. But one area of tension recurs. The PRI and Interior rank their priorities slightly differently. Basically, the PRI needs electoral dynamism in order to generate good candidates and activate the party base. The party might be willing to cede more victories to the opposition in this regard. Also, it might serve the party's interests to allow its congressional delegation a bit more freedom of manoeuvre on legislative matters, since this would better fit their sectorial needs for flexibility. Interior, on the other hand, worries more about maintaining order in electoral matters and about enforcing discipline in the legislative branch and in state and local governments throughout the country. The turf struggle, in turn, may be heightened by the presidential ambitions of both the secretary and party leader.

With regard to tensions between the PRI–government and society, three areas among many are noteworthy. First, it has proven difficult for the party to accommodate itself to the complex and growing middle sectors, especially the intelligentsia, mostly because these groups are less dependent on regime incentives and controls. Also, they apply more stringent standards of competence and democratic practice. Second, the north of the country presents special challenges due to its historical separateness from the centre, higher level of socio-economic development, and proximity to the US, which practices a decentralised form of two-party electoral competition. Finally, party activists frequently comment on their difficulty in attracting and motivating young members, which is of special concern given that over two-thirds of the population is under 25 years of age, and about 5 million new voters were added to the rolls between the 1982 presidential elections and the mid-term elections of 1985.

PARTY AND SYSTEM REFORM PROJECTS

Mexican leaders have experimented with political reform since the late 1950s. My working hypothesis assumes that governing elites act to retain power and to avoid anti-system behaviour such as voter abstention or violence. Political change at the institutional level proceeds along three interconnected tracks: the PRI, the party system and the federal bureaucracy, with the latter taken as a proxy for federal agencies carrying out an overall development strategy. Reformers typically have attempted to use electoral reform to bring pressure to bear on the PRI to modify its internal procedures. Anti-system behaviour acts as the main impetus to reform. As progress along one track encounters obstacles, efforts shift to another track or tracks. Generally, though, while one might argue that system reform has created incentives to select 'better' PRI candidates for the national legislature, little has been accomplished in the way of internal change.

Among the several reasons, especially important is the role of organised labour in providing support during a gruelling crisis; and for reasons of power and policy, labour prefers a centralised, sectorialised party.

As illustrated in Figure 5.2, worker unrest in the late 1950s provided the impetus for Adolfo López Mateos' 1963 'party deputy reform'.[20] Carlos Madrazo's 1965 campaign to rejuvenate the PRI was intended to complement the electoral reform. Madrazo's failure shifted efforts to the bureaucracy track, which was pursued until the political crisis of 1976. That crisis in turn gave rise to the LOPPE in 1977 – which, characteristically, accompanied another effort, – again unsuccessful, – to revitalise the PRI. The oil bonanza of 1977–81 reignited the bureaucracy–development effort, and electoral reform and bureaucratic activity proceeded until the economic collapse of 1981–82. With austerity, De la Madrid attempted at first to continue with electoral reform, but retreated from this after setbacks in 1983. After 1983 emphasis returned to internal reform of the dominant party.

Efforts to strengthen grass roots participation in the PRI by somehow diluting sectorial power have been fiercely resisted. The first step in this direction came in 1946 with Miguel Alemán, who restricted the powers of the sectors and constituted individual membership as the basis of the party. The changes, consistent with Aleman's pro-business, anti-communist emphases, quickly collapsed. 'After four years of unhappy experimentation with the new system the objections of the labor and agrarian leaders won the day, and the party was reconstituted on a sectoral basis in 1950'.[21] Gonzáles Casanova fixes that year as the essential freezing of party reform.[22]

From that point forward the national PRI systematically subordinated its local and regional organisations to the centre. *Caciques* (local busses) continued in many areas, to be sure, but they survived by subordinating themselves to the centre. Over time, the costs of the system became more obvious: apathy at the base, opportunism at all levels, sacrifice of talent and constructive dissent to discipline and loyalty. This legacy confronted Carlos A. Madrazo on assuming the party presidency in December 1964.

MADRAZO'S EXPERIMENT: THE LESSONS AND QUESTIONS OF FAILURE

Carlos A. Madrazo was from Tabasco, and pursued his early education in Villahermosa before attending preparatory and law school

Figure 5.2 Alternative routes for political change in Mexico, 1958–86

Reform route	Significant events
PRI	Madrazo internal elections 1965; Sansores Pérez transparent democracy 1978 – 9; Lugo Verduzco consultations with the grass roots 1983 – 6
Party system	Party deputy reform 1963; Voting age lowered 1970; Party deputy expanded 1973; LOPPE 1977; Moral renovation 1982
Bureaucracy	Stabilising development 1955 – 71; Shared development 1970 – 6; Economic crisis, 1976; Full growth 1978 – 81; 1982 collapse; Austerity 1983 – 6
Causes	
Violence	1958: teachers' and railroad strikes; 1968: student movement; Sporadic protest and violence
Voter abstention	32%; 31%; 37%; 36%; 40%; 31%; 51%; 34%; 49%

1958	1964	1970	1976	1982
Adolfo López Mateos	Gustavo Díaz Ordaz	Luís Echeverría	José López Portillo	Miguel de la Madrid

in Mexico City.[23] He was active on the left as a leader of the Bloc of Revolutionary Youth of the Red Shirts (1933–35) under Tabasco governor Tomás Garrido Canabal. Madrazo was elected to leadership positions in preparatory school and in national youth organisations. He served as private secretary to Luís I. Rodríguez in 1937–38 during the latter's tenure as governor of Guanajuato, and in 1938–39 when Rodríguez moved on to lead the PRM, the forerunner of the PRI. He served in the Chamber of Deputies during 1943–46, where he formed a close friendship with Gustavo Díaz Ordaz, and held several other posts in the federal bureaucracy before reaching the governorship of his home state during 1959–64. Madrazo distinguished himself as an effective politician and dynamic orator. In December 1964 President Díaz Ordaz appointed Madrazo as President of the CEN, with a charge to reform the party.[24]

Madrazo consistently emphasised certain themes. The PRI should attract youth by stressing reform and idealism; the party should establish an identity separate from government; 'natural leaders' should be identified and nominated for office, as opposed to the traditional method of *dedazo*; individual party militancy should be rewarded; corruption should be rooted out; the party should take the lead in identifying national problems and solutions. Another theme stressed was decentralisation by revitalising the 'free municipality'.[25]

To complement the 1963 electoral reform, the strategy to improve the PRI was first to reinvigorate the party apparatus and then to introduce internal party primaries for municipal elections. Madrazo sent special groups of delegates from the CEN to each state to look into local-level demands, reinforce militancy, promote programmes for women and youth and renovate local and state leadership.[26] The delegates were to analyse the party from the bottom upwards.

The first states affected were Morelos, Baja California, Michoacán, Chihuahua, Durango, Guanajuato and San Luís Potosí. Following this, local party militants were to elect their leaders in free voting in local assemblies all over the country on 25 July 1965. It was not clear how these elections were to be carried out, and in some cases they took on the appearance of ratification of decisions reached earlier. Important to note is that Madrazo used the CEN to bypass state governors, presumably to ensure that the reforms were indeed implemented. Sceptics noted that this tactic provided Madrazo with additional patronage to distribute among his own followers.[27]

The next step in reform was primary elections to select the PRI's candidates for municipal president and councilmen. Customarily, the local party supplied the state committee with the names, qualifications and petitions of support of the several candidates. The state committee, after study and comment, passed the nominations on to the CEN where the final slates were drawn up, including at times a presidential approval. Special delegates from the state committee or even from the CEN were occasionally despatched to verify information or to resolve problems. In reality, the state governors were the primary deciders of municipal nominations. This was due to the centralist assumption that the governors could work more harmoniously with their own municipal presidents, just as the President could best work with governors of his own choosing.[28]

The system of primaries was put into effect in the municipal elections in Baja California. The new procedures generated unwonted public interest and – although it was evident that existing powers could continue to influence the elections – the close race in Ensenada showed that the primaries introduced new elements in local contests. Elections in other states showed the co-existence of the two systems. Thus:

> In order for the old system to maintain its dominance, it had to develop new methods to subvert the institutional democracy. Although these methods were effective in most areas, the exceptions proved that the old system would have to evolve eventually to accept the change. Madrazo was being pragmatic in allowing some subversion of the *elecciones*, but his pressure for upholding its purpose was being felt, and in some areas CEN control was able to force the regular power structures to reduce their hold on the *municipios*.[29]

Even in the best of circumstances, changing long-established patterns of power would be difficult. Complicating this experiment was Madrazo's willingness to use the CEN and party discipline to override state and local objections. That style would inevitably create opposition. The governor of Sinaloa, Leopoldo Sánchez Celis, a product of the old school of Mexican politics, was quite willing to challenge Madrazo. The specifics involved tainted primaries in September 1965 in two cities of Sinaloa. Madrazo overturned the decisions, and the governor then entered his same candidates as independents in the October general elections, winning both races. Madrazo evidently persisted in objecting; the case apparently was decided by Díaz Ordaz; and Madrazo resigned on 17 November 1965.[30]

Clearly Madrazo's opponents had triumphed. Certain governors were opposed, including – in addition to Sinaloa – those of Guerrero and Chihuahua, in which the reforms had allowed victories by independent *priístas*. But governors of other states also took comfort from Madrazo's fall. Besides the governors, certain cabinet members, and especially Interior Secretary Luís Echeverría, could feel some relief, first with the elimination of a rival for the succession, but also with the reaffirmation of presidential dominance and the continued ascendency of the bureaucracy over the party.

The episode teaches several lessons. First, it was clear that Madrazo wanted to create his own power base in the party, and Díaz Ordaz was simply behaving logically in firing him. Second, the failure demonstrated the system's rigidity; young reformers could take little comfort about their prospects of rising in the PRI. Third, following events showed that reform would more likely come from other quarters, initially through violent protest, as with the student movement of 1968, then through the bureaucratic apparatus, with new programme and interest representation structures, and later through renewed electoral reform.

Other questions remain unanswered. First, President Díaz Ordaz probably encouraged Madrazo's opponents at some point, and did little to defend the party leader once the counter-reform got underway. The question, though, concerns the limits on presidential power: How much reform can any Mexican President force on unwilling governors and party notables? Second, it is far from certain that the party base was ready for internal elections, especially if these were to be introduced across the board throughout the country. Have attitudes changed over the past twenty years? Third, as a progressive *priísta* formed in the *cardenista* period, was Madrazo the last best hope of reforming the PRI? Did Echeverría's emphasis on youth, bureaucracy and technocrats foreclose the possibility of party reform?[31]

THE LOPPE AND 'TRANSPARENT DEMOCRACY'

Luís Echeverría took office in 1970 in the aftermath of the 1968 student movement, encountering an economy in recession, university protests, guerrilla movements in different parts of the country and a rapidly changing international order. His statecraft emphasised the bureaucracy and youth over the PRI and party veterans, aggravating in the process the tensions between *políticos* and *técnicos*. Minor adjustments were made in 1973 in the electoral system, expanding the number of party deputy seats available and lowering the percentage vote required to win them.

As PRI President during 1971–75, Jesús Reyes Heroles concentrated largely on healing the wounds between the party and those intellectuals who were alienated by the brutal repression of 1968. In that regard, for example, he sponsored an international conference in 1974 to protest at the military intervention in Chile. Later in the *sexenio* he convened a party commission on a basic plan, recruiting several well-qualified thinkers to grapple with national problems. He also attempted, unsuccessfully, to involve the party more fully in the succession process. With respect to internal party organisation, Reyes Heroles continued to push for changes in candidate selection that would strengthen the base, but without altering the basic structure of the party. Padgett concluded that 'despite the party reform, the principles of hierarchy and discipline directed from above were maintained. Most importantly, the all powerful role of the CEN was reaffirmed on every level'.[32]

Echeverría's populist revival culminated in the political and economic crisis of 1975–76, which set the stage for the LOPPE. As discussed in Chapter 3, the LOPPE was a component of a more comprehensive strategy, and one which may prove historically more significant.

With regard to system reform, the appointment of Reyes Heroles as Interior Secretary in 1976 signalled renewed efforts. The initial appointment of Carlos Sansores Pérez to lead the PRI, however, showed more the continuing influence of Luís Echeverría and disinterest, if not opposition, with respect to internal party reform.[33] The firing of Reyes Heroles in May 1979 seemed to signal a retreat from the system reform; and Sansores' replacement in February 1979 by Gustavo Carvajal reflected more the 'take charge' attitude of López Portillo than an internal party policy. Behind this speculation is the received wisdom that political changes are best implemented early in the *sexenio*, before pressures mount for the presidential succession.

The electoral reforms of 1963 and 1973 covered basically three aspects: lowering the voting age from 21 to 18 and lowering the minimum age to run for congress, easing requirements to register parties for national elections and providing an easier way for them to win seats in the Chamber of Deputies.[34] The 1977 law went beyond the earlier reforms in promoting the opposition. Reyes Heroles had supported the previous efforts, first as a national deputy in 1963 and later as PRI President. His main concern was to create legitimate channels for opposition activity to prevent an accumulation of pressure that might explode in violence and reawaken what he often called 'México bronco' (violent Mexico). His consistent rationale was that the PRI needs institutional opposition: 'The PRI's main fear is to find itself in an institutional vacuum, of not having parties to debate with. "That which opposes assists", is what the CEN president constantly likes to proclaim.'[35]

The 1977 reforms provided that:

1. Parties might qualify to run candidates by registering a minimum number of members in states or electoral districts; alternatively, they might seek provisional registration, and if they received at least 1.5 per cent of the vote in the subsequent national election, their registration would be made permanent (unless their vote in the future dropped below the minimum);
2. The Chamber of Deputies would set aside 100 of 400 seats to opposition parties, to be won by proportional representation in at-large races; and
3. Opposition parties would receive free access to media, the postal frank, as well as subsidies for party expenses.

Also important was a general amnesty granted in 1978 to those convicted of political crimes and the government's commitment to allow greater public access to previously restricted information.

While the purpose of the 1977 reforms was to encourage citizen participation through legitimate channels, a subsequent goal was to stimulate the growth of the left to re-establish equilibrium in electoral politics, given the more impressive growth in influence of the PAN on the right. We can find this notion of the PRI as the centre balance as far back as the electoral law of 1946. It might be argued that the reforms succeeded in increasing electoral participation, as was apparent in higher voter turnouts in 1982, but abstention reappeared at near-record levels in the 1985 mid-term elections. Also, the left never really achieved coherence, either as a party or as a coalition of parties, and the prospect of bipartisan competition with the PAN increased as a threat.

One might also make a case that the 1977 reforms upgraded congress' role and led the PRI to nominate congressional candidates who were more articulate and adept at parliamentary manoeuvring.

Certainly a number of prestigious individuals were nominated by the PRI for the 1979 congress. Also, the addition of around 100 new single-member districts worked to the advantage of the popular sector (as seen in Table 5.2), thus strengthening the presidency and improving the potential for greater electoral competitiveness.

Quite apart from electoral politics, it might be argued that the major accomplishment of the reform was to make dissent routine. Under Díaz Ordaz, and to some degree under Echeverría as well, labour strikes and student demonstrations were often seen as direct challenges to government authority. With López Portillo, strikes could more easily be legalised and resolved through routine bureaucratic procedures. Further, writers enjoyed greater freedom of expression. Little, however, was accomplished with respect to internal party reform. This was evident from the outset of López Portillo's *sexenio* with the appointment of Carlos Sansores.

Carlos Sansores might be considered a successful, disciplined *priísta* of the old school. He entered national politics with Miguel Alemán in 1946, serving as a national deputy. Subsequently, he was elected to the Chamber on three occasions, to the Senate twice and to the governorship of his home state of Campeche. He also held several party posts before his appointment as President of the CEN in December 1976.[36] If one is to believe the critics, Sansores' alliance with Echeverría dates at least from the Madrazo episode and includes Echeverría's support in reaching the governorship of Campeche in 1967.

López Portillo's selection of Sansores to lead the PRI reflected the balancing style discussed in Chapter 3. Reyes Heroles was certainly no *echeverrista*, having feuded with the then-president in 1975–76. Creating a counterweight to Reyes Heroles might have seemed useful. Also, the courting of business interests in the early stages of the Alliance for Production implied debts to labour. Labour was apprehensive about reform, fearing a reduction of its influence within the PRI as well as difficult challenges for control over unions by left opposition parties.[37] Sansores could reassure both Echeverría and labour, and his appointment could contribute to a smooth transition. But Sansores was clearly out of step with the reform project, and his confirmation at the IX Party Assembly of August 1978 left the reformers frustrated.[38]

Even so, Sansores sponsored internal party reforms that came to be labelled 'transparent democracy' (*democracia transparente*), which appear similar in some respects to Madrazo's programme and which will reappear in 1984–85 in a subsequent form as 'consultation with the grassroots' (*consulta a la base militante*).

PRI statutes call for internal nomination processes to be congruent with the varying levels of political, social and economic development of the various regions of the country. Thus, the particular nominating mechanism (*auscultación*, party assemblies, primary elections) for the varieties of elections in each state is left to the decision of the party president, who generally consults with the delegate, the state governor and others. Transparent democracy thus implied an option, not a requirement.

In a July 1977 press conference, Sansores characterised the policy as a flexible process being implemented gradually, in which nominations for local-level offices were chosen by secret ballot in party assemblies. As to the success of the nominees in the general elections, he claimed that some 20 600 municipal posts had gone up for election by that time and – with the exceptions of Puebla and Oaxaca – the PRI had won them all. Counting the three additional states that would hold elections by the end of the year, general elections would be held in 1489 municipalities. Furthermore, he believed that the new nominating process worked to fortify internal democracy and to lessen voter abstention in the general elections.[39]

How much of these claims should be accepted is questionable. We lack a serious study of the effort.[40] It was also clear in the reporters' questions, though, that tensions were rising between Sansores and Reyes Heroles. The press had been attacking Sansores and raising doubts about his continuing as party president. The association-by-question of Sansores with Carlos Hank González, the popular Mayor of the Federal District and presidential contender, though constitutionally ineligible, must have been damaging as well.[41]

Whatever the case, Sansores and transparent democracy disappeared in February 1979 with the arrival of Gustavo Carvajal. With mid-term elections only five months ahead and the second half of the *sexenio* thereafter, Carvajal – and his two successors – needed to emphasise stability and control. Internal party reform would have to await a new *sexenio*.

MORAL RENOVATION AND CONSULTATION WITH THE GRASSROOTS

Miguel de la Madrid began his term with poor relations with the PRI and with a commitment to bring 'moral renovation' to the electoral arena. After setbacks in 1983 and several rounds of difficult encounters with organised labour during 1983–84, the President appeared to pull back from party system reform and to cede greater influence to labour and PRI regulars. During this same period, however, the PRI leadership introduced reforms in candidate selection that came to be labelled 'direct consultations with the grassroot.

De la Madrid's nomination provoked tensions not seen since at least 1952. PRI President Javier García Paniagua openly indicated his irritation; and Fidel Velázquez conditioned labour's support to a series of demands. During the campaign rumours abounded of tensions between party regulars under PRI President Pedro Ojeda Paullada and the candidate's own team. Throughout 1983 the new administration dealt harshly with the CTM, occasionally supporting a rival bloc, the CROM. Tensions persisted into 1984 and complicated the timing and agenda of the PRI's XII Ordinary Party Assembly.

The first assembly convened under a new administration is especially important because personnel changes are ratified and ideological and programmatic directions are announced. The XII Ordinary Assembly was originally scheduled for June, but subsequently was postponed until August, reinforcing rumours of discord and the possibility of dramatic changes. One rumour had it that the sectors would be eliminated and the party renamed. In the event, the assembly produced no dramatic change, but did reassert – among several planks – a commitment to revive direct participation of party militants in the nominations process.

What came to be called 'direct consultation with the grassroots' originated in July 1983 from problems with a specific city: Salina Cruz, Oaxaca. There, several factions struggled to control nominations to municipal posts. The recommendation of the PRI's Director of Assemblies, Maximiliano Silerio Esparza, was to attempt a direct vote of party members, which produced an acceptable candidate. Another experiment was conducted in May 1984 in Nayarit, significant because of the governor's affiliation with the PRI's labour sector. The results were sufficiently encouraging that the idea was adopted by the XII Party Assembly. The cumbersome label eventually given the process was intended to distinguish it from previous reform efforts, Madrazo's internal elections or Sansores Pérez' 'transparent democracy'.

Though with some experimentation, the basic process of direct consultation involved six steps:

1. Convocation of municipal party members, including sectors and sections, to explain procedures;

2. Circulation of petitions by those seeking nomination to office;
3. Study of the petitions by the national PRI's Coordinator of Assemblies to ascertain that the aspirants fulfil legal and party qualifications;
4. Random assignment of candidates' names with photographs on ballots;
5. Establishing voting tables at the neighbourhood level, each with representatives of the three sectors, the nominess, and CEN;
6. Collection and tabulation of the vote, with appeals processes stipulated [42]

The principal formal requisite to implement a consultation is that the CEN's Secretary of Organisation certify that the municipality's sectional committees have been restructured, that the party rolls are complete and that credentials – which are required for the vote – have been issued to party members.

Table 5.3 shows the record of implementing the direct consultation in local elections after Nayarit.

Direct consultations confront strong vested interests at the local level. Though with many variations, municipal governments are frequently controlled by cliques or families, party sectors, labour unions, business interests or some combination of these. Futhermore, the state governors seek to control *at a minimum* the capital city as well as their own particular power bases in the state. Governors' ambitions often exceed the minimum.

The diversity of the various states noted in Table 5.3 complicates the analysis, but two hypotheses might be suggested to explain the implementation of direct consultations: gubernatorial style and opposition strength. Governors enjoy considerable autonomy on political matters and retain power as long as they contain problems within state boundaries.[43] Thus, the governor's decision on consultations is paramount. Also, where opposition party strength is considerable, direct consultation *might* weaken the PRI in the general elections. However, one can conceive of situations in which consultations might strengthen the PRI. A review of contrasting cases, Tabasco and Nuevo León, reveals conditions that facilitate or limit reform.

In Tabasco the PRI has received on average over 86 per cent of the congressional vote during 1970–82. Governor Enrique González Pedrero is considered a progressive and nurtures ambitions to someday become PRI President. The consultations for the 17 municipalities of 10 September 1985 produced surprises: four of the governor's

Table 5.3 PRI's use of 'direct consultations' in choosing municipal candidates, 1984–85

State	*Date of General Elections*	*Number of municipalities*	*Number of consultations*
Nayarit – May 1984		19	12
Yucatán – November 1984		106	104
México – November 1984		122	11
Coahuila – November 1984		34	12
Hidalgo – December 1984		84	33
Morelos – March 1985		33	0
Querétaro – July 1985		18	0
Sonora – July 1985		69	39
Veracruz – October 1985		203	57
Tlaxcala – October 1985		44	39
Nuevo León – October 1985		51	0
Tabasco – November 1985		17	17
Colima – November 1985		10	10
Chiapas – November 1985		111	0
Campeche – November 1985		8	7
Guanajuato – December 1985		46	0
Jalisco – December 1985		124	10
Zacatecas – December 1985		56	55
San Luís Potosí – Dec. 1985		56	55

Source: Interview material, November 1985.

candidates were defeated. Interestingly, the outgoing mayors exercised influence in the selections, which led some to speculate that if the reform continued the mayors might become the key actors at the municipal level. 'Normal' politics seemed to hold in other cases. A candidate in Cárdenas was able to use the governor's endorsement to deter opponents, and in Paraíso the local section of the oil workers union used money and PEMEX vehicles to bring workers in from other areas to elect its candidate. In the state capital of Villahermosa a former congressman faced no opposition after PRI members learned he had the support of Interior Secretary Manuel Bartlett Díaz.[44]

Nuevo León presents stark contrasts. There the PRI has won an average of 74 per cent of the congressional vote during 1970–82, but the opposition has increased in recent years. The gubernatorial elections of 7 July 1985 produced strong protests and minor violence due to the PAN's claim that the PRI had resorted to extraordinary levels of fraud. Outgoing governor Alfonso Martínez Domínguez, a leading 'old school' *priísta*, is thought to seek a leadership role in strengthening the party's *político* faction. Martínez' personal candidate for the governorship was overriden by Mexico City, and some concessions were owed. He was granted considerable sway in shaping the state's congressional delegation as well as a free hand in the *municipios*. The PRI's mayoral candidate for Monterrey, Luís M. Farías, was a party veteran cut from the same cloth as the outgoing governor. In a surprisingly low turnout in the October 1985 municipal elections, Farías won easily, but amid renewed protests of official fraud.

In a 1985 year-end speech PRI President Adolfo Lugo summed up the party's policy on direct consultations: the commitment to the process remains firm; consultations will be attempted flexibly, according to the specific conditions in each state; the indispensable conditions are unity and internal discipline; the process will proceed gradually with political realism; and 'despite the great deal that has been accomplished in deepening democratic life in the heart of the party, that – due to the survival of local fiefdoms [*cacicazgos*] – we encounter obstacles and resistance'.[45]

Party officials stress the success of the direct consultations in producing candidates that in turn can win in general elections. A recurring problem, though, is that the consultations appear in some cases to divide the party internally and to reduce voter turnout in the general elections. Losers in the consultations may not give full support to the winning candidate, and there have been cases of losers defecting to opposition parties. In a way similar to the Democratic party in the 'Old South' of the United States, the important decisions are taken in the primary with the general election held merely as ratification. This puts the PRI in jeopardy in cases where the opposition is strong, and one finds repeated exhortations to *priístas* to turn out and vote.[46]

WHAT FUTURE FOR PARTY REFORM?

The easiest conclusion about party reform is scepticism. Certainly, complaints in 1986 by a disgruntled PRI official in San Luís Potosí leaves one chary:

> We can't show our faces. No one believes us. Everybody listens to us with a smirk [*sonrisa burlona*]. One wants to convince the

> people – the way I was – that there is a different, democratic attitude, but one ends up thinking they were right: the PRI doesn't evolve, it's always the same.[47]

More interesting, however, is to make cases both for and against party reform and then consider the likelihood of each. Supporting party reform is that the regime needs a response to the almost universal scepticism about moral renovation and widespread criticism of the government's inept response to the earthquakes of September 1985. The continuing hardline rejection of the PAN argues against electoral system reform. Also, the consultations process is limited to the municipal level and is being implemented flexibly. Over time, as perhaps the Tabasco example suggests, support for continuing the consultations might acquire a certain momentum. Conceivably, some set of circumstances might reduce labour opposition, either a passing of the present leadership or a trade-off in some other area.

Arguing against reform is the conventional wisdom that the party returns to its foundations during the second half of the *sexenio*. Fifteen states hold gubernatorial and/or local elections in the fourth year, including cases in which the opposition counts (Chihuahua, Durango, Sinaloa, Tamaulipas) or which have especially conflictive histories (Guerrero, Oaxaca, Puebla, Veracruz). One searches the list in vain for a case hospitable to consultations. Even in terms of limited personnel, the party would be hard-pressed to implement consultations in most nominations contests. The problems of debt and economic opening complicate reform.

Thus, some scepticism about continued reform seems justly warranted. But that scepticism should be tempered with the knowledge that significant reform currents remain alive within the party and that the rhythm of Mexican politics will provide opportunities for renewal.[48]

6 Interest Group Politics and Government–Business Relations

In everyday language the labels *sector público* (public sector) and *iniciativa privada* (private sector, sometimes given simply as I.P.) denote two distinct sub-cultures that have increasingly come into conflict since the early 1970s. The single most important domestic issue confronting the Mexican government in the 1980s is the renegotiation of a workable set of government–business agreements that will overcome mutual distrust and clear the way for resumed domestic investment, assuming that investible capital becomes available in the continuing liquidity squeeze.[1] A renewed pact is critical because growth was a requisite of the previous order and there is no other obvious source of investment: petroleum revenues are highly mortgaged to interest payments on the foreign debt, there is little likelihood of substantial voluntary foreign private lending and increased direct foreign investment will be insufficient.

The main participants in these negotiations include the Mexican government (presidency, bureaucracy and party), the business community (both domestic and foreign) and certain closely involved groups, especially labour unions and the national intelligentsia, each of which operates with complex and conflicting agendas as well as significant resources and constraints. The simultaneous equations to be solved are a mutually acceptable government–business pact, and agreement on Mexico's foreign trade and investment policies. A solution depends upon external factors as well: regional peace, manageable debt and increasing opportunities for exports. The devastating earthquakes that struck central and western Mexico in September 1985 further complicated the calculations, as did the oil price collapse after November of that same year.

We should begin the analysis by recalling critical features of the setting. Population growth on the order of 2.6 per cent annually, with even faster growth of the labour force (perhaps at an annual rate of 3.5 per cent), constitutes the critical parameter. Though not measurable in any valid way, increasing expectations of new entrants to the job market matter as well.

Both a cause and consequence of population growth is extreme income inequality. Mexico ranks as one of the most unequal nations in Latin America with respect to income distribution and – although much controversy marks the research in this field – the inequality probably worsened with the inflation and unemployment after 1981. Faced with the intractability of inequality, government has constructed complex webs of subsidies and services, erecting what has come to be called a 'fictional economy'. Along with an extensive informal economy, this support web has served to channel limited benefits to the lower strata. The mechanisms of these transfers were designed in turn to reinforce support for the PRI–government. For example, urban immigrants who seized land to construct precarious dwellings were frequently provided services and enrolled in PRI-affiliated organisations.

Except for the Monterrey and Puebla business groups, the Mexican private sector was in effect invented by government in the post-World War Two period of ISI to constitute the engine of growth in a mixed economy. As a gross generalisation, business and industrial firms comprised relatively small-scale enterprises and tended to adopt a concessionary mentality, stressing limited production volumes and high profits over the short term. As a promoter, government granted generous protection and subsidies. These arrangements, as with ther poor, reinforced government control throughout society and worked to the satisfaction of most parties until the Echeverría government.

This pattern of growth produced structural deformities. Business firms operated largely with reference to the domestic market and neglected export opportunities. Protection through import licences, price controls and other measures inhibited efficiency and innovation. Especially important, government failed to construct a tax system that could finance desired levels of public expenditures. Much of this failure was due to the conviction that low taxes would promote private capital formation. A structural constraint here is that with the US market next door Mexican business demands a stiff premium for its investments. As Roger Hansen put it: 'In a less developed country, especially one with no restrictions on capital outflows, only the continuously demonstrated capacity of the political system to ensure stability and profitable economic opportunities can induce growing rates of private domestic investment'.[2]

Discord grew in the 1970s as Echeverría revived populism to co-opt the left and emphasised 'revolutionary nationalism', a variant on social democratic ideology. Revolutionary nationalism, in turn, was seen as threatening by business groups, whose perspectives were shaped by traditional liberal and Catholic social values. Business groups grew stronger but also more vulnerable during the oil boom of the late 1970s and early 1980s. The López Portillo government's mismanagement of the oil price collapse and the bank nationalisation reinforced a growing disillusionment with the competence of the political class, but the foreign debts of many significant firms made these increasingly dependent upon government assistance.

The De la Madrid government inherited the difficult situation of profound structural distortions at a time when many segments of the business community were deeply alienated from the political system. In the renegotiation of the government–business pact, opening the economy means that international standards of efficiency and productivity must increasingly shape business decisions. This is turn implies a less preponderant role for government in promotion and regulation and greater autonomy for market forces. Expanding the market means reducing government's influence at the same time that social pressures rise as subsidies and protection are modified or – in some cases – dismantled. In the policy debate, critics of statist practices correctly call for market-oriented reforms; equally correctly, critics of neo-liberalism denounce the vices of the Mexican private sector and emphasise the harm that will befall Mexico as market forces take hold: loss of national control over the economy and worse privations for the lower classes. Hard-liners and moderates populate both camps.

Mexico's foreign debt figures importantly in the debate as external actors, principally the US banks and government, push the Mexican government to diminish its role and promote economic efficiency. The US government can enlist international financial institutions such as the IMF and World Bank in this campaign. For its part, the Mexican government has recognised the need to implement reforms and has taken steps to trim the size of the public sector and to promote efficiency. But pressures persist to extend the changes, and behind US complaints about drugs, illegal migration, corruption and authoritarianism some Mexicans suggest that the real agenda is to liberalise laws on trade and foreign investment.

In these complex debates one hears extreme and moderate voices both within Mexico and abroad. Within the country, hard-line minorities attempt to force a dialogue of dichotomies: either the traditional presidential system or real democracy; either socialism or free markets. Moderates on both sides search for alternative forms of accommodation. In the United States, actions range from provocative senatorial hearings and vigilante threats to police the border to more sensible pleas for constructive negotiation. Throughout, De la Madrid has reiterated his position: difficult changes are being implemented in the context of Mexican institutions, and foreign pressures will not dictate the course of Mexican domestic policy.[3] Whether such a stance can be sustained in the face of debt, oil prices and trade pressures is problematic.

Thus, the stakes of the controversy are high. What kind of economy can evolve that can generate sufficient growth and employment, compete on world markets, locate principally outside the Central Valley and remain under Mexican control?

This chapter reviews generalisations about interest group politics in the light of trends since the early 1970s. It then examines government and allied groups from the perspective of interest politics. The following section analyses the business communty and its representation through peak associations. The concluding section reviews the debates within and among these groups over the past decade about the proper course of economic development. The working argument is that the rupture of the government–business pact is so severe that it will require several years, certainly beyond the De la Madrid *sexenio*, to repair. Relations between government and business are further complicated by the policy of foreign investment and trade liberalisation pursued tentatively under López Portillo and more consistently thereafter.

INTEREST POLITICS AFTER 1970

Authoritarianism has served as the reigning interpretive model for Mexican politics since the mid-1960s, replacing the previous and short-lived image of that nation as evolving toward something like pluralist democracy. Juan Linz's influential framework stresses that authoritarianism should be viewed as an enduring regime type, not as one necessarily evolving toward either liberal democratic or totalitarian opposites. Interest group politics in authoritarian systems are characterised by limited pluralism, low subject mobilisation and a state interest. That is, groups are recognised but their behaviour is closely constrained by political authorities; independent and active movements are discouraged; and government is guided by an elite consensus on more or less coherent programmatic goals.[4]

Subsequent work on authoritarianism in Latin America stressed the class bias of most of these systems, in which most active controls are exercised over labour, peasant and dissident middle sector groups, with middle and upper strata interests as well as most producer associations enjoying greater independence and state support.[5] It was also shown that complex patterns of state penetration of interest groups coexist with group penetration of government bureaucracies. The later work was more attentive as well to the historical setting and the dependent status of the Latin American countries.

The authoritarianism model led to more accurate and suggestive analyses of interest politics in Mexico. It more fully accounted for patterns of state initiative and apparent group passivity. With some critical revision[6], this approach allows one to sum up in a rough *ad hoc* fashion a set of propositions about interest politics in Mexico:

1. The state during the 1930s–1940s was the major force in shaping Mexican society;
2. A system of interest representation was constructed by government in a top-down fashion through the bureaucracy and official party to include most organised groups;
3. The formal system encompasses perhaps a majority of Mexican society, but a much smaller proportion, limited largely to a minority of middle and upper-strata urban dwellers, participate actively in interest politics;
4. Labour, peasants and middle sector groups (including some businessmen) are represented in both the PRI and the government bureaucracy;
5. Diverse producer and commercial interests are organised into both mandatory chambers, as well as into voluntary associations;
6. The formal system of representation is structured along quasi-corporatist lines, with functional criteria such as labour, producer, peasant generally more significant than geographical boundaries;
7. Government most closely controls lower-strata groups and grants preferential status to producer interests, upper and middle sector groups and such elites as university students and intellectuals;
8. Government bureaucracy is coherent and responsive to presidential control, but a degree of autonomy and bureaucratic politics affects policy-making;

9. The formal system of interest representation is supplemented with complex informal networks of friendships and patron–client ties that guide benefits to the privileged and permit communications with outgroups, for example, the Catholic Church and foreign investors;
10. A coherent state interest sets out programmatic goals, which each administration can translate into concrete programmes;
11. In general, policy initiatives originate in the executive branch, involving the presidency at some point, and interest groups are largely limited to reacting to government;
12. In policy-making, the formal architecture of interest representation may be active in policy formulation, depending on the attitude of the presidency, but the tendency is to focus on consultation during policy implementation; the informal networks concentrate on policy implementation;
13. Interest associations, reflecting government structures and processes, are also centralised; and
14. The legitimacy of the Revolutionary projects of nationalism, liberalism, welfare as well as continuous economic growth provide a consensus that supports interest politics.

Formulated during the 1960s–1970s, the wisdom about interest politics has not yet fully registered the significance of change since Echeverría. Part of the reason is that the Linz model itself is most useful in static comparative analysis, and this limitation was sometimes exaggerated by insufficient attention to the historical dynamic of Mexican politics. The argument throughout the book holds that the basic pacts that underpinned interest politics in Mexico since the 1940s are now being challenged and may be substantially modified. Thus, the received wisdom about interest politics may prove a poor guide during this period of transition.

PRESIDENCY, BUREAUCRACY AND STATE INTEREST

In some respects the Echeverría presidency hastened trends already underway in Mexican government. Government planning and state participation in the economy had been increased in tentative fashion under President Díaz Ordaz. Echeverría's interpretation of the political crisis of 1968, joined with the economic downturn of 1970–71 and expressed in his own abrasive style perhaps explain some of the frenetic pace of change during his *sexenio*. With oil income, the López Portillo government renewed the statist trends following the retrenchment of 1977–78. The rate and nature of change in public sector activity during 1970–85 shown in Table 6.1 convey a central aspect of the present government–business tension.

Echeverría began his administration with essentially good relations with the private sector, despite his revolutionary nationalist rhetoric. Businessmen were long accustomed to politicians' populist rhetoric belied by practical support, and Echeverría was considered initially a conformist product of the system. The creation in 1971 of a National Tripartite Commission (government, labour, business) to concentrate on defining and resolving national, as opposed to sectorial or specific issues, seemed to provide a new channel of representation for business. Echeverría continued to subsidise and protect Mexican business during most of his term, but relations with the private sector deteriorated. Causes included the President's sponsorship of tax reform, controls on foreign investment and technology transfer, the pace of expansion of public enterprises into production and commerce and his increasing alliance with organised labour. The assassination by terrorists in September 1973 of Eugenio Garza Sada of the Monterrey group, who had acted as mediator between business and government, proved a pivotal turning point toward worsened relations. By 1976 charges and counter-charges between government and business associations led to significant capital flight and the government's land expropriation in Sonora and Sinaloa. Business groups emerged from the episode with a new and independent peak organisation, the Business Coordinating Council (CCE, formed in 1975), and a more radicalised anti-government orientation.[7]

López Portillo also began his term with essentially good relations with business groups. By emphasising political reform to guide dissent into legitimate channels and administrative reform to bring coherence to an expanded and unwieldy bureaucracy, López Portillo was able to make government planning and legalisation of left parties less objectionable to business interests. His Alliance for Production attempted to enlist both business and labour in a pact to control wages and prices to support the IMF-negotiated austerity programme. With the massive new petroleum discoveries for financing, López Portillo first worked to reestablish business confidence, then opted for high growth after 1978. A series of assumptions about oil prices, interest rates, and rapid international economic recovery proved incorrect. When signs of an oil glut appeared in May 1981 the

Table 6.1 Expansion of public sector activity, 1970–83

	A	*B*	*C*	*D*	*E*	*F*
1970	419	83	91	8	4.3	–
1971	452	91	100	11	4.5	–
1972	565	105	127	23	5.1	–
1973	691	138	172	37	7.1	8.4
1974	900	190	240	52	10.1	6.1
1975	1100	251	338	101	14.4	5.5
1976	1371	317	444	139	19.6	4.3
1977	1849	436	531	96	22.9	3.5
1978	2337	587	708	130	26.3	8.2
1979	3068	794	1017	232	29.8	9.1
1980	4277	1181	1520	333	33.8	8.4
1981	5858	1581	2426	865	53.0	8.1
1982	9417	2887	4600	1740	56.6	–0.5
1983	17429	5849	7662	1680	73.4	–4.7

A. Gross domestic product in billions of current pesos
B. Public sector income in billions of current pesos
C. Public sector expenditures in billions of current pesos
C. Financial deficit in billions of current pesos
E. Foreign public debt in billions of current US dollars
F. Percentage growth in GDP in 1970 pesos

government delayed cutting oil prices, then adopted a series of inadequate responses. Inflation accelerated, as did deficits in the balance of payments and of trade as well as in public sector financing. Watching developments with growing concern, many in both government and the private sector began to speculate against the peso, increasing the pace of capital flight. Events reeled out of control by mid-1982, culminating in the currency controls and bank nationalisation of August and September.

By rupturing the 'mixed economy' pact that had governed relations between government and business since 1925, the abrupt changes in banking policy thoroughly traumatised many elements of the private sector and the middle strata generally. Not only were the banks a significant source of investment capital for Mexican industry, the major chains served as the hubs for industrial groups. The banks also provided a source of leadership for the private sector in its dealings with government. The initial reaction by business leaders to the bank seizure was surprisingly muted, perhaps because of the assurance of adequate compensation and the substantial public support shown for the President's dramatic move.[8]

Table 6.1 (continued)

	G	H	I	J	K
1970	–	19.8	21.7	1.9	–
1971	5.7	20.1	22.1	2.4	4.7
1972	5.0	18.6	22.5	4.1	13.3
1973	11.4	20.0	24.5	4.1	39.2
1974	22.4	21.1	26.7	5.8	40.8
1975	16.9	22.8	30.7	9.2	44.0
1976	15.9	23.1	32.5	10.1	36.1
1977	29.0	23.6	28.7	5.2	16.8
1978	17.4	25.1	30.3	5.6	14.8
1979	18.2	25.9	33.1	7.6	13.3
1980	26.4	27.6	35.5	7.8	13.4
1981	27.9	27.0	41.4	14.8	56.8
1982	58.9	30.6	48.8	18.5	6.8
1983	101.9	31.5	44.0	9.6	29.7

G. Percentage annual increase in consumer price index
H. Public sector income as a percentage of GDP
I. Public sector expenditures as a percentage of GDP
J. Financial deficit as a percentage of GDP
K. Percentage annual increase in public foreign debt

Sources: Jose López Portillo, *Tercer informe de gobierno, Anexo* I (1979); *Sexto informe de gobierno, Sector política económica* (1982); Miguel de la Madrid, *Segundo informe de gobierno, Sector política económica* (1985); Inter-American Development Bank, *Economic and Social Progress*, 1976, 1981–82, 1982, 1986.

The bank action, combined with deteriorating confidence and the high savings interest rates in the US, acted to spur capital flight. Previous bouts of flight – as in 1960–61 and 1976–77 – aimed at influencing government policy or were linked to over-valuation, and quickly subsided. The situation after 1982 was distinctive due to the volume, perhaps as much as $50 billion in US financial instruments alone, and apparent permanence. It would seem obvious that Mexico cannot tolerate for long a capital haemorrhage of this magnitude and that such resources would figure importantly in a sustainable recovery. One estimate shows that Mexico's foreign debt as of 1986 would total $12 instead of $97 billion if there had been no capital flight. In contrast to nearly 90 per cent in the Mexican case, Brazilian capital flight amounts to only 7 per cent of that nation's $106 billion foreign debt. Private US banks have balked at extending fresh credit that seems to finance continued flight. This must be seen as disingenuous since much of the flight returns to those same banks. Regardless, the rates and directions of capital movement serve as something of a barometer of business confidence.[9]

As presidential candidate, De la Madrid indicated reservations about López Portillo's 'economic populism' (at least as much as the official candidate can), and as President-Elect, he showed little enthusiasm for the bank nationalisation. He moved promptly to arrange compensation and divestiture of corporate shares held by banks as loan collateral. But two factors worked to complicate his government's relations with the private sector. By introducing amendments in December 1982 to raise planning, state tutelage of the economy and the notion of a 'social sector' to constitutional status, he provoked criticism.[10] More important, though, was his support for opening the Mexican economy toward greater foreign trade and investment. If the bank nationalisation ruptured the old pact, economic opening pointed the way towards a new order, one which the majority of businessmen viewed with great trepidation.

With this background, two aspects of state behaviour merit comment: the significance of 'revolutionary nationalism' as state ideology and the general policy orientations of the government bureaucracy with respect to the desirable form of mixed economy. In a highly statist system, official ideology carries extra weight. And the government bureaucracy will influence how government–business relations are managed.

The 1917 Constitution contains both statist and market provisions, which have been implemented pragmatically under the catch-all label 'mixed economy'. The statist tradition is embodied in such provisions as Articles 25–28 and implemented in policies such as the petroleum nationalisation of 1938 and restrictions on foreign ownership of land within Mexico. At the same time, Article 123 explicitly recognises private firms in outlining government's role in supervising labour–management relations. In the postwar period the statist tradition was tempered with political pragmatism and consistent support for the private sector. Businessmen perceived this pragmatism to be rejected by Echeverría's revolutionary nationalism.

Essentially, revolutionary nationalism follows the mainstream of modern social democratic ideology, positing a mixed economy under state tutelage, central planning of the indicative sort and increased welfare. López Portillo tended to play down the ideology, appearing at times even to toy with the formulae of nationalist revolutionary, revolutionary nationalist. President De la Madrid embraced the ideology throughout his campaign, in his inaugural address and again in the opening paragraphs of his first annual report to Congress. But his formulations of the ideology stress a balance of individual liberties with equality and social justice.[11]

Revolutionary nationalism also shares much in common with populist ideologies elsewhere in Latin America. The core notion is that the Mexican experience has given rise to a unique programme of ideas particularly suited to that country. In this programme a strong state is needed to defend the national territory and the welfare of the weak. The government assumes the rectorship of a mixed economy and exercises leadership through democratic planning. It exercises broad regulatory powers to set wages and prices and exercises a monopoly in defined areas. A closely related notion is 'integral democracy'. As set out in Article 3 and elsewhere, democracy means much more than parties and elections narrowly considered. Rather, 'the 1917 Constitution conceived of democracy as a political structure, a juridical regime and a way of life founded in the constant social, economic and cultural improvement of the people'.[12] Furthermore, 'integral democratisation' requires grounding political power in the basic consensus of the majorities as represented in the PRI, and exercised through a state bound by respect for the law.[13] Thus, while social democratic ideology may be compatible with electoral democracy, revolutionary nationalism equates rule by the PRI with integral democracy.

Many in the private sector hold a 'devil theory' explanation of revolutionary nationalism. To them, it was introduced by the Marxist Vicente Lombardo Toledano in the 1950s, subsequently smuggled into the PRI in 1972 by Jesús Reyes Heroles, where it was adopted by Echeverría and further propagated by party theoretician Enrique Ramírez y Ramírez. It is seen as Leninist in origin, serving as a covert strategy of the socialist international for the construction of socialism in developing countries. Especially significant are the adoption of government planning and the expansion of the government bureaucracy into spheres claimed by the private sector. De la Madrid is seen as firmly committed to the programme, and his advocacy of planning and the state rectorship of the economy is proof that the socialist project continues apace.[14]

The 'devil theory' is symptomatic of the profound distrust businessmen feel towards government. Distrust is nurtured by lack of political sophistication in a sector which for many years had left politics to the PRI and only recently has felt motivated to participate. The centralised and secretive nature of Mexican politics reinforces conspiracy theorising.

The central government bureaucracy, dominated by the presidency, is the main source of public policy. Public sector personnel are recruited largely from the middle strata, but study different fields in comparison with private sector businessmen. Also, as might be expected, public sector personnel tend to adopt more statist views than their private sector counterparts. The sum of these factors gives the relatively great social distance between public and private sectors, in contrast to the cases of Columbia and Brazil, for example, where there is greater migration between camps.[15] The phenomenon of the old-style politician–businessman provided a bit of a bridge between sectors, although the political entrepreneurs tended to favour such activities as construction rather than industry. With the rise of the technocrats, whose careers depend more completely on the growth and importance of the public bureaucracy, this social distance has probably increased.

On the other hand, one might argue that with the expansion of the state enterprise sector, managed by *técnicos* – some holding advanced degrees in business administration – there might be greater convergence of public and private sectors as the *técnicos* experience at closer range the tribulations of the business world. Furthermore, there is evidence that government increasingly recruits its better trained *técnicos* from elite private universities, such as ITAM, Ibero-Americana and Anáhuac, thus eroding the virtual monopoly of the UNAM economics faculty. One might infer from this trend a kind of infiltration from the right, as more eclectic neo-keynesian approaches replace the statist thinking of the National University.[16]

However, it seems to me that state enterprises operate with substantially fewer constraints than private firms with respect to credit, profits, taxes, import restrictions, labour relations and government regulations. Also, state-sector managers are thoroughly integrated into the overall system of political recruitment and circulation, with their careers riding less on agency performance than on group ties and luck. But all this is speculative. More research is required to determine the new synthesis of elite recruitment and agency orientations.

Lacking a career service and marked by high rates of turnover at the policy-making levels, the central bureaucracy is still reasonably coherent and responsive to presidential leadership. Mexican 'bureaucratic politics', as shown in Chapter 4, are different from those of the United States. Rather than 'iron triangles' made up of interest group, congressional subcommittee and agency subdivision, one finds rather formalistic interest activity, virtually negligible congressional involvement, and much diluted agency and sub-agency orientation. The President's attitude sets the tone of agency orientations. Nonetheless, agency orientations are identifiable to some extent and do count in policy-making. Such orientations count in the President's effort to build a consensus for policy. This is especially the case when the policy touches on the nature of the government–business pact.

Taken in the context of a strong state as rector of a mixed economy, one can say that a pro-private sector outlook characterises the Bank of Mexico, Treasury and SPP. A more complicated and ambivalent outlook characterises SECOFIN, which is charged with regulating many aspects of market transactions and with promoting industrial development, and SARH, which tends to represent the larger-scale agri-business interests. Both agencies supervise large public enterprises and naturally share certain statist attitudes. Also, their strength derives in part from administering webs of market regulations. SEMIP tends to adopt an anti-business outlook, largely because its main constituency is government enterprises. For example, businessmen complained that when they sought precise information from SEMIP on state enterprises presumably available for purchase they encountered mainly delays and obfuscation.[17]

Still, it is inaccurate to adopt a bureaucratic politics perspective, because there is a high degree of personnel turnover and limited career services, which tend to disrupt interest group linkages with bureaucracy. Also, there is a tendency to place officials with different perspectives on policy questions in the same agency.

BUSINESS GROUPS AND IDEOLOGY

Given the pervasive role of government in creating and sustaining development, as well as the complexity of the business community, the term 'private sector' is a bit of a misnomer, but convenience dictates a kind of shorthand.[18]

Much simplified, since the 1940s the Mexican business community has been divided into two broad factions: the 'northerners', who tended to adopt more radical stances against government activities, and the 'centralists', who generally followed a more moderate line. The northern faction dates from the last half of the nineteenth century and has its epicentre in Monterrey, with allies in other states, Chihuahua, for example. Consolidated during the Porfiriato, the northern faction is based in industry, commerce, agriculture and mining; it has a strong sense of its own class identity and demonstrates a combativeness with respect to the state that emerged from the Revolution. This faction has clashed periodically with government, especially on questions involving agrarian reform and the *ejido*, official unionism, state intervention into the economy and statist rhetoric. Proximity to and closer commercial contact with the United States reinforces impatience with Mexico City. Led by large firms, the northern bloc has participated actively in the public debate, taking leadership positions in COPARMEX and helping found PAN to counter *cardenista* populism. Through these organs, and also from leadership positions in the National Chambers of Commerce and Industry (CONCANACOMIN, the forerunner of the current industrial and commercial organisations), the northern faction has sought to organise and speak for business interests nationally.

The other main faction is based in the Valley of Mexico and more specifically in Mexico City. It dates from the 1920s–1930s and is concentrated more in diversified small-scale manufacturing, which took root with the government protection. The central faction co-existed with larger-scale foreign and public firms in the Confederation of Chambers of Industry and experienced a sense of vulnerability to competition and thus greater need for government assistance. During the 1930s this diverse group founded the National Association of Industrialists within the CONCAMIN, and in the 1940s – when the CONCANACOMIN was separated into confederations of industry and commerce – the central faction consolidated itself as the National Chambers of Transformation Industries (CANACINTRA) within the industrial confederation. The central bloc is more fully based in industry and typically senses greater vulnerability to foreign competition and thus greater need for government protection. Its dealings with government are therefore more pragmatic and focused on issues of industry. Also, the central bloc generally accepts more the government's hegemony and participates through pro-business factions of the PRI, such as the *alemanista* group.

As in many countries, much of the significant contact and negotiation between government and business is carried on discreetly. Thus, while PRI–government and business leaders may engage in apparently harsh public exchanges, private conversations may be more cordial. The opposite holds as well. Also, one should not confuse the elected leaders of business associations with 'real' leaders. But, to confound things further, neither should one accept at face value the frequent PRI charges that association leaders are somehow unauthentic spokesmen for business interests. Important aspects of government–business relations are carried on by formal associations, and a review of this aspect is worthwhile.

Six peak business associations are most active in the national level dialogue on government–business relations. This is not to suggest that specialised chambers such as chemicals or foreign trade or certain regional chambers, especially Monterrey, Puebla and Guadalajara, are unimportant. Rather, in the case of the former, they tend to look after the interests of their constituents, while the latter tend to follow the lead of the national groups.

The National Confederation of Chambers of Industry (CONCAMIN) and the National Confederation of Chambers of Commerce (CONCANACO) are obligatory chambers.[19] With considerable inflation over the past decade, even quite small-scale firms qualify for the minimum peso volume that determines membership. The local chambers in turn are affiliated with state and national chambers, providing a percentage of members' dues to support the higher associations. CANACINTRA belongs to CONCAMIN, but has a special identity due to its close cooperation with government during the import-substitution phase.[20] With large and diverse memberships (CONCAMIN claimed some 94 000 members as of 1979, CONCANACO some 400 000) it is difficult for the peak associations to reach clear cut positions on specific issues. Some general concerns, such as support for tax incentives and the protection of Mexico's eligibility under the Generalised System of Preferences programme, would promote unity. A continual tension within these peak associations separates the large *versus* small-scale enterprises.[21]

The Mexican Employers' Confederation (COPARMEX) is significant as a voluntary association which embraces virtually all fields of enterprise, including finance. Legally organised under labour legislation as an 'employers' union', COPARMEX claims some 18 000 members, most of whom belong also to one or another of the obligatory chambers. COPARMEX tends to take a harder line in government–business relations, reflecting more the Monterrey mindset of its founders. Another voluntary association, the Mexican Council of Businessmen (CMHN), is an elite group of some 30 or so top Mexican entrepreneurs who own and operate their own firms. Formed in 1958 to combat erroneous foreign perceptions of Mexico, the CMHN is not well known. Basáñez is probably correct in depicting it as a kind of politburo of the CCE.[22]

The CCE was created in 1975 to orchestrate a business response to Echeverría's anti-business rhetoric and actions. Comprised of the peak associations noted above (plus the Mexican Association of Insurance Companies, AMIS) the CCE tends to stress the general issues of trends in the economy and overall government policies. With the Private Sector Centre for Economic Studies (CEESP) and the Centre for Sociological Studies (CES), the CCE generates a steady stream of information to its members, government and the media.

In general terms, business leaders tend to rotate frequently from one to another of the associations, with little important distinction drawn between industry and commerce. There is some minor movement of leaders from the business associations to government, for example, the Cano Escalante brothers, but there is virtually none in the other direction. Government tends to exercise greater influence in the leadership selection in the obligatory chambers (CONCAMIN, CANACINTRA, CONCANACO) than in the voluntary associations. But even in the latter groups, government exercises some degree of influence if only by members' anticipation of government response. Patterns of leadership selection indicate trends in government–business relations, as the candidates' views on these issues are generally known.[23]

The groups perform important representation functions for their members, and surveys show that business firms cite participation in chambers and associations as a principal activity.[24] In their periodic public meetings with government officials, as well as in a variety of public statements, the associations set the tone of business–government relations. They provide data about economic and political trends, which is especially helpful to their smaller-scale members. And they provide ideological guidance as well. The associations strictly observe a policy of non-partisanship, but insist that individual businessmen should take part in political activity as a civic duty.

In general terms, a moderately critical stance toward government is adopted by CONCAMIN and CANACINTRA. Hard-line criticism characterises COPARMEX and CONCANACO. The other main associations (CCE, CMHN, AMIS, the National Confederation of Cattlemen – CNG, and CAMCO) oscillate between moderate and hard criticism. Two other groups, the National Confederation of Small Farmers (CNPP) and the National Confederation of Small

Merchants (CNPC) belong to the popular sector of the PRI and typically support government.[25]

Business ideology draws on classical western liberalism and Catholic social thought of the early twentieth century.[26] The individual is the basic unit of society, and individual freedom and dignity are the principal ends of the state. Private property is a natural right, not one conceded by the state, and the defence of property against state encroachment is critical in order to prevent totalitarianism. Property should serve a useful social purpose by generating wealth and employment. Employers should observe responsibilities to their workers in keeping with the goals of human freedom and dignity. The mixed economy is desirable, with government attending to public order, essential services and activities beyond the capacity of private enterprise. Generally, the principle of subsidiarity should be observed, such that social functions should be performed by the smallest capable units, that is, individual, family, private firm or local government, with national government strictly limiting its involvement.

LABOUR AND THE NATIONALIST INTELLIGENTSIA

Labour unions influence the renegotiation of a government–business pact, because the unions constitute the backbone of the PRI, which in turn serves as a critical pillar of support for the presidency. The nationalist intelligentsia, for want of a better term, also influence the debate, because elite opinion carries weight in policy-making, and in this instance the majority of commentators express anti-business views.

The Congress of Labour (CT) was formed in 1966 and consists of some 34 unions with an estimated membership of about 5 to 6 millions.[27] Formed during the populist government of Lázaro Cárdenas, the labour movement preserves something of the class-struggle ideology and rhetoric, although this was tempered by the expulsion of Vicente Lombardo Toledano from the CTM in the mid-1940s and the more pragmatic bent of the new leadership of the Fidel Velázquez group. The CTM may act independently and on behalf of the presidency in government–business exchanges.

Workers generally have borne much of the sacrifice of the economic crisis of the 1970s–1980s, and the CT reported that wages and salaries as a percentage of GDP declined from 48.1 in 1975 to 30 in 1984. Labour also maintains that the minimum wage is insufficient to sustain a family of five and that an estimated 60 per cent of the workforce earn less than the minimum.[28] Faced with economic stagnation, union leaders have concentrated pragmatically on the broader concept of the social wage (food subsidies, employer contributions to social security, housing and the like)[29] and political concessions. However, a more recent and significant demand is the 'social sector', which is of special concern to business leaders.

The concept of the social sector, if not the term itself, first appeared in the 1917 Constitution with reference to the *ejido*, or cooperative farm. It reappeared in vaguer form in the vocabulary of the 1970s, for example, in government planning documents, referring to the mixed economy as consisting of public, private and social sectors. The latter referred ostensibly to the *ejidos* and cooperatives, principally union cooperatives. By 1980, union theoreticians, such as Arturo Romo, began to advocate greater government support for the social sector as a means of correcting the flaws of the mixed economy. The unions were unhappy with De la Madrid's nomination, and as part of the price for their support for him and for the austerity programme, they sought and received constitutional status in Article 25 for a broader conception of the social sector. In March–April 1985 the CT won commitments from government to implement legislation and provide funds to support the social sector.[30] Businessmen oppose the social sector on the practical grounds that the government will subsidise a variety of union enterprises, thus fortifying the union leadership and creating yet another front of disloyal competition, in addition to the public enterprises. They also oppose the theoretical justification of the social sector as a realistic step toward a more humane society.[31]

Striking by its absence from the mainstream of Mexican intellectual discourse is an articulate advocate for Mexican private enterprise. At the level of elite opinion, the prevailing bias of the more influential Mexico City dailies, for example, *Excélsior*, *Unomásuno*, *La Jornada*, *Universal*, as well as opinion and cultural magazines such as *Proceso*, *Nexos* and *Vuelta* is anti-business. Business finds sympathy and defenders in the electronic media, especially those controlled by Televisa, in conservative newspapers and magazines such as *Novedades* and *Impacto* and in some provincial newspapers (Monterrey's *El Norte* is a good example). In general, however, business finds it difficult to articulate a persuasive case and then to penetrate the intellectual mainstream of the capital. The obvious implication is that government and labour enjoy a mobilised bias in their dealings with business. At the same time, this mindset makes it difficult for government to take a more supportive public stance toward business.

GOVERNMENT–BUSINESS RELATIONS UNDER DE LA MADRID

Two sets of logic struggle to define the meaning of 'mixed economy'. Reduced to symbiology, government works to equate Revolution, nationalism, state rectorship of the economy and state enterprises with PRI hegemony as the party of the majorities. The private sector links strong civil society, genuine democratisation and modernisation with real checks and balances needed to cleanse and revitalise Mexican society. As in any political struggle, some in either camp want simply to keep or get power.

The period since 1982 has been characterised by the private sector's search for guarantees of its interests within the Mexican political system. Various avenues have been tested, including membership in the PRI (rebuffed by labour), the formation of a business party and even constitutional amendments to limit presidential power. The international dimension counts as well. For example, from business' perspective, GATT membership may present difficulties, but at the same time it may constrain government arbitrariness. The most prominent avenue has been the use of the PAN in electoral politics. In this respect, some private sector leaders appear to be pursuing a double, flexible strategy of continued electoral pressure while at the same time holding out for the possibility of better relations and pragmatic cooperation with a reformed PRI–government. In this strategy, the ascension to PAN leadership of *neopanistas*, a group closely identified with business interests, has converted the party to some degree into an instrument in the business community's effort to renegotiate its relationship with the government. The electoral system is clearly a weak link in the PRI's armour, and business support for the PAN has been perceived in government circles as part of a strategy to pressure concessions.

To simplify, it is useful to adopt a business perspective and to divide government–business relations into economic and political categories and also into 'normal' *versus* 'exceptional' relations. Table 6.2 summarises the result of such an exercise. Clearly, all issues are ultimately political, but some deal with the day-to-day concerns of

Table 6.2 Business perspectives on business–government relations

Normal relations	Exceptional relations
ECONOMIC	
Normal relations	*Exceptional relations*
Long-term predictability of government policy; Inflation control; Realistic exchange rates & price controls; Generous protection & subsidization; Light taxation; Reduced bureaucratic controls; No disloyal competition from government enterprises.	Economic opening should be predictable (priority issue, splits both government & business); Fewer controls on foreign investment; Privatization of parastatals, including the banks.
POLITICAL	
Normal relations	*Exceptional relations*
Real consultation with business; Labor peace; Political pragmatism (no populist rhetoric; no scapegoating business); Pragmatic foreign policy (emphasize relations with U.S., avoid divisive adventures).	Limit presidential power (constitutional change, institutional constraints); Constitutional status of state rectorate of economy; social sector; Businessmen in partisan politics; Real electoral competition (honest elections); Freedom of instruction; Privatization of the *ejido*.

business. The division between normal and exceptional comes at different times for different businessmen, but the bank nationalisation of 1982 is a clear divide. The key theme to stress is that the De la Madrid government apparently concluded that further growth, employment creation and greater efficiency cannot be achieved through continued expansion of the public sector. Rather, progress must come from a reinvigorated private sector, one more fully integrated with the international economy.

To an outside observer, it would seem that the De la Madrid government has made considerable efforts simply to preserve the private sector, and then to win its confidence. From the business perspective, though, the President receives mixed ratings with respect to normal economic relations. In December 1982 De la Madrid introduced his Immediate Programme for Economic Recovery (PIRE), putting the fight against inflation at the top of the agenda. He also accomplished reforms that had eluded his predecessors by eliminating 'bearer shares' (stocks held anonymously to avoid taxation) and consolidating sources of income into one tax schedule. What seemed to be a determined course of 'economic realism' and austerity during 1983 and early 1984 gave way in the latter part of the year and the first quarter of 1985 to rapid deficit spending, inflation and overvalued exchange rates. The maxi-devaluations of July–August 1985, along with budget cuts, bureaucratic trimming and government layoffs, were offered by government as evidence of a continued commitment to austerity. They were seen by critics as necessary adjustments for previous policy errors. Later in 1985 the government suffered two blows in succession. In September a series of massive earthquakes struck the western and central regions of the country; and in November oil prices began a sustained skid from around $25 to an average of about $12 per barrel by July 1986, which was followed by a fragile price firming as OPEC sought to stabilise the market. The earthquakes cost the economy more than $4 billion in direct loss of plant and equipment. The government's effort to downplay the loss of life and its hastily improvised property expropriations reduced its credibility with the population generally, and with business specifically. The oil price collapse cut export earnings from about $16 billion in 1985 to an estimated $9 billion for 1986, reducing government revenues by a third.

De la Madrid might get high marks on his normal political dealings with business. He has attempted to open channels of communication with business groups and has taken a generally firm line on wages. He also has consistently avoided the anti-business rhetoric of his predecessors. While some businessmen still might criticise Mexico's leadership in the Contadora Group, De la Madrid's approach to the Central American crisis has sought a lower profile in a multi-lateral effort. But even with respect to normal relations, the government's relaxation of austerity during 1984 sent a chill through many in the business community, who were watching for a replay of the two previous governments, which began each *sexenio* with firm policy and ended it in chaos.

The more difficult issues involve the extraordinary relations (Table

6.2), those that would transform the Mexican political economy. Here, the question of economic opening rearranges the coalitions that dispute normal relations. The presidency, parts of the bureaucracy (Treasury, SPP, Bank of Mexico, SECOFIN), and a minority of businessmen (ANIERM, CONCANACO, COPARMEX, and the larger-scale firms of CONCAMIN) favour a policy of gradual opening, including entry into GATT. Opposing this policy are other parts of the bureaucracy (Foreign Relations, SEMIP), the majority of small to medium-sized industries (represented especially in CANACINTRA), as well as the vocal intelligentsia. Throughout the first half of his term the President moved toward opening, however erratically, preparing public opinion and attempting to generate support. Negotiations on Mexico's entry into GATT were concluded in August 1986.[32]

Equally firmly, the De la Madrid government has resisted efforts by some business leaders to transform Mexico's presidential system. These disaffected leaders maintain that the PRI–government system constitutes the major impediment to the modernisation of Mexico. Even if De la Madrid proves to be a steadfast and competent leader, his immediate predecessors showed the extreme dangers of capricious abuses of power. Thus, to restore business confidence, it is necessary to limit presidential power. This should be done through constitutional reforms, bolstered with real decentralisation, greater citizen participation and vigorous opposition parties competing in honest elections.[33]

The President has indicated repeatedly that important structural changes are being carried out under difficult circumstances *in the context of Mexican democratic institutions*.[34] The message seems clear enough that the PRI–government will create political spaces for opposition currents and will permit free expression. However, the system will not tolerate business interests working through the PAN in an effort to create 'a new majority', especially if these interests are seen to ally themselves with the Republican Party and US federal executive branch. Business support for the PAN in the Chihuahua local elections of 1983 seems to have been a turning-point in government attitudes. In 1984–85 the PRI leadership took a hard public line against *neopanistas* and their anti-national, anti-revolutionary programmes. An even harder line was taken when necessary by the CT and CTM. One might interpret the official fraud perpetrated in the Sonora and Nuevo León elections in July 1985, and in Chihuahua in July 1986, as yet another message that this President will not permit changes in the presidential system.

In general terms, the tensions between government and business seemed to increase during late 1984 and early 1985, in part due to the congressional elections of July 1985 in which several business leaders apppeared to support the PAN, either as candidates or as party activists. After March 1985 the government appeared to reduce its criticisms of business. Then in November 1985 government pressures against business participation in politics resurfaced, in this instance against Rogelio Sada of the Monterrey VITRO group. The 'dialogue' is complicated to follow through the media, because it involves the PRI and occasionally the CTM taking a hard line on the government side, with COPARMEX reciprocating for business, while the President, cabinet officials, and most of the other business associations, typically appear more conciliatory in comparison.[35]

The principal question raised by these developments is the extent to which the private sector is willing to push its breach with the PRI. Business 'hard-liners' are convinced that the only way free enterprise can be preserved is through a democratisation permitting opposition counterweights to the PRI. 'Soft-liners' prefer not to challenge PRI dominance and care less about democracy than about recreating a stable and profitable business environment. For them, the PAN is a useful tool with which to pry concessions from the PRI–government.

The private sector's ambivalence about democracy intensifies a dilemma for the PRI. *Priístas* complain privately that should they open the political system and accept losses, then some business interests would perceive this as a loss of control, and investor confidence might decline. On the other hand, when the PRI practices a 'complete sweep' electoral policy, other business interests complain about the authoritarianism that inhibits innovation and decentralisation, and investor confidence suffers.[36]

Should the PRI–government offer sufficient guarantees of security and profits to business interests then the soft-liners might prevail, leading to a withdrawal of some business support for the PAN. Some point to the PRI's business-oriented nominees to the governorships of Sonora, Nuevo León and Chihuahua in 1985–86 as indicative of efforts to reassure the business community. The promises delivered by PRI candidate Félix Valdés to Sonoran businessmen shortly before the July 1985 election played a role in weakening the PAN. In Nuevo León, however, the situation appeared more complicated. On the day before the inauguration of Jorge Treviño as Governor, the PAN held a protest rally that attracted some 40 000 persons. Conspicuously absent at the inauguration were important senior members of the local business community and representatives from the state chapters of national business interest associations. Yet the attendance by Bernardo Garza Sada from ALFA and Eugenio Garza Lagüera of VISA are reminders that both conglomerates have been hard hit by the economic crisis and look forward to continued government assistance. The central question that must occupy government leaders is how to guarantee security and profits while opening the economy, and how to minimise costs to labour and the dependent poor.

In all, if a government–business reconciliation emerges, the PAN's electoral push might lose steam in 1986–88. If the tensions persist and the business hard-liners prevail, continued electoral pressure can be expected.

7 Political Parties and Electoral Politics

Mexican authorities after 1983 repeatedly invoked *bipartidismo*, roughly two-party competition, as an undesirable, exotic notion promoted largely by the United States and other hostile forces to eliminate the left and undermine national sovereignty. The historical record – not only in Mexico but in other countries of the region as well – shows that the United States sees no inconsistency in both favouring democratisation and using out-parties to pressure governments. Throughout the Mexican Revolution the United States played one faction off against another, now granting or now withholding recognition, in order to advance its interests. Although this vivid memory coincides nicely with the PRI–government's project of maintaining hegemonic power, realism suggests that the United States would work through a major opposition party in Mexico. This should be kept in mind when we consider the PRI's special efforts to prop up the partisan left as a political counterweight to the PAN and the threat from the right.

As the Mexican government finds it increasingly difficult to continue improving living standards for its population, it has relied more for legitimation on two other revolutionary projects: liberalism and nationalism. Chapter 5 discussed the political reform of 1977 and noted that the reform of the PRI and that of the electoral system were conceived to go hand in hand. That is, increased electoral competition was viewed as a means of promoting changes within the PRI that would permit the party to compete in a more democratic system. Democratisation in turn, along with decentralisation and greater efficiency, were seen as changes important to the continued success of the PRI–government system. During the López Portillo government, considerable progress was made in registering new parties and – even though most observers stressed its limited nature – the reform was seen to go beyond previous efforts. But the chaotic policy miscalculations, and the corruption and frivolity of the López Portillo government, had the dual effect of delegitimating the regime in the judgement of many and of strengthening the opposition, especially that on the right.

The De la Madrid government attempted to advance the political reform, including it under the umbrella of 'moral renovation'. After a promising start, however, moral renovation met setbacks in the electoral arena. The 1982 presidential elections produced the desired result for the PRI: a plausible claim to represent the majority.[1] But the state and local elections of 1982–83 produced some surprises as the opposition won seven major cities, including five state capitals. Particularly striking was the PAN's strength in the north, where it won the capital cities of Hermosillo, Durango and Chihuahua, and in the central states of Guanajuato and San Luís Potosí. Not until Baja California Norte in September 1983 did the PRI halt the opposition. There, amid the typical claims and counter-claims of fraud, the PRI held the state governorship, thus preserving intact its monopoly of governorships since 1929. In the sexennial election calendar, 1984 was a relatively quiet year with no governorship up for election. In 1985 the President and Interior Secretary assured opposition parties that the July elections of seven state governors and 400 national deputies would be clean. But the official fraud perpetrated against the PAN in Sonora and Nuevo León, and to some extent in Chihuahua and Baja California Norte, was of a scale and style of the early 1950s, and the fragile credibility of moral renovation suffered further, especially in the eyes of foreign observers. The Chihuahua state elections of July 1986 reconfirmed the government's hard line.

Of the various explanations offered to account for the apparently deliberate fraud in the north, most convincing is politics as the choice among lesser evils. President De la Madrid possibly concluded at some point in 1983 that honest elections would produce serious setbacks for the PRI, that such would create even more insecurity in an already difficult situation and that the party needed to maintain the support of its labour constituency and local bosses. This was especially the case if the government were committed both to austerity and economic opening on the one hand and to a more accommodative posture toward the United States on the other. Political reform thus fell victim to political necessity.[2]

This chapter first discusses various meanings of elections in Mexico and then describes the registered parties as of 1986, dividing them into satellite and opposition parties with respect to the PRI. Electoral trends during 1976–86 are analysed to show areas of PRI and allied party strength, as well as opposition party strength. Finally, the 1985 mid-term elections are discussed at some length to identify clues about the regime's survival strategy.

My argument is that elections in Mexico generally have not been credible exercises in the sense of honest balloting to select governments from competing parties. This reality was insignificant as long as elections served to validate the PRI as the expression of a successful revolution. As difficulties have accumulated, some have called for genuine democracy as the route to transcend the system.[3] However, government leaders show little inclination to risk losing power in electoral contests. After the 1983 experience they appear more intent on revising arrangements so that the PRI relies to a greater extent on its allies and works to weaken and divide the 'real' opposition. But these should be considered short-term defencive tactics. Still unclear is the longer-run regime survival strategy.

ELECTIONS IN THE MEXICAN CONTEXT

Anglo–American and Western European readers are accustomed to elections serving as mass choices among competing elites to structure government and implement policies. In this sense, elections serve as a check on government, and voting is studied for clues about tendencies in mass opinion. In the Mexican setting, elections have served more to reaffirm longer term and more abstract ends than as the instrumental expression of preferences about policies or candidates.[4] Elections also allow the PRI to demonstrate to potential adversaries such as the United States, the Catholic Church, business interests and left groups its ability to mobilise support. Padgett has suggested that in a society long characterised by hierarchy and tradition, elections have become a modern ritual to legitimate choices that are made within a closed elite.[5] Craig and Cornelius also stress the symbolic nature of the vote, but note an element of pragmatism as well:

> When voting, the average citizen appears to respond to official exhortations to participate, viewing his activities on behalf of the official party as an opportunity to express gratitude for assistance received from previous or incumbent administrations as well as his solidarity with the goals of the Mexican Revolution and its heirs within the PRI. Others reason that by supporting the PRI, one (or one's local community) stands a better chance of receiving additional benefits from the government or preserving the gains already realized. Government coercion, real or feared, appears to be a relatively insignificant factor in voter turnout.[6]

We might speculate that these sentiments continue to motivate many in the lower social strata, but Mexican society is changing rapidly.

Urbanisation is a significant force in undermining support for a one-party system. Booth and Seligson, for example, argue that their survey data show stronger support for democratic practices than that suggested by the received wisdom. Their sample, however, was drawn from Guadalajara and from northern industrial cities, precisely areas of regional sensitivities and greater critical awareness.[7] Thus, one is left willing to rethink the issue, but wanting to compare their findings with those from central Mexico, smaller cities and rural areas. The dearth of survey data hampers the discussion.

In Mexico's presidential system, elections also serve as a mechanism of elite circulation which – as we have seen – contributes to discipline, recruitment and socialisation of new participants and the continuous renewal of expectations. At the same time, elections can inform the government about trends in popular support as reflected in both abstention rates and in votes for the PRI. Elections also can send protest signals to central government authorities, either by defeating official candidates, violently protesting vote manipulation or by not voting at all.

Molinar identifies four different phases of electoral competition since the Revolution. The underlying logic is that each phase contributed to the formation of a durable PRI–government regime, which has been able to replace an exhausted system when necessary.

1. 1917–33 was characterised by several hundred local and regional clubs, cliques and parties, led by *caciques*, who enjoyed some autonomy from the centre and joined fluid and changing coalitions to influence national policy;
2. 1933–38 brought the formation of a dominant-party system, which began with the dissolution of parties allied with the PNR and ended with the corporatist architecture of the PRM, both forerunners of the PRI;
3. 1938–50 saw the government create and recognise opposition parties and work to legitimate elections, as opposed to violence, as the route to office;
4. Mid-1950s to the 1980s has witnessed a consolidated PRI–government system using the power of government to manipulate elections and fine-tune coordination between party and bureaucracy to win votes.[8]

Constitutionally, Mexico is a federal republic; thus, federal law prescribes rules for deputy, senatorial and presidential elections.[9] In brief, deputy candidates must be native-born citizens, resident of the state from which elected (or of a neighbouring state) and have completed 21 years of age by the date of the election. Senatorial candidates must meet the same requirements, but must have completed 30 years of age by election day. Presidential candidates must be born in Mexico of native-born parents and at least 35 years of age. Re-election is prohibited. The Constitution requires republican forms for the states and prohibits the immediate re-election of state officials. State statutes govern elections for governorships and state deputies (*diputados locales*) and also for mayors (*presidentes municipales*) and municipal councillors (*regidores*).[10]

With regard to national elections, of greater interest in this discussion, the key policy-making body is the Interior Secretariat's Federal Electoral Commission (CFE). Since the first post-Revolutionary electoral law of 1946, the CFE has operated under Interior's control. This is guaranteed by its composition in which in June 1985 the PRI controlled five votes to the 'real' opposition parties' four.[11] The Interior Secretary can cast an additional vote, presumably in favour of the PRI or its allies, in cases of ties, but such a situation would demonstrate a precarious grip on the body. The CFE decides the specific rules by which national elections will be held: forms of ballots and balloting, hours of voting, numbers and boundaries of voting districts and the like. After the election, the Commission also judges protests about fraud or voting irregularities, forwarding the cases it considers valid on to the Electoral College of the Chamber of Deputies.

The President and senators are chosen by direct popular vote at the same time (the first Sunday of July, 1976, 1982 and 1988) and serve six-year terms. Beginning in 1994 the election will be held on the first Sunday of September, this to reduce the period of the 'lame duck' President. A mixed system is employed for the national Chamber of Deputies, with 300 deputies elected directly on a plurality basis from single-member districts and another hundred chosen on a proportional representation basis in at-large multi-state electoral districts.[12] The CFE establishes the numbers and boundaries of the districts prior to each election. In practice the mixed system means that voters deposit two ballots, one for the single-member district candidate and another indicating party preference in the at-large district. Electoral law stipulates that a party winning 60 or more plurality districts loses its eligibility for the at-large seats. Since the PRI wins the great majority of the single-member districts, the law effectively reserves the 100 at-large seats for opposition parties. Thus one can see that *priístas* regard nomination to the at-large districts more as an unpleasant duty than a real prize. The nominations may be useful, though, to reward militancy at the grassroots.

Article 53 of the Constitution prescribes that the 300 single-member districts should be allocated among the states 'taking into account the last general census of the population', but that each state should receive at least two deputy posts. Within the states, however, the districts vary widely in numbers of registered voters, as shown in Table 7.1. At the low end, in 1982 the 19th District of the State of Mexico held some 35 500 voters, while in 1985 the 40th of the Federal District registered almost 375 000. Nearly two-thirds of the districts fell in the range of 80 000 to 120 000 registered voters in 1982. Population growth produced a 'bracket creep' so that the same proportion of districts in 1985 fell between 90 000 and 140 000. It is not clear what accounts for the variation, although if Mexico follows universal norms one would expect the government to design electoral districts to its own advantage.[13] Similarly, the at-large districts varied in size in 1982 from 5 million voters in the fourth to 6.8 million in the first. Here more clearly the rationale was to dilute the voting strength of the PAN. With the creation of an extra district in 1985, the numbers were evened out a bit, with 3.2 million registered in the second district and 4.0 million in the fifth.

Table 7.2 shows the sexennial calendar of national, state and local elections. The logic of presidentialism groups the elections towards the middle two years of the *sexenio*, presumably the peak of presidential power. Thus, of the 155 state and local elections (governor, state deputies and municipality), nearly half (70) occur during the middle third, with 39 elections during the first biennium and 46 in the last. Included among the 70 elections falling in the middle of the *sexenio* are 20 of the 31 governorships, with five more chosen in the first half of the fifth year. 'Difficult' states are spread over the course of the *sexenio*, and the term ends with such 'easy' states as Colima, Morelos and Tabasco.[14] Congressional elections at the mid-point of the *sexenio* are less important to the citizenry than presidential or municipal elections, in which the candidates are known and the implications comprehensible. Nevertheless, the mid-term elections contribute to the President's consolidation of power and open a more heated phase of the succession process.

By and large, the pattern at the state level is for the governor, state deputies and municipal offices to be elected simultaneously (17

Table 7.1 Variations in numbers of registered voters in single-member congressional districts, 1982, 1985

Numbers of registered voters (in thousands)	*Numbers of single-member districts*	
	1982	*1985*
>250	1	1
240–249	0	1
230–239	0	0
220–229	0	0
210–219	3	2
199–209	0	0
190–199	0	5
180–189	0	3
170–179	3	3
160–169	3	9
150–159	2	13
140–149	8	12
130–139	18	33
120–129	29	54
110–119	58	47
100–109	46	40
90–99	48	36
80–89	38	17
70–79	20	10
60–69	11	7
50–59	7	4
<50	5	3
Total	300	300

Source: Compiled from CFE, *Reforma política, gaceta informativa de la Comisión Federal Electoral*, *Tomo IX* (México, D.F.: 1982); 'Documento definitivo', (México: 1985).

states), or for the governor, often with the deputies, chosen slightly before the municipalities (11 states).[15] This timing allows for the complicated balancing to be calculated among the party sectors and permits the gubernatorial nominee some influence over nominations to municipal offices, which can be important for state–municipal cooperation. Tlaxcala, Veracruz and Zacatecas follow a different pattern, with municipal elections slightly preceding the gubernatorial. The Federal District, with some 12 per cent of the national population, is governed by a presidential appointee (the *regente*) and appointed delegates in its sixteen precincts (*delegaciones*).

Table 7.2 The sexennial election calendar, 1983–88

	1983	*1984*	*1985*	*1986*	*1987*	*1988*
Aguascalientes			*	G		* *
	D			D		
	M			M		
Baja Calif. N.	G					
	D			D		
	M			M		
Baja Calif. S.				G		
	D			D		
	M			M		
Campeche			G			
	D			D		
			M			M
Coahuila					G	
			D			D
		M			M	
Colima			G			
			D			D
			M			M
Chiapas						G
			D			D
			M			M
Chihuahua				G		
	D			D		
	M			M		
Durango				G		
	D			D		
	M			M		
Guanajuato			G			
			D			D
			M			M
Guerrero				G		
	D			D		
	M			M		
Hidalgo					G	
		D			D	
		M			M	
Jalisco						G
			D			D
			M			M
México					G	
		D			D	
		M			M	
Michoacán				G		
	D			D		
	M			M		
Morelos						G
			D			D
			M			M

	1983	1984	1985	1986	1987	1988
			*			* *
Nayarit		D M			G D M	
Nuevo León			G D M			D M
Oaxaca	D M			G D M		
Puebla	D M			G D M		
Querétaro			G D M			D M
Quintana Roo		D M			G D M	
San Luís Potosí		D	G M		D	M
Sinaloa	D M			G D M		
Sonora			G D M			D M
Tabasco			D M			G D M
Tamaulipas	D M			G D M		
Tlaxcala	D		M	G D		M
Veracruz	D		M	G D		M
Yucután		D M			G D M	
Zacatecas	D		M	G D		M

Table 7.2 (continued) The sexennial election calendar, 1983–88.

* Federal Deputy elections
** Presidency, senate, deputy
G = governor
D = state deputy
M = Municipal

Source: Compiled from CFE, Registro Nacional de Electores, 'Calendario electoral 1983–88'.

Juan Molinar put perhaps most trenchantly the significance of voting in Mexico after 1977. Since 1929 the PRI has operated as a hegemonic party, utilising elections as referenda on the legitimacy of the Revolution and conceding posts to the opposition based more on a calculus of preserving a degree of democratic legitimacy than on what opposition parties actually won at the polls. The PRI–government could act accordingly given its impressive record of growth and stability. With the economic crisis after 1981, however, the PRI no longer could legitimate itself through material progress; thus, democratic opening might provide another avenue of legitimation, with elections taking on new meaning. Given its undeniable strength, the government might eschew electoral 'alchemy' and begin the transition from a hegemonic party system to a dominant party system, one in which opposition strength is recognised, but with the dominant party retaining control. The cases of India's Congress party and Japan's Liberal Democratic party come to mind.[16]

The challenge of moving to another phase, however, is fundamental. As Vernon reminds us: 'One must bear in mind that there has not yet been an instance in the history of modern Mexico in which the "outs" have succeeded the "ins" by legitimate means; hence, no president of modern Mexico can fail to be uneasy in the face of opposition.'[17] Recent electoral trends show that the government has rejected opening in favour of preserving PRI hegemony by modifying details.

THE PRI'S ALLIES AND OPPONENTS

The 1977 LOPPE succeeded in bringing diverse ideological groups into the formal party system, thus helping to re-legitimate the regime's claim to rule. In this sense all the parties discussed here subscribe to system rules. But among the parties, one can distinguish those that assist from those that resist the PRI, even though specific circumstances may alter general party behaviour. By and large the PRI can count as allies the Partido Popular Socialista (PPS) and the Partido Auténtico de la Revolución Mexicana (PARM). The Partido Socialista de los Trabajadores (PST) is less reliable, although it has cooperated at times. The PRI's real opposition consists on the left of the Partido Socialista Unificado Mexicano (PSUM), Partido Revolucionario de los Trabajadores (PRT) and the Partido Mexicano de los Trabajadores (PMT) and on the right of the Partido Demócrata Mexicano (PDM) and the PAN.

Table 7.3 summarises current data on the registered parties, divided into the categories of allies and opponents with respect to the PRI.[18]

Beginning with allies, the PPS claims the legacy of Lombardo Toledano, the CTM leader who split away from the official party at about the time of its restructuring as the PRI in 1946. While claiming Marxism–Leninism as its ideology, its practical strategy has been to support a national patriotic front against US imperialism, lending virtually unconditional backing to the PRI. The case of Nayarit still plagues the party because of accusations that in 1975 the PPS conceded its victory of the governorship for a seat in the senate. The alledged deal split the PPS and damaged its credibility. It can claim some bases of support in Oaxaca, Nayarit, Chihuahua and Sinaloa.

The PST was formed by some members of the PMT who sought to take advantage of the decline of the PPS, adopting some aspects of that party's ideological line (anti-imperialism, socialism) and modernising it. It copies the *priísta* organisational style of compulsory affiliation of groups. Allegedly the PST has been supported on occasion by some left-wing *priístas*. It has some support in groups of settlers (*colonos*) and peasants and in Guerrero and Veracruz. As will be shown, the PST apparently received special government support in the 1985 elections.

The PARM is something of an historical relic, created by a group of dissident military leaders in 1954 to protest at the excesses of corruption under President Alemán. Segovia suggests that the sole reason for the electoral reform of 1973 (lowering the minimum national vote from 2.5 to 1.5 per cent to qualify for 'party deputy' seats) was to preserve the PARM as an ally in the CFE. The party has carved out a regional base in Tamaulipas, where voters can express regional protest without supporting the PAN. 'The PARM appears,

Table 7.3 Characteristics of nationally registered parties, 1986

Party	*Ideology*	*Year founded/ registered*	*Membership 1985**
Partido Acción Nacional (PAN)	liberal democratic; Catholic.	1939/1948	750 000
Partido Revolucionario Institucional (PRI)	social democratic; populist	1946/1946	15 millions
Partido Popular Socialista (PPS)	marxist–leninist	1947/1948	125 000
Partido Auténtico de la Revolución Mexicana (PARM)	national revolutionary; populist	1954/1957	90 000
Partido Demócrata Mexicano (PDM)	democratic	1972/1978	175 000
Partido Socialista Unificado Mexicano (PSUM)	scientific socialism	1981/1982	450 000
Partido Socialista de los Trabajadores (PST)	marxist–leninist	1975/1978	175 000
Partido Revolucionario de los Trabajadores (PRT)	trotskyist	1976/1982	500 000
Partido Mexicano de los Trabajadores (PMT)	democratic-reformist, anti-imperialist	1974/1985	120 000

	Origins	*Geographic bases*
PAN	1920s Cristero movement Catholic intellectuals; businessmen;	Northern border states, Jalisco, D.F., urban areas
PRI	Calles, 1929; restructured in	General; rural; Gulf Coast

	1938, 1946; coalitions of groups from Revolution	
PPS	Lombardo Toledano, with some labour and intelligentsia support	Chihuahua, Nayarit, Oaxaca, Sinaloa
PARM	Former military leaders to protest Aleman government corruption	Tamaulipas
PDM	1920s *Cristero* movement 1930s *Sinarquista* movement	*Bajío*, San Luís Potosí, Jalisco, Querétaro, Michoacán
PSUM	PCM, student movement, MAP, MAUS, PSR, PMT	D.F., Jalisco, México, Nayarit
PST	Left wing of PRI; National Committee of Coordination & Consultation (1971) (intellectuals; labour & student leaders)	Guerrero, Veracruz
PRT	Students, intellectuals	D.F., México
PMT	1968 student movement National Committee of Coordination & Consultation (1971) (intellectuals; labour & student leaders)	D.F.

* Self-declared membership

Sources: P. González Casanova, *El estado y los partidos políticos en México* (México: Ediciones Era, 1982), pp. 78–79; *Excélsior*, 15 April 1985, p. 10–F; J. Klesner, 'Party System Expansion and Electoral Mobilization in Mexico' (paper presented at the XII Congress of the Latin American Studies Association, Albuquerque, 18–20 April 1985), pp. 20–29.

then, like a PRI-less PRI, that is to say with no national idea, no discipline and with a political competence that shines in its nonexistence.'[19]

With respect to the real opposition, several factions combined forces in 1981 to found the major party of the left, the PSUM. The Mexican Communist Party (PCM), which dates from 1919, regained its registration in 1978 and forms the core of the PSUM. Joining with the PCM were forces that grew out of the 1968 student movement

(MAP, MAUS) and factions that split off from the PPS (PSR). The party succeeded in resolving difficult ideological problems, dropping Marxism–Leninism in favour of scientific socialism and supporting proletarian internationalism while condemning intervention. For a brief time, the PSUM appeared to unite disparate leftwing groups into a formidable electoral force, but the party has been riven by ideological, tactical and personal disputes. The PSUM has failed to become more than the sum of its parts, as was shown in the delicate balancing of representatives of factions on its central committee, and the party split again in the 1985 elections. One of the issues dividing the leadership was the relative emphasis to place on electoral politics as opposed to the development of a party of militants dedicated primarily to organisation and education of workers and peasants. The party runs ahead of its national average in Nayarit, the Federal District, Jalisco and the State of Mexico.

The PRT, founded from several small student groups, is the Mexican section of the Trotskyist Fourth International. It considers itself to the left of the PSUM and has succeeded in staking out a distinctive claim with the cause of political repression and the 'disappeared', that is, those individuals whom the government is accused of illegally imprisoning or executing for political reasons. Its 1982 presidential candidate, Rosario Ibarra de Piedra – whose son figures among the disappeared – ran an effective campaign, thus helping the PRT gain permanent registration. The PRT can also claim some support in universities, and in the Federal District and the State of Mexico. One of the several obstacles to left unity is the unrelenting hostility of the PPS toward the PRT.

The PMT was founded by Heberto Castillo, a faculty participant in the student movement of 1968, and Demetrio Vallejo, a militant from the 1958–59 railroad strikes. The PMT is more genuinely radical in its programmes of anti-imperialism and economic reform than the PSUM, but it rejects Marxist analysis and terminology as inappropriate to Mexican reality and warily views alliances with other left parties. It also viewed electoral politics sceptically, and its delay in applying for and receiving registration may have cost some support.

Turning to the real opposition of the right, the PDM might be considered conservative in the sense of its *sinarquista*, Catholic roots. *Sinarquismo*, a powerful anti-anarchist movement which emerged in Spain in the early twentieth century, found a sympathetic response among Mexican Catholic activists who advocated an integral, ordered view of society. But the party's social bases among the rural poor of the Bajio region (Guanajuato, Jalisco, Querétaro, San Luís Potosí and Michoacán) give it something of a populist–reformist bent as well. The PDM can trace its organisational roots to the *cristero* movement of the 1920s and the Union Nacional Sinarquista of the 1930s–1940s, and prior to its registration it ran candidates under various labels, including the PAN and the short-lived Partido Nacionalista de Mexico.

The main opposition party by far is the PAN, which was formed in 1939 by a group of Catholic intellectuals and professionals to counter Cárdenas' social and economic policies and the government party's monopoly of power.[20] PAN's surge to prominence in the 1980s can be understood as the result of internal party politics and the deepening crisis after 1968. The faction advocating electoral confrontation consolidated power after 1977 as López Portillo's populist adventure – the bank nationalisation above all – created a number of new adherents, *neopanistas*, especially among businessmen. PAN's electoral successes in 1983 gave the impression of a strong opposition movement. But the party is neither a coherent organisation, nor is it a national alternative to the PRI. Rather, it has become a collection of disparate anti-government forces with important strength in a few regions and whose real success may be to force modifications in government policies.

From its inception the PAN confronted the dilemma of whether to compete electorally against an unbeatable party–government, thus contributing an undeserved legitimacy to the system, or to abstain and concentrate on educating the public to participate in real democracy at some future time. But abstention frustrated those party members who sought more active forms of opposition. Another cleavage along slightly different lines separated the Catholic intellectuals opposed to the regime's religious and educational policies, from traditional liberals, who sought real electoral democracy. Businessmen comprised a minor force from the outset, but none of the major tendencies was particularly pro-business, and prior to the mid-1970s it would be mistaken to label the party 'conservative', taken to mean a defender of the upper classes or of business interests.

From the early 1940s to the late 1960s the 'loyal opposition' line (advocates of education over electoral confrontation) of party founder Manuel González Morín guided the party. This faction stressed ideological study and teaching, with particular attention to Christian democracy and Catholic social thought. During 1962–68, under Adolfo Christlieb, the party moved a bit to the left, in keeping with the liberalising trends in the Church and more generally. The turmoil of the late 1960s and the Echeverría *sexenio* mobilised new opposition to government and heightened tensions within the PAN. At the same time that Echeverría was reviving populism he also created greater opportunities and incentives for political participation through the reforms discussed in Chapter 5. Party President José Angel Conchello, a Monterrey lawyer, seized the opportunity to promote the electoral confrontation faction, with the result that the party won 25 deputy seats (including four from single member districts) in the 1973 congressional race. Echeverría's 1976 land seizures in Sonora and Sinaloa brought several prominent ranchers, including Carlos Amaya, Adalberto Rosas and Manuel Clouthier, into the PAN, thus reinforcing the controntational line. Efforts by Efrain González Morfín and Christlieb to reassert the loyal opposition tendency during 1975 produced a schism so serious that PAN was unable to nominate a candidate to oppose López Portillo in 1976. Manuel González Hinojosa presided over a divided party during 1975–78. Conchello, allied with Pablo Emilio Madero – grandnephew of Francisco I. Madero and an executive in a Monterrey business firm – led the growing ranks of system opponents to eventually gain the upper hand. González Morfín and others of the losing faction left the party to found 'Solidarism' (*solidarismo*), a study group, leaving behind a much weakend loyalist tendency. The *neopanistas* consolidated power with Abel Vicencio Tovar (1978–84), reinforcing the northern and business orientations.

With the bank nationalisation came another influx of businessmen and a closer alliance with business associations, especially COPARMEX. Business associations take great pains to insist that their organisations are non-partisan, but their call for greater civic awareness and participation after 1982 helped PAN more than PRI. Support from business groups was especially important because of PAN's organisational and financial weakness.

The internal tension remained, however, surfacing in the selection of Party President in early 1984. In general terms, the *neopanistas* supported electoral confrontation, private business, the use of legitimate violence to protect electoral victories and two-party competition with PRI. They also advocated a kind of *foco* theory of winning in a few strategic cities and projecting influence outward from these.[21] The 'solidarists' emphasised education, promoting the formation of intermediary organisations, exhausting all legal remedies to defend electoral victories, a multi-party system and a more broad-gauged strategy to gain support. As candidates for the party presidency, 'solidarist' Sergio Lujambio Rafols lost to Pablo Emilio Madero.[22] The new President, in turn, put the PAN on a more aggressive, confrontational course with the government.

While the PAN lacks a national organisation and following, the party does profess – contrary to the insistence of some *priístas* – a coherent set of principles and a programme of government. To what extent its militants really support the programme is a question that can be put to most parties. Party principles stress the classical liberal project of the 1917 Constitution. In terms of programme, PAN stresses a government of laws, honest elections, separation of powers, effective federalism with strong municipalities and respect for citizens' rights. With regard to welfare, it calls for creating the conditions necessary to attend to basic human requirements of food, housing and education, emphasising above all the primacy of individual liberty. It supports the concept of a mixed economy but opposes the recent expansion of government, advocating instead the paramount role of the private sector. It emphasises raising levels of education, ending government's monopoly in this field and encouraging greater participation by families. In addition, the party calls for greater teacher and parent influence over education and greater access by parties to communications media. The police should be purged of corruption. It rejects the notions that the state and government are the same thing or that any party can claim to embody the revolution to the exclusion of others.[23]

Apart from the PAN the remaining seven parties can claim little electoral support, dividing some 15 per cent of the vote among themselves. In 1983, for example, the combined opposition fielded candidates for only one third of the 1469 state and local posts up for election.[24] The key to party politics is the virtual lock the PRI holds over mass organisations such as labour unions and peasant groups. Even the PAN, which runs well in urban, middle-class neighbourhoods cannot penetrate mass organisations.

RECENT ELECTORAL TRENDS

The difficulty in analysing electoral results in Mexico is that one is far from sure about what actually happened. The opposition begins to charge fraud long before election day, often with some basis, and the government counters with charges that the opposition merely attempts to mask its weakness and deliberately de-legitimates the system in the process, which also has some basis in fact. *Excélsior* columnist José Luís Mejía concluded that both the PRI and opposition bear the blame for fraud and cynicism:

> The PRI because it began to inflate the number of votes received absolutely unnecessarily and even without facing an adversary just to show everyone how popular its candidates and overwhelming its electoral victories are. And the opposition parties, especially the PAN, because for more than 40 years it's been planting in voters' minds the idea that all elections are arranged, that they're fraudulent and dirty, even in those districts where it doesn't have enough members to cover the voting booths.[25]

It might be argued that electoral fraud is functional for both PRI and opposition party leaders in the sense that it reinforces apathy and lowers voter turnouts, which in turn makes elections easier to manage. The opposition also can benefit when the PRI inflates the turnout figures to legitimate its claim as the party of majorities. With inflated totals, the PRI can retain system support by granting opposition parties many more votes than those actually won at the polls.

Discussions about electoral fraud have almost a ritual quality about them. *Priístas* hold that only 75 of the 300 deputy districts were challenged in the CFE in 1985.[26] Their point that the PRI indeed wins majority support in most districts is well taken. On the other hand, opposition parties may be loathe to complain formally for fear of having their own, sometimes shaky, vote claims questioned as well. And less important than the small number of challenged elections is location of those districts and the solidity of opposition forces, as shown in a later section.[27]

In response to suggestions that some elections are fraudulent, *priístas* often resort to peculiar reasoning along two lines. First, they concede that there may be some fraud, probably not more than 10 per cent overall. This is due to complex procedures, over-zealous militants and a variety of local reasons. But the PAN commits much worse fraud by claiming that it wins elections, and thus attempting to de-legitimate the process. Second, if there really had been serious fraud (in this or that election) there would have been violence. Thus, they conclude, the absence of violence means clean elections.

One should keep in mind that the PRI relies heavily on government resources. This means that government vehicles, personnel and budgets are liberally assigned to PRI campaigns. Furthermore, government services are targeted to reinforce electoral support. PRI candidates typically resemble newly elected officials, listening to requests and receiving petitions at each campaign stop. This ability to deliver at least something in the way of services explains much of the PRI's strength in the urban, squatter communities and some rural areas. A *priísta* feels more confident running for office in a fringe community of Mexico City than among the affluent in Lomas de Chapultepec.

A basic condition of electoral fraud is that none of the opposition parties has the membership or resources to cover even a large proportion of the 50 000 or so voting booths. Fraud more narrowly considered might be divided in three phases. Before the election the government might strengthen its hand by inflating the voter list to increase pro-government votes. Other rules pertaining to qualifications of candidates and poll watchers, numbers and locations of voting booths and date of publication of voter lists may be juggled. In this sense the government has the element of surprise on its side, and opposition parties complain that changes are frequently introduced at the eleventh hour.

During the election, opposition poll watchers may be challenged, and sometimes intimidated, boxes may arrive at the polls complete with marked ballots enclosed and mobile groups of party militants may be transported from booth to booth. Union leaders may be present to observe their members' behaviour, but also possible is that members will have been issued marked ballots prior to the election with instructions to return a blank ballot afterwards to show compliance. Still, the PRI holds no monopoly on election vice, and opposition parties – especially the PAN in areas of strongholds – has been accused of irregularities as well.

Election results generally are not announced immediately but rather after a few days or a week. (In Sonora in 1985 a two-week delay was instituted.)[28] Historically time was needed to transport and tally the votes; and in a few cases this still is the case. But the delay serves other purposes. It allows election-day crowds to disband and tempers to cool. In some cases, vote results may be substantially altered. But more typically, it gives government time to assess the meaning of the election and to negotiate with the opposition. Positions may be granted in exchange for acceptance of the general outcome. One can only imagine the tribulations of opposition party leaders who try to maintain discipline in their ranks in the face of government temptations.

Thorough and systematic fraud is practiced in only the most

problematic districts. But government control of the election process and the constant allegations of fraud have eroded the credibility of the electoral process. Just before the 1985 elections a Mexico City poll found that only 13 per cent of the respondents believed state and local election results would be respected by government; 55 per cent held a negative view. In Sonora, 37 per cent of those polled believed that government would recognise opposition victories; 56 per cent believed not.[29] A survey in Nuevo León found that 75 per cent of those interviewed believed the vote would not be respected, up from 67 per cent in 1982.[30]

While electoral fraud may be functional for government and party oppositions, it has become an instrument of pressure for other interests, primarily business, the United States and the Church.[31] In May 1986 US Senator Jesse Helms showed extraordinary talents to irritate by claiming to have data from the Mexican *army* that showed substantial fraud committed in De la Madrid's 1982 victory.

Keeping in mind the 'soft' quality of the numbers, Table 7.4 reports data on presidential and national deputy elections during 1961–85. In schematic terms, the significant trends include:

1. The voting population more than doubled between 1961 and 1985, reflecting rapid population growth;
2. Voter turnout is consistently higher in presidential election years;
3. Abstention (percentage voting of those registered) edged upward from the low-to-mid 30 per cent range in the 1960s to nearly 50 per cent by the mid-1980s;
4. Abstention is generally higher for congressional than for presidential contests;
5. The government made a remarkable effort to reduce abstention in 1982, but a resurgence occurred in 1985;
6. The PRI's general share of the vote declined from the upper 80 per cent range in the early 1960s to the mid-60 per cent range in 1985;
7. The PAN's vote virtually doubled (from nearly 8 to just over 15 per cent) between 1961 and 1985; and
8. The combined left vote increased ten-fold (from less than 1 to over 10 per cent during this same period, but a single major party or stable coalition has not emerged.

In terms of a summary overview of the social bases of party

Table 7.4 National percentages of vote by party for the presidency and Chamber of Deputies (single-member districts), 1961–85 (presidential vote in parentheses) +

Party	*1961*	*1964*	*1967*	*1970*	*1973*	*1976*	*1979*	*1982*	*1985*
PAN	7.6	11.5	12.4	13.9	14.7	8.5	10.8	17.5	15.6
		(11.1)		(13.9)		–		(15.7)	
PRI	90.2	86.3	83.3	80.1	69.7	80.1	69.7	69.3	64.8
		(87.8)		(83.3)		(86.9)		(68.4)	
PPS	1.0	1.4	2.8	1.4	3.6	3.0	2.6	1.9	2.0
		(.7)		(.9)		(3.7)		(1.5)	
PARM	.5	.7	1.3	.8	1.9	2.5	1.8	1.4	1.7
		(.5)		(.5)		(3.0)		(1.0)	
PDM	–	–	–	–	–	–	2.1	2.2	2.7
		–		–		–		(1.8)	
PSUM	–	–	–	–	–	–	4.9*	4.4	3.2
		–		–		–		(3.5)	
PST	–	–	–	–	–	–	2.1	1.8	2.5
		–		–		–		(1.5)	
PRT	–	–	–	–	–	–	–	1.3	1.3
		–		–		–		(1.8)	
PMT	–	–	–	–	–	–	–	–	1.5
		–		–		–		–	
Unregistered	.5	.1	.2	.3	.3	.3	.1	.1	.1
				(.2)		(1.2)		(.1)	
Annulled	–	–	–	3.9	10.0	5.7	5.9	.04	4.7
		–		(1.3)		(5.2)		(4.5)	
Abstention	31.7	33.4	37.7	35.8	39.7	38.0	50.7	34.3	49.3
		(30.7)		(35.9)		(31.3)		(25.2)	
Registered^	10.0	13.6	15.8	21.7	24.9	25.9	27.9	31.5	35.3

+Table excludes PNM, which won .28 per cent of the vote in 1961 and the PSD, which won .19 per cent in 1962
*Vote recorded for a coalition registered by the PCM
^In millions

Sources: CFE, *Reforma política, gaceta informativa de la Comisión Federal Electoral, Tomo IX: Acuerdos, indicadores de opinión pública y estadística electoral* (México: 1982); CFE, *Documento definitivo* (México: 1985).

support, Klesner's analysis of voting trends and state-level ecological data found that

> the PRI receives almost all rural lower-class votes, perhaps a majority of working-class votes, especially unionized working-class votes, and a large percentage but probably not a majority of urban middle and upper-class votes. The PAN does very well among the

urban middle and upper classes, receives some but not much working-class support, and does very poorly in the countryside. The PSUM's base is among intellectuals and disaffected middle-class members, but it probably receives some lower-class support as well. The PDM does very well among the very religious peasants of the Bajío region and receives some support from urban marginals. The social class bases of the PPS, the PST, and PARM, and the PRT are not clear.[31]

In terms of regional bases of support, the PRI is strongest in the Gulf Coast states (Veracruz, Tabasco, Campeche, Quintana Roo) and weakest in the northern states, especially those contiguous with the United States, and west central region (Jalisco, Michoacán and Guanajuato) and centre (Federal District and the state of Mexico). The PRI also faces problems in the Isthmus of Tehuantepec, especially in Juchitán, Oaxaca. Contrary to patterns in most other countries, voter turnout typically is highest in the least developed, most rural states. Here, the PRI's organisational strength pays dividends, with vote fraud also playing some important, but unquantifiable, role.

The paradox often noted is that the PRI is weakest precisely among the groups who have most benefited from recent public policies: the urban middle sectors and the wealthy. In the larger cities, the possibilities for vote fraud or for controlling votes are reduced, and the opposition parties are less restricted by their organisational and financial weakness.

Taken together the trends suggest that the political reform of 1977 enjoyed some success by 1982 but then witnessed a setback in 1985. Several new parties were legalised, thus bringing opposition currents into the electoral arena. Voter abstention, however, reached a new high in 1979. The 1982 elections appear more than a little peculiar, with unusually few votes annulled in the congressional races and a nearly three-million vote (almost 14 per cent) difference between the deputy and presidential races. However, abstention in the presidential balloting was reduced to a new low. The mid-term elections of 1985 represent a setback with the resurgence of abstention.

THE 1985 MID-TERM ELECTIONS

The elections of July 1985 produced surprises, largely because expectations had been created for both a stronger opposition and more honest procedures. In balloting marked by high abstention, the PRI overwhelmed its opposition due to its genuine electoral strength and impressive resources, but in some cases by resorting to a 1950s-style fraud. The immediate casualty was the already fragile credibility of the President's 'moral renovation of society'. Also damaged by both fraud and abstention was the political reform of 1977, which had appeared to open new possibilities for change.

On 7 July 1985 some 17.8 million Mexicans went to 52 931 polling places to choose 400 national deputies, 7 (of the 31) state governors, and 845 of the 2378 municipal presidents. As noted above, congressional elections generally matter less than those for the presidency. Those of 1985, however, were assigned special importance by both Mexican and foreign observers, who expected to see a stronger opposition showing, especially in the northern states of Nuevo León and Sonora, and who were led to believe that the regime would observe correct procedures.

One reason for heightened expectation of opposition strength was economic crisis. It thus seemed plausible that disgruntled Mexicans would register their unhappiness at the ballot box, and that the PRI–government would allow opposition victories to stand as an escape valve. Opposition victories in 1983 supported this reasoning.

Also, President de la Madrid had placed great emphasis on the moral renovation of society as the domestic political banner of his *sexenio*. While not much had been accomplished on this front, many were willing to suspend disbelief and entertain the possibility that the President's reiterated assurances of honest elections (which in themselves implied previous electoral fraud) should not be dismissed out of hand.[32]

Added to this was the electoral violence in two cities of the state of Coahuila in December 1984–January 1985, in which disgruntled *panistas* took to the streets to protest fraudulent elections. An inference drawn by some was that the PRI–government would prefer some electoral losses to the prospect of further violence, especially along the border where US media coverage might prove embarrassing.

Furthermore, the PRI itself had emitted confusing signals in the form of a survey leaked in March 1985, which showed that the party expected significant opposition in some 102 of the 300 electoral districts, largely in the north, but also in the Federal District, Jalisco and other interior states.[33] the PAN leadership's claim that its party would win 176 seats if honest elections were held exceeded even the usual sort of campaign fantasising; but their more conservative estimate of victory in 30-odd races seemed plausible.[34]

Events showed, however, that discontent was relatively isolated and that the PRI retained control over its peasant and labour bases. Austerity translated into electoral discontent less than some predicted, as Loaeza observed.[35] While the 1983 elections showed opposition strength in the north, the PRI's resolute stand in Baja California and in subsequent local elections in 1984–85 was the more important lesson to be drawn. Clearly, moral renovation did not extend to elections, and the better predictor of government behaviour was the hard-line speeches by PRI President Adolfo Lugo, who reiterated that the PRI is the party of the majorities and that Mexico would not be misled by exotic notions of democracy imported from abroad. Rather than knuckling under to threats of violence, as in the case of Coahuila, the PRI leadership perhaps decided on a course of firmness. The confusing signals from the PRI might be explained by the need to motivate its candidates to wage effective campaigns. And most importantly, the PRI–government opted to preserve its hegemonic rule.

With the powerful assistance of retrospect, some clues to the outcome of the 1985 general elections can be found in certain preceding state elections, in the PRI's candidate selection processes and in campaign themes. Opposition parties had themselves adopted strategies to prepare for a hard-line approach.

In early 1984 signs appeared that the PRI was adding talent to the CEN to strengthen its electoral capacity. Francisco Luna Kan, former Yucatán governor, Héctor H. Olivares Ventura and Manuel Garza González represented the battle-tested *político* wing. Olivares, son of former Interior Secretary Enrique Olivares, had been a high official in the CNC, under-secretary for administration of SRA and a special party delegate in more than fifteen states.[36] Garza González became adjunct general secretary with responsibilities of supervising party delegates.

The state and local elections in 1984, especially in the cases of the State of México, Puebla and Michoacán brought renewed charges of fraud from the opposition. Puebla especially appeared to signal to *panistas* that the PRI would maintain a hard line.[37]

One of the reforms introduced in the 1984 PRI assembly called for greater grassroots participation in party nominations. Yet with respect to the 300 national deputy nominations, a common impression was that the process followed its customary top-down style. The lists were composed by the President, Interior Secretary and party president. If anything, De la Madrid was even more closely involved than his predecessor.[38] With regard to the gubernatorial nominations, the results – as shown in Table 7.5 – indicated a careful effort to satisfy several party constituencies and to attend to business and middle-strata interests in Sonora and Nuevo León.

The tone of the PRI's campaign was set by party president Lugo in his 12 March charge to the candidates. Mexico's history demonstrates that in the absence of unity and order, foreign interests will intervene. The fate of the nation is at stake and the party rejects anti-Mexican provocations. He emphasised that 'nothing justifies adventurism or irresponsibility against the country', and that Mexicans 'are not disposed to sacrifice on the whim of some experiment the political system that's given us a half century of stability'. Furthermore, in Mexico democracy is not the prerogative of privileged minorities 'but rather an accord [*sistema de conviviencia*] in which the majorities determine the route of transformation'.[39]

These themes were echoed in campaign slogans emphasising order and nationalism. Sub-themes raised included Church and US attempts to meddle in internal politics. The President stayed pretty much at the margin of the electioneering in the early weeks, travelling abroad on diplomatic business, but became more involved as the election approached. He also used code words to hint at a tough line against the right. For example, at a conference on federalism in Tlaxcala, the President indicated that the revolution needed to redistribute power 'but he rejected any transformation that signifies a setback and the turnover of power to old and new oligarchies'.[40]

Left opposition parties faced a dilemma. They opposed government fraud; but they also opposed the PAN, likely the main beneficiary of clean elections. Several efforts to unify the left came to little, The parties agreed to cooperate in single-member district campaigns in the Federal District, which they stood virtually no chance of winning, but ideological and personality disputes impeded broader cooperation. As a practical matter, competition for spots near the top of the at-large tickets produced tensions in the parties and contributed to a split in the PSUM.[41]

With the *neopanistas* in charge, the PAN adopted a strategy of direct confrontation. They sought to nominate 'natural leaders' for office, rather than militants chosen on the basis of seniority. Party leaders wanted articulate ideologues to take up posts in Congress in order to capitalise on a forum made more important by the LOPPE.

Table 7.5 Characteristics of PRI gubernatorial nominees, 1985

State	*Candidate*
Querétaro	**Mariano Palacios Alcocer**
(Age 32. Lawyer, university professor, state university rector; mayor of Querétaro, federal senator; state and national youth leader, CEN Secretary of Political Training. New generation *político*).	
Sonora	**Rodolfo Félix Valdés**
(Age 63. Engineer, UNAM professor; career service in federal bureaucracy including public works and water resources. Veteran *técnico*).	
San Luís Potosí	**Florencio Salazar Martínez**
(Age 54. Lawyer, journalist, state university professor; federal deputy and senator; president of state PRI, extensive experience as CEN delegate. Veteran *político*).	
Colima	**Elías Zamora Verduzco**
(Age 49. Public administrator; former mayor of Colima. Emphasis on competent local administration).	
Campeche	**Abelardo Carrillo Zavala**
(Age 45. Accountant, union leader; city council member, federal deputy; state and national party leader in union affairs. CTM nominee).	
Guanajuato	**Rafael Corrales Ayala**
(Age 60. Lawyer; extensive background in political agencies of federal bureaucracy (Interior, Presidency); federal deputy; Secretary General CEN/PRI, 1956–58. Veteran *político*).	
Nuevo León	**Jorge A. Treviño Martínez**
(Age 50. Lawyer, public administrator (specialist in fiscal affairs); Nuevo León state government, federal government delegate in Nuevo León, federal deputy. *Técnico*).	

Sources: CEN/PRI/Sec de Divulgación Ideológica, *Partido Revolucionario Institucional* (1985), pp. 29–31; R.A. Camp, *Mexican Political Biographies* (Tucson: University of Arizona Press, 1982); Presidencia de la República, *Diccionario biográfico del gobierno mexicano* (México: 1985).

They also wanted to form a corps of full-time politicians to replace the amateurs who had served in the past. Furthermore, PAN leaders under the rubric of human rights sought to enlist international media criticism of vote fraud as a means of bringing pressure against the government.[42] Finally, on the heels of the anti-fraud violence of Puebla and Coahuila, PAN leaders took up the theme of using violence as a legitimate defence of election victories.[43] *Panistas* expected fraud but appeared to bet on voter turnouts of sufficient magnitude to overwhelm 'alchemy'. Close elections were unwinnable, but what Madero and others called the 'knockout' could succeed.[44]

The PAN's strategy and rhetoric appeared to play into the government's hands. While courting foreign media meant little in the north, in the capital it grated on xenophobic nerves. Linking clean elections to human rights also irritated nationalists. And invoking the spectre of violence simply reinforced the PRI's slogan of '50 years of peace'. Whatever the logic that produced the strategy, the PAN was roundly defeated. In Sonora, where expectations were raised of a strong PAN showing, the party lost all 69 municipalities. In Nuevo León, the PRI swept to the governorship and all eleven deputy races.

If we reconsider Table 7.4 in terms of blocs made up of allies and opponents, the apparent pattern is to preserve the PRI's dominant position, to strengthen its allies (which collectively increased their vote by 1.1 per cent), and to weaken the leading parties of both right and left, PAN and PSUM, which suffered losses of 2 and 1.2 per cent respectively.

Interesting ideological trends are discernable also in the single-member district results and are reinforced in the at-large vote as well. Conservative parties (PAN and PDM) experienced an overall decline of 1.5 per cent, while the left (PSUM, PST, PPS, PRT, PMT) emerged with an increase of 1.1 per cent. This pattern might be attributable to an interest in halting the advance of the right and along with it any possible development of a two-party dynamic in the electoral system.

The thesis of structuring the opposition becomes even more apparent when the at-large results, as shown in Table 7.6, are analysed in terms of the PRI and its allies *versus* the opposition. Prior to the elections, leaders of the major PRI-controlled teachers' and oil workers' unions allegedly instructed their members to vote for the PRI on the single-member district ballot and for the PST on the at-large slate. This quite rational voting logic was probably encouraged on a wider basis and appears as a pattern in the at-large results.

In Table 7.6, Sub-column A shows the percentage won by each party within the at-large district; and Sub-column B shows the percentage difference between the vote received in the at-large race and the single-member district race. For example, in Column 2, Sub-column A shows that the PST received 4.4 per cent of the at-large

Table 7.6 Chamber of Deputies, 1985: Single-member district and at-large vote compared

	At-large District			
	1		*2*	
Party	*A*	*B*	*A*	*B*
PAN	20.9	2.2	19.1	4.8
PRI	54.0	–.5	65.1	–9.2
PPS	2.9	21.6	1.7	126.0
PDM	3.3	6.3	4.4	3.8
PSUM	6.2	4.5	1.5	12.6
PST	3.6	18.7	4.4	104.4
PRT	3.0	14.0	1.5	169.1
PARM	2.0	28.2	2.0	182.0
PMT	4.0	5.7	.3	21.8

A = Percentage vote in at-large district
B = Percentage variation of at-large vote in comparison with single-member district vote in the same geographical region

Source: COPARMEX, 'Las elecciones de la crisis (quinta y última parte)', (México: n.d.), pp. 18–19.

vote; Sub-column B shows that this is 104.4 points above the PST vote in the single-member district races in the same geographic area. The overall pattern here is for the PRI to receive fewer votes in the at-large races and for opposition parties to receive more. Within this pattern, the PRI's allies (PPS, PARM, PST) tend to do better on the average (about a 25-point gain per party) than do its foes (about 7.5 per cent).

A reasonable hypothesis to account for this pattern is Molinar's suggestion that the system punishes parties that entertain expectations for real electoral strength.[45] This is probably more the case with the PAN, which had held out the possibility of winning a governorship in the north as well as a large number of deputy seats. The PSUM suffered internal fissures prior to the elections, destroying in the process the left's hope for a unified front.

Finally, the overall thrust of the results was to reduce congressional representation of the stronger opposition parties by encouraging the proliferation and survival of micro-parties. Table 7.7 reports the vote results in terms of deputy seats won. We see here that opposition party victories in single-member districts rose from one in 1982 to ten in 1985. With regard to the at-large races, however, critics had charged that the creation of five districts (in contrast to four in 1982

Table 7.6 (continued) Chamber of Deputies, 1985: Single-member district and at-large vote compared

	At-large District					
	3		*4*		*5*	
Party	*A*	*B*	*A*	*B*	*A*	*B*
PAN	10.1	.7	21.4	1.3	12.9	5.2
PRI	73.9	–5.7	63.7	–3.2	66.8	–3.3
PPS	3.0	15.4	1.7	22.5	3.6	16.5
PDM	1.5	13.5	3.3	–.0	2.7	1.8
PSUM	2.3	6.5	3.3	3.4	4.2	.6
PST	3.7	25.5	2.3	24.9	3.3	24.5
PRT	1.0	71.8	.6	12.0	2.0	5.2
PARM	4.0	23.4	9.6	41.8	2.5	37.6
PMT	.5	11.7	1.8	4.3	1.9	5.3

A = Percentage vote in at-large district
B = Percentage variation of at-large vote in comparison with single-member district vote in the same geographical region

Source: COPARMEX, 'Las elecciones de la crisis (quinta y última parte)', (México: n.d.), pp. 18–19.

and three in 1979) penalised the larger parties, the PAN and PSUM, and rewarded the smaller ones. Each party (except the PRI) is entitled to one deputy in each of the five regional districts; that is, each party is automatically allotted five seats upon attaining its registration by winning a minimum of 1.5 per cent of the vote nationwide. With eight parties qualifying, 40 of the 100 seats allotted for proportional representation are distributed immediately, leaving fewer seats to reflect the relative weight of the stronger opposition parties. The critics' charges were borne out, with the PAN losing 18 seats and the PSUM five in relation to the 1982 tally, while the smaller parties gained 23 overall.

Quite apart from the numerical results is the question of fraud, which goes to the heart of political reform in the sense of recognising a legitimate opposition. There obviously is no way to measure electoral fraud with precision, but the Mexican and foreign press reported an impressive array of techniques ranging from the semi-sophisticated (inflating the voter rolls by an estimated 10 per cent, switching and counterfeiting vote packets from ballot boxes), to the crude (stuffing boxes with 'tacos' of votes, stealing boxes at gunpoint).[46] The fraud seemed targeted primarily on Sonora and Nuevo León, but complaints were registered at several other sites as

Table 7.7 Deputy seats won by party, 1979–85

	1979		*1982*		*1985*	
	A	*B*	*A*	*B*	*A*	*B*
PAN	2	39	1	50	9	32
PRI	298	–	299	–	289	–
PPS	–	11	–	10	–	11
PDM	–	10	–	12	–	12
PSUM*	–	18	–	17	–	12
PST	–	10	–	11	–	12
PRT	–	–	–	–	–	6
PARM	–	12	–	–	2	9
PMT	–	–	–	–	–	6

A = Single member district seats
B = At large seats
*Ran as PCM in 1979

Source: CFE, *Documento definitivo* (México: 1985).

well. Since expectations had been created that the PRI would either have to concede victories or resort to fraud and then confront a violent reaction, the silence from Sonora (with the brief exception of San Luís Río Colorado) was puzzling. The more anguished outcry came from Nuevo León, where defeated *panista* candidate Fernando Canales Clariond led as many as 40 000 in demonstrations to protest the election of *priísta* Jorge Treviño. More puzzling, at least to foreign observers, is why the PRI resorted to fraud at all – much less of 1952 vintage – given its apparent overwhelming strength as well as the unusual degree of foreign press coverage.

If Molinar's hegemony thesis seems to account for the numerical results, a variety of contending explanations have been offered to explain the bare-knuckle style. An explanation that requires qualification is that of the reformist President, sometimes given as reformist *técnicos*, losing out to a traditionalist PRI, bastion of the *políticos*.[47] Distinguishing usefully between *tećnicos* and *políticos* is difficult to begin with, and then drawing equivalencies to 'reformist' and 'traditionalist' respectively is questionable. One of the President's closest collaborators, Senator Adolfo Lugo (arguably a *técnico*), leads the PRI and exercises fairly effective control over the party. The explanation might be strengthened if one narrows the focus to the PRI's labour sector, which is hard-line indeed on matters of the political reform and the PAN. Another notion, attributed to Alan Riding, is that the *técnicos* face the need to fix elections in some cases but lack the skills to do it well.[48] There may be something to this, but the PRI had despatched two of its most able and experienced militants to act as general delegates in Nuevo León and Sonora (Norberto Mora Plancarte and Maximiliano Silerio Esparza respectively). Other explanations involve *grilla* or varieties of manoeuvring by individuals to make others look bad for one reason or another. This may be of some minor importance, but the patterns were too widespread in the north for individual politicking to explain much.

A more plausible explanation is that the President and his advisors concluded that it was necessary to control the political situation in order to manage the severe economic crisis.[49] Reinforcing a political base in the PRI by acceding to the labour sector and local-level *priístas* might better allow the President to implement difficult economic policies, such as austerity and trade liberalisation.

Hypotheses consistent with this explanation are that the President might have been surprised by the PRI's setbacks in 1983 and faced the necessity to back-track on the policy of honest elections. Also consistent is what might be termed the 'domino' or 'slippery slope' notion. As put by Castañeda, the PRI–government could not allow the real opposition vote to stand in the north, or anywhere for that matter, because such would transform the nature of elections from a ritual to the real choice of officials. Such a change would shatter the apathy that has grown over past decades, bring out large numbers of voters, and present the PRI–government with a difficult situation.[50] Orthodox organisation theory might also account for some of the PRI's behaviour. That is, whatever the President's preferences for electoral propriety, local-level *priístas* see their careers riding on their ability to deliver the votes. Faced with uncertainty about real opposition strength, their efforts might have become a bit exuberant. A final speculation is that De la Madrid may have wanted to send a message to Ronald Reagan, the US Embassy and the Republican party to cease efforts to bolster the PAN.

BEYOND THE MID-TERM ELECTIONS: HARDENING AND CO-OPTING

The July 1985 elections represented an apparent setback for the process of political liberalisation set in motion by the political reform of 1977. They clearly signalled that in the short term the reform would remain limited in scope and unlikely to serve as a vehicle for a more meaningful opening. The Chihuahua state elections of July 1986 were closely watched to determine if the hard-line would continue. While Nuevo León and Sonora had pockets of *panista* strength, Chihuahua – with its major cities under PAN control during 1983–86 – was an opposition stronghold. Furthermore, PAN gubernatorial candidate Francisco Barrio generated a strong personal following. The pattern seemed familiar. Complaints of fraud were raised before, during and after the election. In reaction to government victories militant *panistas* resorted to a variety of protests, including hunger strikes and blocking international bridges. But the government held firm, apparently preferring criticism to defeat.[51]

Official control over elections debilitates the emerging party system by provoking internal divisions over what strategy to adopt in response. Recall the split in the PSUM between the factions that favour participating in elections as opposed to those who argue for more attention to organisational effort. Within the PAN, a large faction led by former presidential candidate Pablo Emilio Madero has favoured continued negotiation of electoral results with the government, a larger faction advocated abstention from voting as a way to register protest and a small splinter sought confrontation with the government.[52] Also, local opposition party leaders become more vulnerable to the temptation to disregard election results and to bargain with the authorities. More fundamentally, it becomes difficult to maintain viable political parties over the long term as both the electorate and party leaders increasingly question the meaning and value of the electoral exercise.

Indeed, the political reform and apparent counter-reform have intensified contradictions within the Mexican political system as a whole. On the one hand, the opening encouraged the formation and strengthening of opposition parties. On the other hand, the resulting increase in political competition has been met with a hardened official response. Meanwhile, increased press freedom permits greater public scrutiny of government electoral fraud.

The intensification of such contradictions resonates most among those sectors of the population which the PRI finds most difficult to control, that is, intellectuals, entrepreneurs and growing middle sector groups generally. One might speculate that although the events of 1985–86 did not produce an *electoral* watershed, they may have precipitated a *perceptual* watershed in public awareness of the gap between political myth and reality. This heightened awareness promises to grow more acute in the future, with further erosion of regime legitimacy a probable consequence.

But political reform remains an open subject, and one needs to consider the PRI–government's efforts to retain legitimacy. For example, the PRI's 1986 nominees for the governorship of Chihuahua and the mayoralty of Juárez, Fernando Baeza and Jaime Bermúdez respectively, signalled an opening to business and interests and greater concern about regional fatigue with corruption and Mexico City domination. At the same time, in Sinaloa a reform technocrat replaced a scandal-plagued *político*. And in Veracruz one of the most capable of the old-school political bureaucrats succeeded one notably less adept. At the national level, another round of discussion about reform in official circles has already begun.[53]

8 Conclusions: The Politics of Economic Transformation

Mexican government officials sometimes label as *catastrofistas* those doomsayers who see unacceptable futures fraught with violence or increasing misery for their country. A hard look at the future might indeed lead some to dabble in disaster scenarios. But this sort of attitude merely contributes to self-fulfilling prophecy. It is more useful to assess what has been shown about Mexican institutions and policies in the light of the government's commitment to restructure the economy. Such a restructuring involves several dimensions and implies challenges for the socio-political order. Outdated industrial, commercial and agricultural arrangements must be altered to produce more efficiently. Important to achieve this is economic opening, which implies new policies to promote foreign investment and new lines of exports, especially in labour-intensive products.

Economic transformation resists easy deciphering, because several critical variables lie beyond the control of Mexico, or any other nation for that matter. Most importantly, the Mexican government and economy are virtually paralysed by the burden of debt. The sorts of changes needed to promote transformation are prevented by lack of resources. Outsiders tend to fix on the nearly $100 billion foreign debt, of course, but the internal debt has grown so onerous that the great bulk of internal bank savings have been channelled to finance it, thus crowding out business borrowing needed to preserve the private sector. Recall how decentralisation was slowed by lack of resources and even privatisation suffers because the sorts of improvements needed to make public enterprises saleable cannot be funded. Financing the debt adds considerably to government outlays, creating in the process a kind of 'perpetual inflation machine' which further distorts the economy. As for the foreign debt, pressures have mounted within Mexico to seek relief, and the way in which this issue is resolved will shape the course of Mexican politics over the short term and, conceivably, over the long term as well.

Given the several unknowns, this chapter posits a series of assumptions and considers the more probable courses open for the polity and economy through the presidential succession of 1987–88 and into the next *sexenio*. Obviously, this sort of exercise cannot make precise predictions. Its value rests more on sketching policy emphases and in considering the implications of choices. Much depends on the interplay of domestic and foreign forces and on skillful statecraft.

I proceed from the assumption that the present PRI–government system can survive in different forms in several imaginable futures, and that its survival is more likely than its replacement by some radically different form of political system. Governing elites have directed reform efforts in the bureaucracy, party and electoral politics toward adapting and preserving a hegemonic-party system that has endured several shocks since 1970. Three broad routes towards transformation are probable. First, the government might attempt some version of state-led development, much along the lines advocated by Mexico's 'nationalist' school. While attractive in some respects, this route is least likely for several reasons. The second option is to avoid choosing, to drift along in hope of beneficent automatic adjustments. Drift holds out the benefit of smaller mistakes in the short term. The third option is to pursue economic opening with one or another degree of intensity. This direction is reinforced by the thorough internationalisation of the Mexican economy in the postwar era and promotes modernisation in several respects. From a regime perspective, opening presents the greatest political challenge: how to restructure its clientele support and recast its ideological formulae in ways consistent with a modern economy.

In these conclusions I shall touch upon a related argument advanced by the 'nationalist' school. That reasoning suggests that political democratisation can be made consistent with a relatively closed economic system and that the opening advocated by the 'neo-liberal' school causes or reinforces authoritarianism, as has been claimed with respect to certain South American cases.[1] Rather, it would seem to me that the nationalist route implies retaining a hegemonic-party system, which – even in modified form – is consistent with continued authoritarianism. It might also imply, however, a party that is sensitive to the needs of its principal constituent groups. In contrast, economic opening by no means guarantees greater democratisation in the sense of freedom of participation as members of organisations or as individuals, and it will likely be accompanied by greater overt tensions. But it does hold out greater possibilities for liberalisation in the sense of party competition over the long run.

THE CURRENT SETTING: DETERIORATION

Few would still dispute the notion that Mexico is presently in the throes of its worst systemic crisis since the Great Depression. Aggravating the crisis is an erosion of confidence in the political system. It is debateable whether this scepticism focuses solely on the *técnicos*, whose lustre has tarnished since López Portillo and De la Madrid, or whether it extends to the PRI–government system as a whole.[2] Worth contemplating is the irony that a return to power of the old political class might rejuvenate political life, at least in the short term. But it is delusion to expect that the crisis would melt before the presumed skill of the veterans.

Another feature aggravating the current crisis is the worsening of the age-old problem of inequality. A recent study concluded that

> Mexico has one of the most unequal distributions of income of all LDCs [less developed countries] – of those 16 other countries for which recent and roughly comparable results are available, only Brazil, Peru, and Honduras are clearly worse – and that Mexico's distribution has not changed much from 1963 to 1977 (while real per capita GDP increased by 45%).[3]

Subsequent bouts of inflation and recession have worsened inequalities.

Too often this reality is simply ignored or slighted by outsiders who would advocate one or another recovery policy. But many Mexican officials worry about the pressures that have accumulated due to inequalities. As we review aspects of the setting the common denominator is that the poor are relatively – and in some cases absolutely – worse off than before. Also, many in the recently expanded middle class face the prospect of a painful slide backwards in status.

As we have seen, the features that for 40 years gave the Mexican political system its resilience included constant economic growth and optimism about the future, efforts to find places in the PRI–government for various tendencies, periodic rotation of elites and prudent leadership. Since 1970 the system seems to have closed in on itself in the sense that the presidency has accumulated even greater power, political appointees are drawn from a more homogeneous base and Mexico City dominates the hinterland even more fully through a stronger and more active state. The ascension to power of the second and third generations of the Revolution, the *cachorros* or 'cubs', has decreased the scope of rotation of elites, thus clogging channels of recruitment, piqueing social class sensitivities and sewing resentment in the *político* wing of the dominant party as opportunities are reduced. Further, while scepticism and cynicism about political matters have long been staples in Mexican society, it would seem that these traits have intensified since the mid-1970s. One senses an increasing disregard for political authorities.[4]

With respect to the mixed economy, events have conspired to undermine the private sector but without replacing its productive capacity with an effective alternative based in the public sphere. A pernicious push-pull dynamic has acted to drive capital – and, more recently, capitalists themselves – out of the country. Also hampering the economy is a dearth of entrepreneurs, the nagging lack of risk-takers, innovators, and integrators, whether state or private. If the state enterprise system has shown inadequate efficiency or innovation, the majority of Mexican industrialists have done little better. Even if substantial amounts of flight capital can be retrieved and a government–business pact negotiated, the prospect of restoring the old-style mixed economy gives little comfort.

In the broad category of society, demographic trends are most troubling. The Mexican government changed from a pro-birth policy to one of 'responsible parenthood' in late 1973, and substantial progress was recorded subsequently in lowering birth rates. Nevertheless, the transition was begun relatively late in comparison with other Latin American countries.[5] By the mid-1980s, the combination of a 2.6 per cent growth rate on a base estimated at 81.6 millions calls attention to the phenomenon of demographic 'momentum'.[6] That is, even with a lower birth rate the large numbers of young couples reaching child-bearing age means absolute increases will remain large. Thus, 'the net result may well be a growth rate of at least one per cent well into the 21st century. With a population exceeding 100 million by then, the annual population gain would exceed one million and the growth of the labor force would also be considerable'.[7]

This combination of demographic forces produces an age profile geared towards the young, with about two-thirds of Mexicans under the age of 25, and the immediate problem of generating employment for the nearly one million who will enter the job market annually over the next 15 years. The relationship between overall economic growth rates and job creation cannot be precisely stated because of variable labour productivity. The practical complication, however, is that rapid economic growth generates other problems. In the period

1979–81 annual GDP growth rates in excess of 8 per cent absorbed most new job entrants but quickly generated disequilibria, as seen in inflation, overvaluation and balance of payments deficits. For this reason it would seem that a sustainable rate of growth, perhaps 6.5–7.5 per cent, implies a continuing annual labour surplus over the foreseeable future. This, of course, is tragically irrelevant to the reality of an average annual GDP growth rate of about 2.5 per cent during 1980–86.

Among the various other social phenomena of current interest, two merit comment. First, one must question how long attitudes of passive resignation to poverty and inequality – the legendary capacity to endure – can persist. Even with the cushion of a parallel, informal economy, the pace of mobility and exposure to media must have made some difference.[8] Second, social disorganisation, especially the rising incidence of crime, has become a serious political problem. This appears in the growing concern among the middle strata about insecurity and police abuses, and in the influence of drug traffickers in different regions of the country.[9]

Also, environmental problems must be considered. This involves both resource depletion and pollution. To cite an important example, petroleum reserves are estimated to last some 50 years at current rates of exploitation, but higher growth implies faster depletion.[10] Soil erosion has become increasingly troublesome, especially in the southern states. Land and water pollution afflicts several regions of Mexico, as it does many countries, while air pollution has reached levels hazardous to public health in the Mexico City metropolitan area. Worrisome about all this is that high growth rates must override concerns about the environment.

This gloomy litany, which could be elaborated *ad infinitum*, should be tempered with the recognition of Mexico's impressive human and natural resources and with the demonstrated capacity of its political system to absorb conflict and manage change. Assuming that over the short term the government will be able to manage events to some degree, we might review basic assumptions that affect choices.

ASSUMPTIONS ABOUT CHANGE

It seems most plausible that the present governing elite will attempt to preserve itself by making minimum adjustments to the most urgent pressures. This survival axiom, along with the weakness of political oppositions in Mexico, leads me to expect the persistence of the present regime, in one or another form into the foreseeable future.[11] In terms of dramatic possibilities, the defection of some elements of the labour sector from the PRI, or the greater involvement of the army in government, would seem more likely than the growth of party opposition to the status of a national counter-elite.

Another assumption concerns continuity of US policy, especially with respect to migration and the border with Mexico. The passage of the so-called Simpson–Rodino bill in October 1986, which provides for, *inter alia*, expanded employment of foreign workers in agriculture, limited amnesty for some illegal aliens, employer sanctions against hiring illegals and additional resources to police the US–Mexican border, came as a surprise. Similar legislation had been derailed several times since 1982, because of conflicting group pressures. The revised law provides for ample lead time for educating affected groups, and my impression is that the relevant US bureaucracies will interpret the legislation flexibly to avoid unnecessary hardship. This is important, because abrupt changes in immigration policy could strengthen elites that might push Mexico onto a course that heightens internal and bilateral tensions. For this analysis, I shall assume a gradual, incremental adjustment on questions of migration and the border.[12]

The international economic environment invites less cautious speculation. Oil prices, critical to foreign exchange earnings, have behaved erratically since 1973. After the market softening of 1981–82, prices drifted gradually lower. Then they collapsed from an average around $25 to about $15 per barrel between November 1985 and June 1986, wreaking havoc on public finance. Prices recovered slightly by the end of 1986. Of the many implications, it should be obvious that Mexico's foreign debt must be renegotiated to permit relief on balance of payments. This must be the case, given lags in timing, even if a growth cycle results from lower oil prices and trade protectionism in the United States subsides. That is, more foreign exchange must be released from interest payments to permit the higher levels of imports needed to accelerate growth. In sum, if the future holds only more acute doses of austerity over longer periods, the PRI–government system will likely be forced towards more open coercion, which creates possibilities for confrontation and miscalculation. The agreement Mexico concluded with the IMF in July 1986 recognised this by linking repayment terms to oil prices and allowing greater fiscal stimulus to growth than orthodox formulae.

Finally, the evidence throughout the book points to one or another form of mixed economy under firm government tutelage, and the pertinent question concerns the relative political space the government grants, or surrenders, to the private sector. Whatever the solution, the challenge will be to devise an overall policy that will generate sufficient growth to absorb at least a substantial portion of new entrants on the job market and at the same time will achieve the degree of technological modernisation and efficiency that can make selected Mexican products competitive on world markets. The least likely option to achieve such outcomes is state-led growth.

OBSTACLES TO STATE-LED GROWTH

State-led growth appeals to many in the intelligentsia and business community who view free markets with suspicion. Such suspicion may be rooted in several factors. A careful reading of the Mexican experience shows that economic liberalism produced distortions during the eras of the *Reforma* and the *Porfiriato* in the mid and late nineteenth century. Market-oriented adjustments in the present setting will increase hardships to the poor as subsidies to mass consumption (for example, transportation, food and health care) are reduced. Also, government intervention and active planning appeal to the intellectuals' preference for central rationality over automatic market operations. Many businessmen simply yearn nostagically for the security and comfortable profits brought by ISI.

The state-led option holds out several positive features in principle. Foremost among these is the possibility of adjusting markets to reduce inequalities in a way that can stimulate continued growth. Much prescriptive thinking on this has been done, for example in the 'modified basic human needs' approach.[13] Agriculture and rural development generally offer the greatest opportunity for investment, and raising incomes in the countryside can make the quickest and most significant step towards generating employment and reducing inequalities.[14] In a state-led option, the government might emphasise infrastructure investments that generate relatively high returns, such as feeder roads, irrigation, credit and marketing assistance. The obvious prerequisite to agricultural development is modification of the *ejido* system and the legalisation of land titles in ways that reduce insecurity and attract new capital from the private sector.[15]

Another area of priority investment involves urban infrastructure.

If joined with policies of decentralisation, investment in cities in the range of 10 000 to 250 000 inhabitants in housing, potable water, sewerage, education and health care could have the combined effects of relieving pressures on Mexico City and the major secondary cities, such as Guadalajara and Monterrey, and of stimulating a variety of domestic private industries through both income and backward linkage effects.[16] Such policies have the added benefit of relative labour intensiveness.

The state-led option could also promote export growth. In the state sector, examples such as petrochemicals, fertilisers and plastics come to mind, with many additional fields of export manufacturing open to the private sector in both the *maquiladoras* and regular industry. The *maquiladoras*, for the most part export-oriented assembly plants located largely along the border with the United States, qualify for special tariff exemptions and expanded dramatically after 1982. Tourism offers a variety of possibilities for public and private cooperation. Whatever the specific investments, the requisites are stability and predictability, with profits averaging some acceptable margin over savings interest rates in the United States.

A revitalised form of state-led growth would imply significant changes in existing arrangements. The logic would be to implement minimum reforms that would preserve the PRI, but would also allow for greater productivity and efficiency. Policies then would seek the limits of change that would expand support and improve performance, but without threatening the collapse of essential existing support. Indeed, corruption would continue but would be reduced to levels that permit greater administrative efficiency. In fact, anti-corruption campaigns would be well received in the middle strata. At the same time, islands of corruption could be permitted in strategic places. Patronage would remain useful to the party, but the limited civil service system could be expanded to recruit and retain professionals in technical fields such as agronomy and hydraulic engineering, and in such core administrative functions as budgeting and planning. Over the longer term, an ethic of public service would be required as part of an increasingly professionalised public career service.

To support these changes, the PRI might be restructured to strengthen the farm sector (both *ejidatarios* of the CNC and small farmers in the CNPP) and selected public unions (teachers and social security workers, for example) while weakening other unions in selected public enterprises and the centralised sector. Along with administrative decentralisation, the PRI might move more aggressively on decentralisation of candidate selection. This could have the effect of revitalising local party sections and perhaps creating support to counter opposition at the national level.

The state-led option fits best with time-honoured ideological themes. Greater efficiency, decentralisation and revitalisation of the agrarian sector all recognise the imperative to modernise the country in order to participate effectively in a changing world order. Yet, the changes would be crafted within the traditions of the Mexican Revolution. This direction would generate greatest support from the nationalist intelligentsia, whose major concern would then centre on the need to democratise politics. It would remain for the *priísta* leadership to somehow channel the support for democratisation into its project of reviving the party. Helpful here would be to equate the PRI with Mexico and to mobilise nationalist sentiment against real and perceived foreign intervention, or a more intense version of the 1985–86 practice. This logical sequence leads me to argue that the 'nationalist' route offers least possibility of democratisation in the sense of genuinely competitive party politics and elections. It would also follow that the party–government would tighten its grip over organisations.

However attractive state-led growth might appear, several interrelated obstacles render it unlikely. The business pact, and the style of presidentialism that guaranteed it, has been damaged – probably beyond repair. This means that the state would have to supply the bulk of financing. But there is no obvious way to finance state-led growth that avoids high inflation. Further, this style of mixed economy requires a highly effective public administration with an extensive career service and considerable autonomy. Such administrative structures would take several years to implement and would undermine presidentialism in the process. Finally, the history of PRI since 1946 provides little to encourage reformers, and state-led growth implies a top-down approach that reinforces centralisation. In short, to implement state-led growth would require social mobilisation virtually equivalent to a war effort.

DRIFT AND LIMITED RISK

Economist Abel Beltrán del Río has painted a difficult future for Mexico, even if austerity succeeds. Basing projections on the assumption of a Mexican government determined to combat inflation as part of a transition to a gradual, sustainable economic recovery, he foresaw an economy growing annually at 5 to 6 per cent, but with higher levels of unemployment (16 to 17 per cent) and of inflation (25 to 27 per cent) than was the record of the 1960s. However, the experience of 1984–85 showed a politically more sensitive government taking decisions that left inflation hovering in the mid-60 per cent range and edgeing beyond 100 per cent in 1986. Beltrán's alternative prediction thus assumed greater relevance:

> If, however, the internal and external assumptions behind this projection do not materialize, the route that Mexico will probably follow will be one of stop-and-go, partial abandonment of orthodoxy, further enlargement of the role of the government in the economy, and a slowdown in the processes of administrative decentralization and political democratization.[17]

This projection seems consistent with the hypothesis that the De la Madrid government has been incapable, perhaps for reasons of political survival, of sustaining difficult policies and that the maximum goal is a peaceful transfer of power in 1988. What might such policy drift imply for the economy? Following Beltrán, the likely pattern would be erratic growth beset by structural bottlenecks that reduce possibilities for sustained growth in the future.

With this pattern, a peaceful succession would imply some effort to revive the economy in 1987. Lacking substantial new private investment, the stimulus would come from public sector spending with the hope that a private sector 'echo' of investment might take effect, perhaps in a sequence similar to that of late 1984-early 1985. Such a deficit led growth spurt triggers the familiar cycle: inflation, overvaluation, deficits in the trade and payments balances and economic relapse of greater or lesser proportions, accompanied by further capital flight. This sequence implies overall levels of inflation and unemployment higher than historic averages, but without generating structural changes that might over time produce correctives. Closer integration with the US economy might accompany such a pattern, as one of the more dynamic areas of investment would be the *maquiladoras* (in-bond industries). Given the uncertainties of short-term calculations, there would likely not be an overall improvement in exports of manufactures.

This sort of stop-go and generally sluggish performance could persist for several years, even though each cycle would likely leave higher levels of inflation and unemployment. The essential requisite would seem to be subsidised health care and nutrition to ensure minimum levels of subsistence. While lacking grand vision, the option holds out the benefit of minimum risk.[18]

Policy drift implies the essential preservation of existing arrangements. Even with some erosion of support among the monied groups and middle strata, and seen especially in northern Mexico, the PRI–government has shown an impressive capacity to retain control over the rural poor, organised labour and the more significant marginal groups (for example, urban squatter communities). The system can continue to manage oppositions by granting minor concessions to those willing to negotiate and directing coercion against those who will not.[19] This option might best be managed by old-school *priístas* from the *político* wing of the party. Drift would also permit the maintenance of the system's labour core of strength, since government could grant symbolic and material concessions, depending on the phase of the business cycles. When one considers that the PRI claims some 14 million members, a number that could be multiplied with respect to votes, its staying power becomes more evident.[20]

What sorts of ideological revisions might help legitimate drift? With the slow-down in growth, the rhetoric of progress and improved welfare becomes more difficult to sustain. Even so, the government can channel resources more carefully and can take advantage of growth spurts to rekindle expectations. Greater stress on nationalism would likely evolve, with the most prominent reflections in foreign policy. Mexico's search for a new accommodation with the United States on Central America might be de-emphasised, replaced by a more aggressive posture, though one still within Mexico's historic 'right to differ'. Essentially, there might be left–nationalist rhetoric, accompanied by the appointment of officials acceptable to business and the urban middle sectors. For example, this seems to be the case with the gubernatorial selections in Nuevo León, Sonora and Chihuahua. The interesting unknown here is whether the legendary Mexican nationalism has remained vital over recent years such that the government can count on nationalism as a reliable foundation.[21]

Even drift holds out possibilities for political creativity of the traditional sort. The PRI can pursue different tactics simultaneously in different contexts. That is, in the northern states the party might attempt to promote candidates and policies to attract support from business and the middle strata, thus undercutting the PAN. There its rhetoric might stress economic realism and modernisation. In the central states, it could continue its complex balancing of various tendencies, rotating candidacies in different settings to satisfy groups in serial fashion. A political language of nationalism and the need for a strong state might generate support. And in Oaxaca the party might seek selective openings to the left, but without confronting the more important *caciques*.

This sort of stretching and balancing could be accomplished over the short term, that is, through the next presidential succession, given skillful leadership. In fact, these kinds of complex adaptations could come about naturally as the party attends to pressures on an *ad hoc* basis. The question is whether drift might set the basis for a transition to a more sustainable development project, either with renewed state leadership or a greater role for the private sector.

ECONOMIC OPENING

Remaining within the assumptions of an active state and a mixed economy, the Mexican government might pursue a course in which the state grants greater political space to private entrepreneurs and limits itself more to infrastructure traditionally considered and to a minimum range of strategic goods production. Even so, the sorts of public sector administrative reforms mentioned above (efficiency, market pricing policies) remain essential.

Market-led growth, with the sorts of stable pacts that such implies, offers some possibility of repatriating significant quantities of flight capital. Such an option would also encourage greater inflows of foreign investment. An important assumption, obviously, is that market and labour conditions will make Mexico an attractive investment opportunity in comparison with other countries. Here as well, attractiveness would imply predictable government policies, manageable labour relations (that is, controlled unions) and favourable profit margins. Market-led growth also assumes increased integration with the global economy in order to attract investment, technology, promote efficiency and generate export opportunities.

Much of the market thinking has already been done as well, in this case by the CCE, which has outlined its recommendations for economic liberalisation:

1. Anti-inflation policies, primarily through reduction of the public deficit, which in turn would promote trade liberalisation;
2. Realistic exchange rates (preferably through the gradual elimination of exchange controls);
3. The generalised liberalisation of the external sector, including not only private but also public sector enterprises;
4. A gradual, phased liberalisation, following some agreed-upon calendar and logic about which categories of production will be exposed to competition and which will continue to be protected, and accompanied by an appropriate package of policies;
5. The elimination of price controls;
6. Administrative simplification to reduce red tape in import-export matters;
7. Public investment in infrastructure to promote exports; and
8. An updating of labour legislation that might make Mexican producers competitive with others.[22]

As the CCE recognises, increased state investment would be required in economic opening, as would non-inflationary sources of financing. For example, to promote exports, the state would be required to improve highways and seaports, increase electricity and water supplies and modernise education. Also, public enterprise reforms of the sorts described above would be needed, but perhaps with subsidies policies designed more in favour of business interests. Direct government intervention through public enterprises would decline in favour of fiscal incentives, differential lending interest rates, marketing assistance and the like. Fiscal reform might target tighter controls over professions, luxury goods taxation and forms of turnover taxes. The market-led option perhaps holds out greater possibilities of renewed borrowing abroad, fitting as it does with both private and public lenders' philosophies.

The interests favoured by this option include the national middle and upper classes and foreign commerce.[23] With sustained growth and reduced inflation, lower income groups would benefit as well. The instruments chosen (for example, fiscal incentives) would reinforce market mechanisms. The state, however, could still pursue active programmes in rural modernisation and development of urban infrastructure, which would have the effect of complementing private investment.

A market-led option nevertheless assumes a state active in planning and coordinating development, although with different mixes of instruments. It would also admit of some continued state activity in direct production. The political calculus involves creating broader spaces for participation by business interests, including greater access to, if not membership in, the PRI. Trends in northern Mexico in 1985–86 are especially interesting with regard to ways in which the PRI might accommodate business interests. The party's gubernatorial selection in Nuevo León has family ties with state business elites; in Sonora, the candidate, an experienced and respected technocrat, was acceptable to business; and in Chihuahua, the PRI's choice of a candidate acceptable to business has succeeded in splitting the opposition forces that had coalesced around the PAN. In no case did the party make dramatic concessions, such as formal incorporation of business groups into one or another sector.

An obvious difficulty of a market opening is how to manage the labour sector as presently comprised. That is, attracting business by granting concessions and creating confidence will antagonise certain labour leaders, some perhaps to the point of rebellion. Adjustments would be needed similar to those of the mid-1940s, when Alemán forced the replacement of the militant leftist *lombardista* faction of the CTM with more pragmatic leaders, including Fidel Velásquez. If such a manoeuvre were attempted, some elements of the current labour leadership would be encouraged to defect and either create or strengthen an opposition party on the left. Such a defection could be balanced by reconstituting the CTM on a different arrangement of private sector enterprises and enlisting the strength of favoured public unions, such as the SNTE and STRPRM.

The market option also involves greater opening towards foreign investment, which in turn suggests a reduced direct involvement of the state in regulation and promotion and greater reliance on indirect and automatic mechanisms such as tariffs and tax administration. Taken together, such changes imply that the business sector would itself be forced through a difficult transition to achieve greater efficiency and competitiveness.

The market-led option would be compatible with opening the system such that the PRI would be forced into party-dominant politics. That is, restructuring the party to attract business interests and channel dissident labour groups to the left would fit as pieces of a strategy to shift bases of constituency support while dividing the opposition.

Such would imply that the PRI would cease to be everything to everyone, becoming instead a more centrist force. Such change might retard or even reverse the growth of the right, as seen in the PAN, and would bolster the left. But the chronic inability of left parties to unify would limit their effectiveness.

Ideological adjustments to support this direction would be the revival of the liberal and welfare projects, with the PRI reassuming the role of the modernising, democratising force. Mexico has long claimed to promote a mixed economy, and legitimating private enterprise could be done in terms of economic realism in a world of failed socialist experiments. Only by liberating creative forces and using government as the mechanism to moderate the abuses of monopoly capitalism can Mexico generate the growth necessary to sustain a workable nation–state. Foreign investment would continue to be welcomed to the extent that it conformed to existing law and contributes to balanced, equitable growth.

This policy route signifies the most difficult sort of political creativity, amounting to a high-stakes gamble. The present system relies strongly on organised labour. The CTM and other major unions only reluctantly support economic opening and have opposed political liberalisation. One can see how some elements of labour might be provoked to the point of rebellion. Far from obvious, though, is what the alternative basis of support might be. That is, the newly emerging system would be led by some altered form of the current political class based on a core of public unions and supported by newly attracted business interests and an emerging rural entrepreneurial stratum. In the best of circumstances, the evolving arrangement would require considerable time and skilled leadership to take root and achieve some success in self-legitimation. This implies a period of tension, uncertainty and – probably – coercion.

It is easier to imagine a more troublesome sequence, one in which the government was able to attract some business support and provoke a split in labour ranks. But rather than a successful transition to a modified system, the political leadership failed to consolidate new bases of support and was compelled for survival to rely more completely on coercion over a longer time. This 'downward spiral' suggests greater possibilities for hardening with more likelihood of involvement of the armed forces.[24] Military involvement, and the heightened concern with internal security, complicates internal governance by reducing the party's flexibility in choosing candidates, policies and rhetoric to suit diverse situations. Furthermore, should military involvement bring increased overt coercion, diffuse support for the regime would likely deteriorate, creating sympathy in turn for the almost inevitable resistance by the left. Although miniscule, the left could provide a mind and voice to channel broader discontent.

The discussion to this point has focused on factors internal to Mexico. We need to consider as well how external events might influence policies. Especially important are US policies with regard to external debt, the border and Central America. Also, the short-term performance of the US economy will weigh heavily on Mexico's future.

THE INTERPLAY OF EXTERNAL AND INTERNAL FORCES

A combination of circumstances could render the state-led option attractive if not compelling. The continual renegotiation of Mexico's debt after 1982 has been a saga of brinksmanship and improvisation. In the absence of creative and enduring solutions that provide some form of debt relief, the continual renegotiations simply invite problems. Pressures for a moratorium have mounted within Mexico, partly spontaneous and partly labour orchestrated, and in the tensions of debt negotiations, the government might be tempted or forced towards a populist response.

Successful resolution of the debt problem is by far the key external concern. Two other issues might also facilitate or hinder a move toward the state-led option. If the United States moves abruptly and in a unilateral fashion to impede illegal migration, such would contribute to internal 'hardening'. Also, US military intervention in Central America could prove a popular, consensual rallying point within Mexico for popular frustrations, spawning a movement which a weak government managing the succession might find tempting to join.

Any of these external contingencies could tip the balance toward the state-led option. Should a malevolent fate inflict all three at once, the concern would perhaps be less this or that policy strategy than the maintenance of governability.

What external conditions might favour the market-led option? Again, the primary concern is terms acceptable to both the Mexican government and the banks with respect to the debt. If this is achieved, considerable space will be opened to the Mexican government to craft medium-term policies. Such improved conditions would prove useful to those who need to demonstrate the wisdom of continued participation in a reformable, flexible capitalist order.

A renewed growth cycle in the United States, with an easing of import sensitivities, would also contribute to supporting a market-led option. Along with this a slight reflation of the US and other OECD economies, which is a probable side-effect of bank regulatory reform, could help ease debt servicing while stimulating growth and trade.

Finally, a gradual intensification of pressure on the border to contain illegal immigration would signal serious changes in the rules of bilateral understandings, but without creating an emergency situation. Incremental shifts in immigration policy would also permit time for adjustment for those US businesses that rely on illegal immigrant labour.

With these considerations about external concerns, how might the succession process itself affect policy directions?

THE DE LA MADRID SUCCESSION

A positive assessment of the De la Madrid administration might emphasise the President's determination to stay the course of austerity and to avoid radical policy shifts, especially those that might rekindle the sort of populist adventures that marked the second half of Echeverría's term and the last months of López Portillo's presidency. Critics on the right complain about the expansionist policies that fed inflation in late 1984 or about the property expropriations in Mexico City following the September 1985 earthquakes. But on the whole, this administration has made significant concessions to business concerns, incurring political debts – it would seem – with labour and the nationalist left.

Furthermore, De la Madrid has shown greater openness and tolerance for dissent than his predecessors. Early in the administration, business leaders voiced harsh criticisms, and in the early months of 1986 the petroleum workers' union adopted a threatening tone toward the President. PRI officials suggest that such incidents are more theatre than reality, that the President exhibits confidence and serenity. Moreover, the return to normalcy will require several years, and this President can make the greatest positive contribution by avoiding gambles and confrontation.[25] By serving out his term, managing an orderly succession, and returning to his home in the Coyoacan neighbourhood of Mexico City, De la Madrid can help restore the confidence essential to the preservation of the system.

A less generous assessment might conclude that this administration gives every appearance of weakness and indecision. Neither the President nor individual cabinet members seem to provide a sense of action and direction. More striking is a feeling of opportunities lost:

drug scandals and moral renovation; mid-term congressional elections and party reform; the earthquakes and decentralisation. The fairly routine sorts of cabinet shuffles designed to relieve the infirm and keep forces off balance materialised late in the *sexenio*. Barring a series of deft moves that belatedly demonstrate the President's mastery of events, the image of weakness could complicate the succession.[26]

The succession process is the period of greatest systemic vulnerability. During this time the incumbent President's powers are waning and the successor is not yet named. The various actors in Mexican politics, such as business, labour, the United States (government, business, banks, Embassy), regional interests, the Catholic church, mass media and the army and security apparatus can become openly aggressive in order to influence the choice of the candidate or to put conditions on policies to be pursued in the next *sexenio*.[27] The succession to De la Madrid in September 1981 was unusual in revealing the labour and party leadership's cool reception of the candidate. De la Madrid's low-key style subsequently prompted speculation about the succession even earlier in the *sexenio* than usual. These factors in turn feed the recurring speculation that this government may find it necessary to speed up the succession process.[28]

Granting the possibility that De la Madrid's government is weaker than its predecessors and that the succession process might be more difficult to manage, what are some possible outcomes? One course might be realignment along the lines of either the state or market-led options discussed above. That is, the various interests might more openly advocate their perspectives and advance their candidates, somewhat in the fashion of the presidential successions during roughly 1934–1952, and the winning interests could begin the restructuring process. This kind of a succession could have the positive effect of airing and resolving basic questions within the dominant party structure. Its likelihood of success would be improved if the troublesome and somewhat artificial *técnico–político* tensions could be set aside by 'rehabilitating' political personalities of both right and left to take active part in the debate.

A more troublesome possibility cannot be rejected out of hand. That is, the party might conceivably split if the succession process were more freely contested than has been the recent practice. Such a split could be facilitated if a change in the labour leadership occurs simultaneously with the presidential succession process, and if the new leaders prove less disciplined.[29]

Notes and References

1 Introduction: Perspectives on the Mexican Crisis

1. Brandenburg, F. (1964) *The Making of Modern Mexico* (Englewood Cliffs, N.J.: Prentice-Hall) pp. 1–18, introduced the notion of the revolutionary family as it has come to be used. Dominguez, J. 'Introduction', in J. Domínguez (ed.) (1982) *Mexico's Political Economy: Challenges at Home and Abroad* (Beverly Hills, CA: Sage) pp. 9–22, presents a recent useful discussion of political pacts.
2. See Almond, G. and Verba, S. (1965) *The Civic Culture* (Boston: Little-Brown) pp. 310–12; and Coleman, K. 'Diffuse Support in Mexico: The Potential for Crisis', Sage Professional Papers, *Comparative Politics Series*, 01–057, vol. 5, pp. 48–52. An experienced observer of Mexican society, Josue Sáenz, stressed lack of optimism as the most significant factor in the present crisis in his comments at the Center for Strategic and International Studies Conference, 'Mexicans Speak Out', 19 September 1985.
3. Mainstream thinking sees the survival of the present system in one or another form, but Martin Needler exudes perhaps the most confidence: 'To my mind, the present crisis or the recently passed crisis did not in any way threaten the continuity of the Mexican political system. . . . [T]his regime is not going to collapse, neither in this crisis nor in the next half dozen crises.' In 'Mexican Politics and U.S. Concerns', in *The Mexican Economic Crisis: Policy Implications for the United States*, Joint Committee Print 98–11 (Washington, D.C.: USGPO, 1984), pp. 94–95. His point that the Mexican system should be viewed as an established revolution, in senses similar to the Eastern European countries, is accurate and important in distinguishing Mexico from the democratisation processes of the Iberian peninsula or other Latin American countries.
4. In Mexico the term 'PRI–government' is usually employed by critics or by opposition party spokesmen and as such tends to irritate government and PRI members. I use it here not to offend but rather to sum up the close integration of party and government in shorthand fashion. To get some idea, 'PRI–government' has about the same irritation value as does 'imperialism' to a US audience. To avoid monotonous irritation, I shall also use the terms 'regime' and 'system'.
5. A useful general introduction to Mexican politics is Levy, D. and Szekely, G. (1987) *Mexico: Paradoxes of Stability and Change*, 2nd edn (Boulder, Colorado: Westview Press).
6. Huntington, S.H. (1968) *Political Order in Changing Societies* (New Haven: Yale University Press) pp. 8–21. For an interpretation that rejects this approach, see Purcell, S.K. and Purcell, J.F.H. 'State and Society in Mexico: Must a Stable Polity Be Institutionalized?' *World Politics*, 32:2 (Jan. 1980), 194–227.

7. For an interesting comment on state autonomy from a gramscian perspective, see Córdova, A. 'La larga marcha de la izquierda mexicana', *Nexos*, 9:9 (June 1986), 17–23. In the Mexican literature on political institutions, especially useful are Cosío Villegas, D. (1973) *El sistema político mexicano: las posibilidades de cambio* (México: Cuadernos de Joaquín Mortíz); and CEI, *Lecturas de política mexicana* (México: El Colegio de México, 1977).
8. In this enormous literature, useful basic contributions include Cardoso, F. and Faletto, E. (1967) *Dependency and Development in Latin America* (Berkeley: University of California Press); Glade, W.P. (1969) *The Latin American Economies: A Study of their Institutional Evolution* (New York: American Book Co.); Hirschman, A.O. (1971) *A Bias for Hope: Essays on Development and Latin America* (New Haven: Yale University Press). Marxists reserve the term 'structuralist' for those who emphasise the relative autonomy of the state, such as Poulantzas. An especially lucid discussion of the Marxist approach in the Mexican case is given in Hamilton, N. (1981) *The Limits of State Autonomy: Post-Revolutionary Mexico* (Princeton: Princeton University Press) especially Chapter 1.
9. This tradition, descended from Machiavelli, tended to fall into neglect in the United States with the behavioural emphasis of the 1950s and 1960s, but was revived as policy analysis in the mid-1960s by, *inter alia*, Ranney, A. (ed.) (1967) *Political Science and Public Policy* (Chicago: Markham) and Anderson, C.W. (1967) *Politics and Economic Change in Latin America: The Governing of Restless Nations* (New York: Van Nostrand . Stashjean, J. 'On Theory of Statecraft', *Review of Politics*, 35:3 (July 1973), 375–85, provides a useful overview.
10. Chile during 1974–83 is the classic case of zealous economic opening. See Sanders, T.G. 'Chile's Economic Crisis and Its Implications for the Future', (*UFSI Reports*, 1983, No. 4, *South America*).

2 The Nature of Mexican Statecraft

1. For example, Riding, A. (1985) *Distant Neighbors: A Portrait of the Mexicans* (New York: Alfred A. Knopf) pp. 1–21, presents lucid and convincing descriptions of subjects he knows well, such as daily politics, but he disappoints when he resorts to the 'oriental' or 'mestizo' ethos to explain behaviour. It reminds one of the now unfashionable 'national character' studies that blossomed in the 1940s–1950s. Among their many defects they were often both static and reductionist, useful in alerting one to important insights, but deadly when employed as single-factor explanations of complex phenomena.
2. Basic works on these themes from quite different theoretical perspectives include Gerschenkron, A. (1962) *Economic Backwardness in Historical Perspective* (Cambridge: Harvard University Press); Cardoso, F.H. and Faletto, E. (1978) *Dependency and Development in Latin America* (Berkeley: University of California Press); and Evers, T. (1979) *El estado en la periferia capitalista* (México: Siglo XXI).

3. Scott, R.E. (1964) *Mexican Government in Transition* (Urbana: University of Illinois Press) and Needler, M.C. (1971) *Politics and Society in Mexico* (Albuquerque: University of New Mexico Press) make the case for democracy. Brandenburg, F. (1964) *The Making of Modern Mexico* (Englewood Cliffs, N.J.:) argues for authoritarianism.
4. Linz, J. 'Notes toward a Typology of Authoritarian Regimes' (paper presented at the Annual Meeting of the American Political Science Association, Washington, D.C., 1972); and Kaufman, S. (1975) *The Mexican Profit-Sharing Decision: Politics in an Authoritarian Regime* (Berkeley: University of California Press).
5. See, for example, Reyna, J.L. (1977) 'Redefining the Authoritarian Regime', in Reyna, J.L. and Weinert, R.S. (eds) *Authoritarianism in Mexico* (Philadelphia: ISHI) pp. 155–72, and other essays contained there; and Segovia, R. (1977) *La politización del niño mexicano*, 2nd edn (México: El Colegio de México).
6. See, for example, Alonso, J.L. (coord.) (1982) *El estado mexicano* (México: Editorial Nueva Imagen) and Rodríguez Araujo, O. (1982) *La reforma política y los partidos en México* (México: Ediciones Era).
7. Purcell, S.K. *The Mexican Profit-Sharing Decision*, pp. 1–11.
8. Glade, W.P. (1984) 'Mexico: Party-Led Development', in Wesson, R. (ed.) *Politics, Policies, and Economic Development in Latin America* (Standford: Hoover Institution Press) p. 106.
9. On the distinction between 'Eastern' and 'Western' revolutions, see Huntington, *Political Order in Changing Societies*, pp. 264–74; Brinton, C. (1965) *The Anatomy of Revolution* (New York: Random House) discusses the revolutionary cycle.
10. The Porfiriato refers to the rule by General Porfirio Diaz, who was elected President for the term 1876–80 and thereafter ruled until 1910 by dictatorial means.
11. Though much diluted over time, the *callista* line was still represented in government as of 1986, most notably by Fernando Elias Calles, a subsecretary in the Interior Secretariat.
12. A seminal study of the development of mass politics during the 1930s is Córdova, A. (1980) *La formación del poder político en México*, 8th edn, (México: Editorial Era). As Camp, R. 'El sistema mexicano y las decisiones sobre el personal político', *Foro Internacional*, 17:1 (September 1976), 51–83, and others have shown, strong Presidents tend to leave behind fairly influential political teams. With time, the individuals may leave government, but the programmatic heritage remains. Individual politicians may compete for the mantle of one or another tradition. Echeverría, for example, styled himself as a *cardenista*. The symbolic rallying figure of the *cardenista* tradition is Cuauhtemoc Cárdenas, Governor of Michoacán (1980–86) and son of the former President.
13. González Casanova, P. (1982) *El estado y los partidos políticos en México* (México: Ediciones Era) pp. 55–59.
14. *Amparo* is a court-enforced writ which combines aspects of *habeus corpus* and injunction. Baker, R.D. (1971) *Judicial Review in Mexico: A Study of the Amparo Suit* (Austin: University of Texas) is a useful introduction.

15. 'Stabilising development' was coined near the end of this period to characterise policies that had evolved quite pragmatically. For extended discussions of these themes, see Labastida, J. (1977) 'Proceso político y dependencia en México', *Revista mexicana de sociología*; O'Donnell, G. (1973) *Modernization and Bureaucratic Authoritarianism: Studies in South American Politics* (Berkeley: Institute for International Studies) and Kaufman, R.R. 'Mexico and Latin American Authoritarianism', in Reyna, J.L. and Weinert, R.S. (eds) *Authoritarianism in Mexico*, pp. 193–232.
16. Anderson, C.W. 'Bankers as Revolutionaries: Politics and Development Banking in Mexico', in W.P. Glade, Jr. and Anderson, C.W. (1963) *The Political Economy of Mexico* (Madison: University of Wisconsin Press) pp. 103–85; and Maxfield, S. 'Losing Command of the Heights: Bank Nationalization and the Mexican State' (paper presented at the Latin American Studies Association Meeting, Albuquerque, N.M., 1985) provide good discussions of the banking system.
17. Reynolds, C.W. 'Why Mexico's "Stabilizing Development" Was Actually Destabilizing, (With Some Implications for the Future)', *World Development*, 6 (1978), 1005–18 provides a useful summary critique of stabilising development. Tello, C. (1979) *La política económica en México* (México: Siglo XXI) gives a critical view, while Newell, R. and Rubio, L. (1984) *Mexico's Dilemma: The Political Origins of Economic Crisis* (Boulder, Colorado: Westview Press) Chapters 4–5 are more sympathetic. Aspra, L.A. 'Import Substitution in Mexico: Past and Present', *World Development*, 5:1/2 (1977), 111–23, is especially interesting with respect to the inefficiencies of industrial development policy; and Purcell, J.F.H. and Purcell, S.K. 'Mexican Business and Public Policy', in Malloy, J.M. (ed.) *Authoritarianism and Corporatism in Latin America*, pp. 191–227, discuss political constraints on tax reform.
18. Stevens, E.P. (1974) *Protest and Response in Mexico* (Cambridge: MIT Press) pp. 185–240.
19. It still is unclear whether Echeverría in his capacity as Interior Secretary ordered the attack, or whether the army acted on its own initiative.
20. An important influence was Patrimony Secretary Horacio Flores de la Peña, whose approach – variously labelled Kaleckian or Cambridge school – gained influence with Echeverría. Flores De la Peña influenced Carlos Tello and José Andrés de Oteyza, who were to hold important posts under López Portillo. See by Flores De la Peña, *Teoría y práctica del desarrollo* (México: Fondo de Cultura Económica, 1976).
21. Basáñez, M. (1981) *La lucha por la hegemonía en México, 1968–1980*, (México: Siglo XXI) is a useful overview of the Echeverría period. Shapira, Y. 'Mexico: The Impact of the 1968 Student Protest on Echeverría's Reformism', *Journal of Interamerican Studies and World Affairs*, 19:4 (January 1977), 557–80, stresses the link between the student movement and Echeverría's reform emphasis. In terms of woeful bad luck, recall that worldwide commodity shortages coincided with a severe drought in Mexico in 1972–73, and oil prices were tripled in 1973 while Mexico was still a net importer of some petroleum products.
22. As one of the incentives of stabilising development, the government

returned to businessmen a portion of taxes paid. Devolution was a bookeeping device, and no money actually changed hands.

23. Acevedo de Silva, M.G. 'Crisis del desarrollismo y transformación del aparato estatal: México, 1970–75', *Rev. mexican de ciencias políticas y sociales*, 21:82 (October–December 1975).
24. Edelman, M. (1964) *The Symbolic Uses of Politics* (Urbana: University of Illinois Press) is a standard introduction to the topic. González Casanova, *El estado y los partidos políticos*, pp. 134–39 and *passim*; and Segovia, *La politización del niño mexicano*, Chapter 5, discuss Mexico. Despite the rise of planners and economists, Mexican symbiology is still largely dominated by lawyers, who debate contemporary politics in the framework of the Constitution and the law.
25. Granados Chapa, M.A. 'El estado y los medios de comunicación', in Alonso, J. (coord.) *El estado mexicano*, pp. 341–56.
26. Alternatively, as one irritated politician put it, journalists sometimes earn more from what they do not write!
27. Camacho, M. 'La cohesión del grupo gobernante', *Vuelta*, 1:11 (October 1977), 28–29.
28. Manuel Moreno Sánchez, *priísta* leader of the Senate in the López Mateos government (1958–64) is an exception.
29. A recent case concerns those made homeless in Mexico City by the September 1985 earthquakes. Government could employ traditional methods against the poor, but ran into greater difficulty from middle-strata groups from the Tlatelolco apartment complex. There government encountered sophisticated leadership with access to bureaucratic decision-making and considerable skill at manipulating media.
30. See Stevens, E.P. 'Legality and Extra-legality in Mexico', *Journal of Interamerican Studies and World Affairs*, 12:1 (January 1970), 62–75.
31. Deliberate violence in the sense of sending a message is used mostly with respect to students, labour and peasants. A form of ritualised violence between security police and independent unions has marked recent May Day parades in Mexico City. An attempt by Federal District police in November 1985 to intimidate *Excélsior* cartoonist Marino Sagástegui, was an unusually crude manoeuvre. 'Low blows' are by definition impossible to verify, but dramatic examples might include the air accident of Carlos Madrazo in 1969 and the assassination of investigative reporter Manuel Buendía in May 1984. This is hazardous terrain for researchers, be they social scientists or journalists. Fiction writers enjoy greater licence and security. So often, the conversations on this topic trail off into 'if you want to understand all this, read Luís Spota', referring to the author of several novels that thinly disguise recent political events.
32. I am excluding from this discussion the apparently intractable problem of police brutality, which ranks high on most Mexicans' lists of concerns. The particularly gruesome discovery after the September 1985 earthquake of torture victims in the basement of the Mexico City prosecuter's building suggests that the recent efforts to clean up the police have fallen short.

3 Presidential Politics: López Portillo and De la Madrid

1. *Proceso*, 478 (2 December 1985), 8–21.
2. Meyer, L. (1977) 'Historical Evolution of the Authoritarian State in Mexico', in Reyna, J.L. and Weinert, R.S. (eds) *Authoritarianism in Mexico* (Philadelphia: ISHI) pp. 3–22; Krauze, E. 'Ecos porfirianos', *Vuelta*, 103, (junio de 1985), 22–23; Paz, O. (1972) *The Other Mexico: Critique of the Pyramid* (New York: Grove Press).
3. The term *Maximato* comes from period 1929–34, when Plutarco Elias Calles – the maximum *caudillo* – ruled through three Presidents.
4. Carpizo, J. (1983) *El presidencialismo mexicano*, 3rd edn (México: Siglo XXI) pp. 25–26.
5. Ronfeldt, D. 'The Modern Mexican Military: Implications for Mexico's Stability and Security', (Santa Monica, California: RAND Corporation, *A Rand Note*, N-2288-FF/RC, February 1985); and E. Williams, 'The Evolution of the Mexican Military and Implications for Civil-Military Relations', in Camp, R.A. (ed.) (1986) *Mexican Political Stability: The Next Five Years* (Boulder, Colorado: Westview Press).
6. Ex-Presidents, however, are fair game and frequently are criticised to make some point about the incumbent.
7. Smith, P. (1986) 'Leadership and Change, Intellectuals and Technocrats in Mexico', in Camp, R.A. *Mexico's Political Stability: The Next Five Years* (Boulder, Colorado: Westview Press) pp. 102–3.
8. Hinojosa, O. 'La clase gobernante se nutre de sus propios cachorros', *Proceso*, 494 (21 April 1986) discusses family connections in the De la Madrid administration.
9. Interview material, Mexico City, November 1985.
10. Tulio Hernández offers perceptive remarks in Chávez, E. (1981) 'El PRI, como escalón al poder, ha sido relegado', in Alisedo, P. *et al.*, *1982: La sucesión presidencial* (México: CISA) pp. 123–38.
11. Zaid, G. 'Escenarios sobre el fin del PRI', *Vuelta*, 103 (June 1985), p. 16, sums the point up by noting that in Mexico, unlike countries with freely elected legislatures, public spending determines rather than responds to votes. Satellite parties, discussed in Chapter 7, typically support the PRI on broad ideological issues and in electoral politics.
12. Hansen, R. (1971) *The Politics of Mexican Economic Development* (Baltimore: Johns Hopkins University Press) pp. 124–31, gives a sensible discussion of corruption.
13. The CEN is the most significant decision body of the party, with the resources to manage the other national as well as state and local organisations.
14. The Interior Secretariat (Gobernación) is the key political agency, which during the heyday of the *políticos* (c. 1946–70), served as the main pathway to the presidency. Though it varies with personalities, the Interior Secretary is generally seen to 'outrank' the party president. As one might imagine, ambitious agendas are brought to the negotiations for offices.
15. See the data reported by Almond, G. and Verba, S. (1967) *The Civic*

Culture (Boston: Little Brown), and interpreted by Needler, M. (1971) *Politics and Society in Mexico* (Albuquerque, N.M.: University of New Mexico Press) pp. 80–1.

16. Segovia, R. (1977) *La politización del niño mexicano*, 2nd edn (México: El Colegio de México) p. 58.
17. Cosío Villegas, D. (1973) *El sistema político mexicano: las posibilidades de cambio* (México: Cuadernos de Joaquín Mortiz) p. 30.
18. The López Portillo administration has not yet been fully studied. A preliminary overview is Newell, R. and Rubio, L. (1984) *Mexico's Dilemma: The Political Origins of Economic Crisis* (Boulder, Colorado: Westview) Chapter 8–10.
19. See Carpizo, *El presidencialism mexicano*, p. 194; and Cosío Villegas, D. (1975) *La sucesión presidencial* (México: Cuadernos de Juaquín Mortiz) pp. 18–19. Whatever mystery still shrouded the process was resolved by López Portillo's private secretary, Roberto Casillas, who declared publicly in 1980 that 'the grand elector of his successor is, without doubt, the president himself'. Reported in *Proceso*, 14 July 1980, and reprinted in Alisedo, P. *et al.*, (1981) *1982: la sucesión presidencial* (México: CISA p. 39. Casillas' observation was seconded by Joaquín Cisneros, Díaz Ordaz' private secretary: 'one knows that in our system the president, and only he, resolves the succession. It is a spoken secret. We shout it out'. (quoted in *ibid.*, p. 83).
20. In good Mexican humour, the lesser version of Calles' *Maximato* was dubbed the *minimato*. Useful discussions of the 1975–76 succession include Cosío Villegas, *La sucesión presidencial*, and *La sucesión: desenlace y perspectivas* (México: Cuadernos de Joaquín Mortiz, 1975) and Smith, P. (1979) *Labyrinths of Power: Political Recruitment in Twentieth-Century Mexico* (Princeton: Princeton University Press) Chapter 10.
21. I exclude B. Carlos Galvéz and Luís Enrique Bracamontes from consideration here as realistic candidates, even though Echeverría had included them in a list announced in April 1975. With Antonio Ortiz Mena at the helm during 1958–70, Treasury was hardly aloof from the succession struggles. But whatever independence Treasury exercised was erased when Echeverría replaced Hugo Margain with López Portillo in 1973.
22. Biographical information is drawn from Camp, R.A. (1982) *Mexican Political Biographies, 1935–1981* (Tucson: University of Arizona Press) pp. 176–77; D. Cadena Z., *El Candidato presidencial* (México: n.p., 1975), pp. 45–48; *Tiempo*, 67:1743, 29 September 1975, 5–8; interview material.
23. The Quetzalcoatl myth involves the visit of a white bearded god-like figure to the ancestors of the Aztecs. The visitor taught the natives valuable skills and morals, but ultimately the natives set upon Quetzalcoatl and drove him away. López Portillo christened his presidential jet 'Quetzalcoatl'. The President's fascination with this subject would appear to be a mother lode for biographers.
24. Smith, *Labyrinths of Power*, p. 288; Camp, R.A. 'Mexico's Presidential Candidates: Changes and Portents for the Future', *Polity*, 16:4 (Summer 1984), 588–605.

25. Echeverría defends himself in Súarez, L. (1983) *Echeverría en el sexenio de López Portillo*, 3rd edn (México: Editorial Grijalbo).
26. Especially helpful for documenting the López Portillo government is Smith, *Labyrinths of Power*, Chapter 10. Interview material, March, April 1979; April 1985.
27. See Castañeda, J. 'En busca de una posición ante Estados Unidos', *Foro Internacional*, 19:2 (October–December, 1978), 292–302.
28. A useful discussion of the policy strategy of this period is Whitehead, L. 'Mexico from Bust to Boom: A Political Evaluation of the 1976–1979 Stabilization Program' (Washington, D.C.: The Wilson Center, Latin American Program, *Working Papers*, No. 44).
29. *LAPR*, 18 August 1978, p. 255.
30. The examples nicely illustrate how corruption serves to reinforce presidential power. It would be used from time to time later in the López Portillo administration, as in the case against the *echeverrista* governor of Chihuahua. See, Flores Tapia, O. (1983) *López Portillo y yo* (Mexico: Editorial Grijalbo).
31. *LAPR*, 7 April 1978, pp. 101–02.
32. Malane Vera, C. (1981) *LA OPEP y la crisis mundial del petroleo* (Caracas: Universidad Central de Venezuela) pp. 153–72.
33. *Latin American Weekly Report*, 14 December 1977, pp. 75–6.
34. Weintraub, S. (1984) *Free Trade between Mexico and the United States* (Washington, D.C.: Brookings) Chapter 4; Grayson, G. (1984) *The United States and Mexico: Patterns of Influence* (New York: Praeger) Chapter 6; and Story, Dale (1986) *Industry, the State and Public Policy in Mexico* (Austin: University of Texas Press) Chapter 6 provide useful discussions of the GATT decision.
35. On planning see Blair, C. 'Economic Development Policy in Mexico: A New Penchant for Planning' (University of Texas–Austin, Institute of Latin American Studies, *Technical Papers Series*, no. 26, 1980); and Bailey, J. 'Presidency, Bureaucracy and Administrative Reform in Mexico: The Secretariat of Programming and Budget', *Inter-American Economic Affairs*, 34:1 (Summer 1980), 27–60.
36. López Portillo was ambivalent about a strategy for agricultural development, veering from an approach of market-complementarity with the US to one of self-sufficiency. At the same time he was announcing SAM, the Mexican government was signing massive grain purchase agreements with the US.
37. Szekely, G. (1983) *La economía del petroleo en México, 1976–82* (México: Colegio de México) is a useful discussion of how petroleum development ultimately worsened rather than helped to correct economic distortions.
38. Lieber, R. (1983) *The Oil Decade: Conflict and Cooperation in the West* (New York: Praeger) Chapter 2, is a useful overview. See Stobaugh, R. 'World Energy to the Year 2000', in Yergin, D. and Hillenbrand, M. (eds) (1982) *Global Insecurity* (Boston: Houghton-Mifflin Co.) for an interesting exercise in forecasting.
39. Servan-Schreiber, J.J. (1980) *El desafío mundial* (Barcelona: Plaza & Janes) p. 49.

40. Szekely, *La economía del petroleo*, p. 96.
41. Figures for inflation and interest rates are taken from US Department of Commerce, *Statistical Abstract of the United States, 1986* (Washington, D.C.), pp. 477, 505.
42. Bailey, J. (1983) 'Mexico', in Hopkins, J. (ed.) *Latin America and Caribbean Contemporary Record*, vol. 1, 1981–82 (New York: Holmes & Meier) p. 464.
43. Useful on the 1981–82 crisis are Grayson, G.W. *The United States and Mexico*, Chapter 8; and Newell, R. and Rubio, L. (1984) *Mexico's Dilemma: The Political Origins of Economic Crisis* (Boulder, Colorado: Westview Press) Chapter 9–10.
44. Interview material, April 1985.
45. Quoted in Grayson, *The United States and Mexico*, p. 177.
46. *Ibid.*, p. 178.
47. Newell and Rubio, *Mexico's Dilemma*, p. 222.
48. This trend is reflected in the increasing attention to foreign relations in the annual reports to Congress.
49. C. Loret de Mola gives an especially interesting critique of López Portillo in *El juicio* (México: Editorial Grijalbo, 1984), as does Krauze, E.(1986) *Por una democracia sin adjetivos* (México: Joaquín Mortiz) pp. 17–43.
50. My 'short list' is subjective. Others might include Fernando Solana (Education) and Enrique Olivares (Interior) as well.

4 Federal Bureaucracy and the Administrative Reform

1. Jesús Reyes Heroles, Secretary of Public Education (who died in office in 1985), Miguel González Avelar, also Education (Senate) and Alfredo del Mazo, SEMIP (Governor of Mexico). It should be noted, though, that Pedro Ojeda Paullada, Secretary of Fisheries, may claim legitimate party credentials, as can Interior Secretary Manuel Bartlett.
2. Sanderson, S.E. 'Presidential Succession and Political Rationality in Mexico', *World Poltics*, 35:3 (April 1983), 316–34, usefully discusses these themes.
3. Employment data are difficult to find. These are calculated from SPP sources cited by Felipe Pazos in *Impacto*, 1834 (25 April 1985), p. 6. Other data are drawn from Tables 4.1 and 6.1 of this volume.
4. According to the Constitution, ambassadors, army officers above the rank of major and high treasury officials are appointed by the President with the consent of the senate.
5. Pichardo Pagaza, I. (1984) *Introducćion a la administración pública de México* (México: INAP) vol. I, pp. 203–6.
6. Pichardo Pagaza, *Introducción a la administración*, I, p. 232.
7. PEMEX and CFE are enormous entities directly engaged in productive activities, yet they would be considered decentralised agencies.
8. See Levy, D. (1980) *University and Government in Mexico: Autonomy in an Authoritarian System* (New York: Praeger) for a useful discussion.
9. M. de la Madrid, *Tres informes de gobierno*, pp. 145, 149.

10. Besides agencies clearly overlapping categories, the analysis might be improved (but rendered much more complicated) if one were to descend to the intra-agency level and classify undersecretariats and general directorates. One agency, the Department of the Federal District, is a large urban multi-purpose government whose functions span several of the clusters described here.
11. Moreno Rodríguez, R. (1980) *La administración pública federal en México* (México: UNAM) p. 210. Technically, the reform was a series of laws passed in December 1976 in the areas of public administration, debt, planning and budgeting. Rorem, M.O. 'Mexico's Organic Law of Federal Public Administration – A New Structure for Modern Administration', *Hastings International and Comparative Law Review*, 1:2 (Winter 1978), 367–88, gives a brief legal analysis; and del Villar, S.I. 'Reforma administrativa: vieja carta de López Portillo', *Proceso*, 12 (22 January 1977), 6–13, provides an excellent political analysis.
12. The following discussion draws especially on Moreno Rodríguez, R. *La administración pública*; Carrillo Castro, A. (1973) *La reforma administrativa en México* (México: INAP); Flores Caballero, R. (1981) *Administración y política en la historia de México* (México: INAP) and Pichardo Pagaza, *Introducción a la administración pública*.
13. Scott, R.E. (1964) *Mexican Government in Transition* (Urbana: University of Illinois Press) pp. 244–94; Gabbert, J.B. 'The Evolution of the Mexican Presidency' (unpublished Ph.D. dissertation, the University of Texas–Austin, 1963).
14. Camp, R.A. 'The Cabinet and the Tecnico in Mexico and the U.S.', *Journal of Comparative Administration*, 3:2 (August 1971). Career services are found as well in the armed forces and diplomatic corps.
15. López Portillo, J. 'La función de control en la reforma administrativa', *Revista de administración pública*, 22 (Jan.–Feb., 1971), p. 93.
16. Solana, F. 'Los marcos de la reforma de la administración', *ibid.*, p. 47.
17. Sectorialisation referred to placing parastatal agencies under the administrative supervision of line agencies. Thus, for example, CONASUPO was placed under Commerce, PEMEX under SEPAFIN, and so forth. In principle, the parastatals were to coordinate their planning-budgeting with their sector head so that sectorial plans might be developed. As one can imagine, the distribution up of so many agencies at one time created tensions. Also, the more powerful parastatals (PEMEX, CFE, CONASUPO) could usually resist control. This is discussed more extensively in Bailey, J. 'Presidency, Bureaucracy and Administrative Reform in Mexico: The Secretariat of Programming and Budget', *Inter-American Economic Affairs*, 34:1 (Summer 1980), 27–59.
18. Pichardo Pagaza, *Introducción a la administración pública*, I, p. 255.
19. The SPP reorganisation reminds one of that undertaken in the US Office of Management and Budget after 1972 when President Nixon, frustrated in his efforts to create super-secretaries ('czars' was the term in vogue), created instead four 'program associate directors' to supervise budgeting in major programme areas.
20. President De la Madrid announced in a speech on 29 March 1983 that more than half the land distributed in the agrarian reform has some form

of title irregularity. Thus, the priority of his administration would be title certification. See Bailey, J. and Roberts D. 'Mexican Agricultural Policy', *Current History*, 82:488 (December 1983), 420–24.

21. The contradiction requires political artistry. Félix Valdés, campaigning in early 1985 for the Sonora governorship, gave out titles of immunity to established ranchers while at the same time promising landless peasants that land would be made available at some future time.
22. The division of labour here is that the executive branch controller monitors continuing administrative and financial practices while the congressional Controller's Office of the Federation conducts the post-audit and concentrates on the legality of expenditures.
23. CONASUPO, for example, which requires flexibility with regard to commodities operations, such as shipping practices or speculation on futures markets, has had difficulties with the Controller.
24. Kelley, G. 'Politics and Administration in Mexico: Recruitment and Promotion of the Administrative Class', (University of Texas–Austin, Institute of Latin American Studies, *Technical Papers Series*, No. 33, 1981) is especially interesting.
25. Grindle, M.S. (1977) *Bureaucrats, Politicians, and Peasants in Mexico: A Case Study in Public Policy* (Berkeley: University of California Press) pp. 40–69. Also useful is Márquez, V. and Godau, R. 'Burocracia y sociedad: una perspectiva desde América Latina', prepared for Oszlak, O. (ed.) *Teoría de la burocracia estatal: enfoques críticos* (mimeo, 1980).
26. None of this is to suggest that personal, informal dimensions of bureaucracy and policy-making are absent from systems that have career services. The significance of informal ties is orthodox wisdom in the US case since the late 1940s. It does suggest that the presence of an extensive career service directed by a top stratum of temporary political appointees produces a different policy-making dynamic, which H. Heclo (1977) captures so well in *A Government of Strangers: Executive Politics in Washington* (Washington, D.C.: The Brookings Institution).
27. Salinas De Gortari by far assembled the most extensive network, placing his people in other secretariats, state governments and the party. So successful was he in the 1985 deputy nominations that some joked that SPP had become the fourth sector of the PRI!
28. Again, this is not to suggest that information and turf are somehow unimportant in systems with merit services. The voluminous US literature on 'bureaucratic politics' suggests otherwise. Rather, in Mexico, with an oversized bureaucracy, many ambitious actors and virtually no job security, a good deal of time is invested in scanning the environment. Given scarce information, administrators often must begin their days with an early political breakfast at which several trusted friends pool their facts and rumours. Thereafter a substantial part of each work day, which usually goes late into the evening, must be dedicated to offensive and defencive manoeuvring with respect to allied and opposition agencies and teams. Skillful plotting (*maña*) is a requisite for survival.
29. See the comparative data reported in Bailey, J. 'Political Bureaucracy and Decision-Making in Mexico', (prepared for Research Workshop on the role of the Military in Mexican Politics and Society, University of California–San Diego, March 1984).

30. Godau, R. 'Mexico: A Bureaucratic Polity', (unpublished M.A. thesis, University of Texas–Austin, 1976).
31. The basis of the turnover rates is to first calculate the number of 'position-years' in the secretariats. This is done by multiplying the number of positions by the number of years the post exists. Taking the incumbents at the outset of the period as given (that is, not counting them), the next step is to calculate the number of *changes* of people in the various posts. The turnover rate is the number of personnel changes divided by the number of position-years, and then multipled by 100 to give whole numbers. A personnel directory for 1982 was not available to me. The turnover rates probably increased in the last year of the López Portillo government.
32. Gutiérrez Barrios' legendary political skills will be sorely tested as governor of Veracruz (1986–92).
33. Smith, P. *Labyrinths of Power*, pp. 160–64, found that since the 1920s about two-thirds of high-level office-holders rotated out of government with each sexennial change. His universe included electoral offices (no re-election) as well as administrative posts.
34. Spalding, R.J. 'State Power and Its Limits: Corporatism in Mexico', *Comparative Political Studies*, 14:2 (July 1981), 139–61; Greenberg, M. (1970) *Bureaucracy and Development: A Mexican Case Study* (Lexington, Mass.: D.C. Heath); Benveniste, G. (1970) *Bureaucracy and National Planning: A Sociological Case Study in Mexico* (New York: Praeger).
35. Purcell, S.K. and Purcell, J.F.H. 'State and Society in Mexico: Must a Stable Polity Be Institutionalized'? *World Politics*, 32:2 (January 1980), p. 218.
36. Mesa Lago, C. (1978) *Social Security in Latin America* (Pittsburgh: University of Pittsburgh Press) p. 222.
37. Graham, L.S. 'Intergovernmental Relations in Mexico: The View from below', (paper presented at the Annual Meeting of the Southwestern Social Science Association, Fort Worth, Texas, 21–24 March 1984), p. 11.
38. *Ibid.*, pp. 11–12. The CUC, for example, involved only limited sums, but it included funds for politically popular works projects. By tying these loose ends into one package, the CUC strengthened the President's hand in negotiating with the governors, at the political expense of the cabinet secretaries. Bath, C.R. and Rodríguez, V.E. 'Mexico's Evolving Decentralization Policy', (unpublished paper, 1985), p. 11, reach similar conclusions: 'All of these efforts at decentralization had very little impact on the powers or lack of power of the state and municipal governments.'
39. See M. de la Madrid, *Tres informes de gobierno* (México: 1986), pp. 52–53.
40. W.P. Glade, 'How Will Economic Recovery Be Managed'?, in Camp, R.A. (ed.) *Mexico's Political Stability: The Next Five Years*, pp. 47–72.
41. Bath and Rodriguez, 'Mexico's Evolving Decentralization Policy', p. 17. Having had the process explained to me at considerable length in Morelos in March 1985, I would concur. The governor of that state was powerful enough to do pretty well as he pleased and call it planning.
42. De la Madrid, M. *et al.*, (1986) *La descentralización de los servicios de*

salud: el caso de México (México: Porrúa) especially the chapters by G. Soberón, J.F. Ruiz and R. Ortega.

43. M. de la Madrid, *Tres informes de gobierno*, p. 29; Trebat, T. 'Public Enterprizes in Brazil and Mexico: A Comparison of Origins and Performance', in Bruneau, T. and Paucher, P. (eds) (1981) *Authoritarian Capitalism: Brazil's Contemporary Economic and Political Development* (Boulder, Colorado: Westview Press) pp. 41–58, stresses welfare and business promotion goals to account for Mexico's costlier parastatal sector.

5 The PRI and the Political Reform Projects

1. Leff, G. 'El partido de la revolución: aparato de hegemonía del estado mexicano', in Alonso, J. (coord.) (1982) *El estado mexicano* (México: Editorial Nueva Imagen) pp. 201–23; and Stevens, E.P. 'Mexico's PRI: The Institutionalization of Corporatism?' in Malloy, J.M. (ed.) (1977) *Authoritarianism and Corporatism in Latin America* (Pittsburgh: University of Pittsburgh Press) pp. 227–58, provide useful brief introductions to party history. See Garrido, L.J. (1982) *El partido de la revolución institucionalizada: la formación del nuevo estado en México (1928–1945)* (México: Siglo XXI) for a more extended discussion. The PRI's Political Training Institute (ICAP) publishes a valuable collection of party documents (seventeen volumes as of 1985), covering the period 1929–83.
2. Huntington, S.P. 'Social and Institutional Dynamics of One-Party Systems', in Huntington, S.P. and Moore, C.H. (eds) (1970) *Authoritarian Politics in Modern Society: The Dynamics of One-Party Systems* (New York: Basic Books) p. 5.
3. Klesner, J.L. 'Party System Expansion and Electoral Mobilization in Mexico' (paper presented at the XII Congress of the Latin American Studies Association, Albuquerque, 18–20 April 1985) pp. 1–2. 'Semi-authoritarian' is hardly precise, but the underlying idea is that the PRI relies on genuinely strong popular support for the most part and resorts to fraud and force only in a relatively few but still significant instances.
4. Molinar, J. 'La costumbre electoral mexicana', *Nexos*, 85 (January 1985), p. 18; see also Loaeza, S. 'El llamado de las urnas: para que sirven las elecciones en México'?, *Nexos*, 90 (June 1985), 13–19; and Peschard, J. 'Los escenarios del PRI en 1985', *Revista mexicana de ciencias políticas y sociales* 31:120 (April–June 1985), 49–64.
5. These themes are developed at greater length in Bailey, J. 'Can the PRI Be Reformed? Decentralizing Candidate Selection', in Gentleman, J. (ed.) *Mexican Politics in Transition* (Boulder, Colorado: Westview Press, 1987).
6. Cordova, A. (1980) *La formación del poder político en México*, 8a edn, (México: Editorial Era) and 'El desafío de la izquierda mexicana', *Nexos*, 18 (June 1979), 3–15, develops these themes most trenchantly.
7. The membership estimate is from *Excélsior*, 15 April 1985, p. 10–F. If we take membership to mean those who suscribe to party goals and vote for party candidates, accurate figures on party membership are not available. The PRI, like the British Labour Party and many others, employs

indirect membership whereby one is enrolled as a party member by virtue of belonging to an organisation which itself belongs to the party.

8. González Casanova, P. (1982) *El estado y los partidos políticos en México* (México: Editorial Era) pp. 108–13, provides a thorough discussion of party functions, especially with regard to mass politics.
9. PRI, *Documentos básicos* (México: Talleres Gráficos de la Nación, 1984), pp. 156–215 gives statutory organisation. See also by PRI/Secretaría de Divulgación Ideológica, *Partido Revolucionario Institucional* (n.p.; n.d.). Much of the following discussion draws on personal interviews carried out in the Federal District, San Luís Potosí, Morelos, Tabasco, Nuevo León, and Sonora in January–June and November 1985.
10. Granados, O. (1983) *Las organizaciones campesinas* (México: Ediciones Oceano) pp. 49–74.
11. Based on congressional directories, 1982, 1985.
12. This was noted recently in Sonora by Encinas, R. 'Políticas públicas y grupos de presión' (paper presented at Seminario sobre Procesos Políticos y Elecciones en Sonora, Hermosillo, 22–23 March 1985), p. 10. The Sonoran labour sector was mightily displeased about losing one of its state assembly slots and leaders threatened to sit on their hands in the July state election.
13. Matamoros, Tamaulipas (1985), Ensenada, BCN, and Ciudad Juarez, Chihuahua (1983), come to mind.
14. PRI, *Documentos básicos*, p. 45.
15. See the discussion of the assembly in *Hispanoamericano*, 2209, 3 September 1984, pp. 10–12.
16. See, for example, his speech to SNTE, reported in *Unomásuno*, 6 January 1984, p. 4. Later that year in Tamaulipas, 'the leader emphasised that *priísmo* has to be the interlocutor between civil society and its governors, and he indicated that whoever didn't feel the passion of being a *priísta* leader ought to know that there are thousands of party comrades who feel this emotion vitally'. *Excélsior*, 26 October 1984, p. 16–A.
17. The survey, reported in *Unomásuno*, 8 February 1984, p. 5, was part of a campaign by the party president to inject partisan militancy into the bureaucracy. See the report of his speech in *ibid.*, 13 December 1983, p. 4.
18. See the opinion pieces in *Unomásuno*, 28 December 1983, p. 2, and 12 February 1984, p. 2. On resistance to dues: 'A few days ago . . . a public servant related his preference to pay not 20 000 but rather 40 000 pesos to not belong to the PRI.' *Ibid.*, 10 January 1985, p. 6.
19. See discussions of the Manifesto in *Unomásuno*, 11 January 1984, p. 3, and 16 January 1984, p. 2. PRI, *XII Asamblea Nacional: las grandes cuestiones nacionales; pronunciamentos del partido* (n.p., n.d.), reports the party's platform. *Proceso*, 439, 1 April 1985, pp. 6–9, reports on the campaign manual.
20. The reform granted minority parties seats in the National Chamber of Deputies based on a formula of five seats each to parties winning at least 2.5 per cent of the total national vote plus an additional seat for each .5 per cent of the vote, up to a maximum of 20 seats.
21. Needler, M.C. (1971) *Politics and Society in Mexico* (Albuquerque, N.M.: University of New Mexico Press) p. 27.
22. González Casanova, *El estado y los partidos políticos*, p. 62.

23. In popular lore, *tabasqueños* are noted for frankness and sponteneity. Some find it convenient to dismiss Madrazo's failure as inevitable given his outspoken and impulsive character.
24. Biographical data from Camp, R.A. (1982) *Mexican Political Biographies, 1935–1981* (Tucson: University of Arizona Press) pp. 182–83, and from interview material.
25. Much of the following discussion draws on Bossert, T.J. 'Carlos A. Madrazo: The Study of a Democratic Experiment in Mexico' (Senior thesis, Department of History and the Woodrow Wilson School of Public and International Affairs, Princeton University, 1968), pp. 21–31 and *passim*. The idea of the free municipality has roots both in the Spanish colonial and modern liberal traditions. Establishing a municipality gave Cortez the legal basis for continuing the conquest; and the municipality figured in the liberal emphasis on federalism. Madrazo stressed it as a strategy to combat hyper-centralisation and the loss of what he valued in Mexican vitality.
26. In this case, sensitive to the sectors' apprehensions, Madrazo assigned to each state a general delegate as well as delegates from each of the sectors.
27. Bossert, 'Carlos A. Madrazo', pp. 51–54.
28. *Ibid.*, pp. 75–76.
29. *Ibid.*, pp. 75–76.
30. *Ibid.*, p. 100.
31. By way of epilogue, Madrazo hovered at the edge of party activity during 1966–69, toying at times with the idea of forming an independent party. He died in an airplane accident at Monterrey, Nuevo León, in September 1969.
32. Padgett, L.V. (1976) *The Mexican Political System*, 2nd edn (Boston: Houghton-Mifflin) p. 88.
33. Middlebrook, K. 'Political Change and Political Reform in an Authoritarian Regime: The Case of Mexico', (prepared for delivery at the conference on 'Prospects for Democracy: Transitions from Authoritarian Rule', sponsored by the Latin American Program of the Woodrow Wilson International Center for Scholars, Washington, D.C., October 1982), pp. 21–3, notes that Sansores worked to block extension of LOPPE to state and local governments.
34. The discussion draws on Middlebrook, 'Political Change and Political Reform', and Rodríguez Araujo, O. (1982) *La reforma política y los partidos en México* (México: Ediciones Era).
35. Segovia, R. (1974) 'La reforma política: el ejecutivo federal, el PRI y las elecciones de 1973', in Centro de Estudios Internacionales, *La vida política en México (1970–1973)* (México: Colegio de México) p. 57.
36. Camp, *Mexican Political Biographies*, pp. 281–82.
37. Middlebrook, 'Political Change and Political Reform', pp. 19–21.
38. See Chávez, E. 'Acatamiento en público, cuestionamiento en privado', *Proceso*, 86 (26 July 1978), reprinted in Chávez E. *et al.* (1980) *50 años de PRI* (México: Editorial Posada) pp. 262–71.
39. PRI/ICAP, *Historia documental del Partido de la Revolución PRI, 1963–68* (México: Offset Altamira, S.A.: 1982), vol. 8, pp. 301–07.

40. Certainly Fidel Velázquez' joke to the effect that transparent democracy is so transparent that no one can see it inspires more than a little doubt.
41. PRI/ICAP, *Historia documental*, vol. 8, pp. 308–13.
42. Information on consultations is based on interview material as well as PRI/CEN/CCC, 'Consulta directa a la base militante', (Secretaría de Divulgación, 1985), and *ibid.*, 'Proceso interno de consulta a la base militante' (mimeo, 1985).
43. Under President De la Madrid 'only' four governors (Yucatán, Guanajuato, Coahuila, Chihuahua) were removed during January 1983–September 1986.
44. This account draws on *Excélsior*, 11 September 1985, 'States' section, p. 4, translated in JPRS–LAM–85–092, 86–88.
45. Adolfo Lugo Verduzco, 'Intervención del presidente del Comité Ejecutivo Nacional del Partido Revolucionario Institucional, en la sesión del Consejo Nacional Extraordinario correspondiente a 1985' (México, 10 December, mimeo), p. 12.
46. *Ibid.*; also, Rodolfo Echeverría Ruiz, 'Los adversarios, situados a la derecha', conferencia nacional de análisis ideológico sobre la Revolución mexicana 1910–85, 7–8 agosto (supplement to *Excélsior*, 18 August 1985).
47. Quoted in Chávez, E. 'En el PRI la lealtad se entiende como servilismo', *Proceso*, 480 (13 January 1986) p. 12. One ought to note that San Luís Potosí was suffering difficult times as the centre worked both to break the grip of a powerful *cacique*, in this case the leader of the SNTE's Vanguardia faction, and also to overcome recent PAN advances.
48. In June–July 1986, for example, Interior convened a round of discussions on electing some Federal District offices.

6 Interest Group Politics and Government–Business Relations

1. The *Miami Herald*, 22 July 1985, reports that 'in a recent poll by the Business Coordinating Council, fully 92 percent of the more than 1000 Mexico City entrepreneurs said that De la Madrid's economic policies had inspired "little confidence". Only 4.9 percent said that the policies inspired "great confidence".'
2. Hansen, R.D. (1971) *The Politics of Economic Development in Mexico* (Baltimore: The Johns Hopkins Press) p. 64.
3. See the President's 'Texto íntegro del IV informe de gobierno', *Excélsior*, 2 September 1986, pp. 2–4.
4. Linz, J. (1975) 'Totalitarian and Authoritarian Regimes', in F. Greenstein and N. Polsby (eds) *Handbook of Political Science*, vol. III (Reading, Mass.: Addison-Wesley) pp. 175–411.
5. An interesting exception to this pattern was the Peruvian populist experiment of 1968–75.
6. See, for example, Spalding, R.J. 'State Power and Its Limits: Corporatism in Mexico', *Comparative Political Studies*, 14:2 (July 1981), 139–61; and Story, D. (1986) *Industry, the State, and Public Policy in Mexico* (Austin: University of Texas Press) Chapter 4.

7. Luna, M. 'Los empresarios y el régimen político mexicano; las estrategias tripartitas de los años setenta', *Estudios Políticos; Nueva Epoca*, 3:1 (January–March 1984), 28–34; also, Basáñez, M. (1981) *La lucha por la hegemonía en México, 1968–1980* (México: Siglo XXI) Chapters 3, 5.
8. Camp, R.A. (1984) 'Mexico', in Hopkins, J. (ed.) *Latin American and Caribbean Contemporary Review*, vol. II, 1982–83 (New York: Holmes & Meier) p. 553, reports results of a public opinion survey on the bank nationalisation.
9. Maxfield, S. 'The Internationalization of Finance and Macroeconomic Management: Mexico and Brazil Compared', (prepared for the Annual Meeting of the American Political Science Association, Washington, D.C., 27 August–1 September 1986), p. 44. On the flight of capital and capitalists, see *The Wall Street Journal* 11 October 1985, pp. 1, 18: 'Mexico's central bank acknowledges that in 1977–84, at least $33 billion flowed out of the country. Other economists say the total could be closer to $60 billion.' Castaneda, J.G. 'Mexico at the Brink', *Foreign Affairs*, 4:2 (Winter 1985/86), p. 296, cites the $50 billion figure.
10. With respect to the state rectorship of the economy, the constitutional amendments were intended to reassure the private sector about new and reliable rules of the game. Also, as secretary of SPP, De la Madrid had authorised the expenditure that helped fuel the inflation of 1980–82. Thus, he suffered something of a 'contamination' effect from the López Portillo administration.
11. M. de la Madrid, *Ideología y partido* (Mexico: 1984), pp. 91–120.
12. M. de la Madrid, *Tres informes de gobierno, 1983–1985* (México: 1986), p. 2.
13. *Ibid.*, pp. 1–2. See also PRI, *Documentos básicos* (México: 1984), pp. 13–15.
14. See 'Qué es el nacionalismo revolucionario?' *Serie cuadernos políticos del DHIAC* (Desarrollo Humano Integral y Accion Cuidadana: México, #1, n.d.).
15. See Smith, P. (1979) *Labyrinths of Power: Political Recruitment in Twentieth-Century Mexico* (Princeton: Princeton University Press) Chapter 7.
16. This argument is developed by Levy, D. 'The Political Consequences of Changing Socialization Patterns', in Camp, R.A. (ed.) (1986) *Mexico's Political Stability: The Next Five Years* (Boulder, Colorado: Westview Press) pp. 24–5.
17. *Proceso*, 'Paraestatales en oferta' 500, 2 June 1986, 10–13.
18. The following three paragraphs draw on the excellent study by Luna, M., Tirado, R. and Valdés, F. 'Los empresarios y la política en México: 1982–1985', (paper presented at the Workshop on Government and the Private Sector in Contemporary Mexico, Center for US–Mexican Studies, University of California–San Diego, 16–18 April 1986), pp. 15–18.
19. Mexican law since the late 1930s requires that business and commercial enterprises register and affiliate with local chambers. This practice, along with the sectorial basis of representation in the PRI, reinforces a corporatist interpretation of Mexican politics. For a useful historical survey of business organisations, see Shafer, R.J. (1973) *Mexican Business Organ-*

izations (Syracuse: Syracuse University Press); Vernon, R. (1965) *The Dilemma of Mexico's Development: The Roles of the Private and Public Sectors* (Cambridge: Harvard University Press) analyses a critical point in Mexican development, the beginning of the Díaz Ordaz presidency.

20. Story, D. 'Industrial Elites in Mexico: Political Ideology and Influence', *J. of Interamerican Studies and World Affairs*, 25:3 (August 1983), 351–76; and 'Enterpreneurs and the State in Mexico: Examining the Authoritarian Thesis', (Austin: University of Texas, Institute of Latin American Studies, *Technical Papers Series*, No. 30, 1980) argues that it is inaccurate to view the CANACINTRA as a government instrument to divide the private sector. His findings show that CANACINTRA members' attitudes closely parallel those of members of the other chambers.
21. Tirado, R. 'Semblanzas de las organizaciones empresariales mexicanas', *Estudios políticos (nueva época)*, 3:1 (January–March 1984), 5–14, is a useful brief overview with membership data on the associations.
22. Basáñez, *La lucha por la hegemonía*, pp. 98–100. Tirado, R. 'Semblanzas de las organizaciones empresariales mexicanas', 5–14, lists CMHN as a member group of the CCE on a par with five others, as does the CCE itself.
23. Arriola, C. 'Los empresarios tras el estado?' *Nexos*, 14 (February 1979), 3–5; *Razones*, 7–20 April 1980, 14–16; 5–18 May 1980, 17–20; 16–29 June 1980, 20–21; 30 June–13 July 1980, 21–22, 31–32.
24. See Story, D. 'Entrepreneurs and the State in Mexico: Examining the Authoritarian Thesis', (Austin: University of Texas, Institute of Latin American Studies, *Technical Papers Series*, No. 30, 1980), and 'Industrial Elites in Mexico: Political Ideology and Influence', *Journal of Interamerican Studies and World Affairs*, 25:3 August 1983) 351–76.
25. Luna, M. *et al.*, 'Los empresarios y la política en México', p. 18.
26. This characterisation draws on 'Ideario del Consejo Coordinador Empresarial', (México: Centro de Estudios Sociales, n.d.).
27. The unions typically inflate their membership claims; thus, accurate figures are not available. Basic information is given in Robinson, C.H. (1985) 'Government and Politics', in Rudolph, J.D. *Mexico: A Country Study* (Washington, D.C.: USGPO) pp. 268–73; Camp, R.A. 'Organized Labor and the Mexican State: A Symbiotic Relationship?' *The Mexican Forum*, 4:4 (October 1984), 1–8; and Carr, B. 'The Mexican Economic Debacle and the Labor Movement: A New Era Or More of the Same?' in Wyman, D.L. (ed.) *Mexico's Economic Crisis: Challenges and Options* (San Diego: UCSD Center for US–Mexican Studies, Monograph Series 12, 1983), pp. 91–116.
28. Dirección de Planeación y Estudios Económicos, 'Los trabajadores ante la situación económica nacional: opciones para el desarrollo', (resumen del documento presentado por el Congreso del Trabajo al Gabinete Económico, Monterrey, Nuevo León, April 1985, mimeo), p. 1. CT 1985 estimates on incomes.
29. Carr, B. 'The Mexican Economic Debacle', pp. 97–98, notes the importance of the social wage.
30. CT, 'Los trabajadores ante la situación económica', p. 2, calls for, *inter alia*, strengthening the rectorship of the state over the economy and, to

instrument social change, the establishment of an integral programme for the development of the social sector.

31. See, for example, Bravo M., L.F. 'Coparmex y la política mexicana', (paper presented at a workshop on Government–Private Sector Relations in Mexico, UCSD, Center for US–Mexican Relations, 16–18 April 1986), pp. 16–21.
32. For extended discussions of the GATT debates, see Grayson, G. (1984) *The United States and Mexico: Patterns of Influence* (New York: Praeger) Chapter 6; and Weintraub, S. (1984) *Free Trade between Mexico and the United States*? (Washington, D.C.: Brookings) Chapter 4.
33. See the comments by business leaders Emilio Giocoechea Luna, *El Financiero* (Mexico City) 21 October 1984, pp. 1, 16; Manuel Clouthier, *El Porvenir* (Monterrey) 18 October 1984, p. 3–A; José María Basagoiti, *El Porvenir* 19 October 1984, pp. 1, 3 (international section); Alejandro Gurza, *El Norte* (Monterrey) 21 October 1984, p. 1; and Alfredo Sandoval, *ibid.*, p. 2.
34. See, for example, President De la Madrid's speech of 19 March 1985, reported in *Excélsior*, 20 March, pp. 1, 20A. The same theme is taken up in speeches immediately following the congressional elections of July 1985, and has been continued. See his remarks to the XLV Annual Ordinary General Assembly of CANACINTRA, 26 February 1986.
35. To get some sense of the exchange during 1985, see the criticisms of government by the CCE, *Excélsior*, 5 February, pp. 1, 12A, and by COPARMEX, *ibid.*, 4 March, pp. 1, 11A; and the response by the CTM, *ibid.*, 19 March, pp. 1, 8A, and by the PRI, *ibid.*, 31 March, pp. 1, 12A. *Proceso*, 474, 2 December 1985, reports on the case of VITRO.
36. Interview material, May 1985.

7 Political Parties and Electoral Politics

1. De la Madrid won nearly three-quarters of the vote of about a 75 per cent turnout of those registered.
2. Baer, D. and Bailey, J. 'Mexico's 1985 Midterm Elections: A Preliminary Assessment', *LASA Forum* (Fall 1985), pp. 7–8.
3. Krauze, E. 'Por una democracia sin adjetivos', *Vuelta*, 85 (January 1985), 4–13; Meyer, L. 'La democracia como proyecto', *Excélsior*, 21 November 1985, p. 74, and 'Los riesgos de la democracia', *ibid.*, 10 December 1985, pp. 7, 10–A; Paz, O. 'Hora cumplida, 1929–1985', *Vuelta*, 9:103 (June 1985) 7–12.
4. Loaeza, S. 'El llamado de las urnas: para que sirven las elecciones en México?' *Nexos*, 90 (June 1985) 13–19.
5. Padgett, V. (1976) *The Mexican Political System*, 2nd edn (Boston: Houghton-Mifflin) p. 115.
6. Craig, A.L. and Cornelius, W.A. 'Political Culture in Mexico: Continuities and Revisionist Interpretations', in Almond, G.A. and Verba, S. (eds) (1980) *The Civic Culture Revisited: An Analytic Study* (Boston: Little, Brown) p. 367.
7. Booth, J. and Seligson, M. 'The Political Culture of Authoritarianism in

Mexico: A Reexamination', *Latin American Research Review*, 19:1 (1984), 106–24. A. Hernández H. also reports data that might be interpreted as showing stronger democratic attitudes in northern border cities than in the Federal District. See 'Actitudes políticas de los jovenes fronterizos' (paper presented at the coloquium on Electoral Patterns and Perspectives in Mexico, Center for US–Mexican Studies, University of California, San Diego, 7–9 November 1985).

8. J. Molinar H., 'La costumbre electoral mexicana', *Nexos*, 85 (Jan. 1985) 19–21.
9. Electoral rules are set out in the *Constitución política de los Estados Unidos mexicanos*, Articles 51–60 for the congress and 81 for the President. The implementing legislation is the 'Ley federal de organizaciones políticas y procesos electorales', *Diario Oficial*, 30 December 1977, usually referred to as 'the LOPPE'; and 'Reglamento de los organismos electorales y previsiones para la ley federal de organizaciones políticas y procesos electorales', *Diario Oficial*, 27 October 1978.
10. The municipality comprises a town or city as well as the surrounding countryside. Perhaps 'county' conveys a similar notion.
11. CFE, *Federal Electoral Process, 1984–1985* (México: Talleres Gráficos de la Nación, 1986), pp. 11–13, discusses the composition of the CFE. I include with the PRI the members from the Chamber and Senate, as well as the PARM and PPS. The PAN, PDM, PRT and PSUM typically oppose the PRI. The PST is a part-time ally, and the PMT had only conditional registration and thus could not vote. (See Table 7.3 for a description of the parties.)
12. In the cases of senators and deputies, the parties nominate a principal candidate (*propietario*) and a substitute (*suplente*) for each seat. The doubling of posts, from 462 to 924, gives the PRI more prestige positions with which to reward discipline. Also, *priísta* deputies and senators are occasionally called upon to serve as party delegates outside of Mexico City; at these times, the substitute can fill in. With respect to the no re-election rule, a *suplente* who has not served as a *proprietario* may be re-elected immediately as the *proprietario*.
13. Segovia, R. 'Las elecciones federales de 1979', *Foro Internacional*, 20:3 (January–May 1980), p. 408, mentions re-districting in Puebla and Culiacán designed to dilute the PAN's strength in the urban vote by adding rural constituencies.
14. Lists would vary, of course, but I would include as difficult states Baja California Norte, Chihuahua, Nuevo León, Sonora, Guerrero, Puebla and Coahuila. Another state that can be difficult, Jalisco, does fall in the last year.
15. Recent literature on state and local elections is thin. Arreola, A. '1981: elecciones en el Estado de México', *Estudios políticos (nueva epoca)*, 1:1 (October–December 1982), 25–32; and Guadarrama, R. and St Clair, A. 'La oposición conservadora en Sonora', (paper presented at Seminario Procesos Políticos y Elecciones en Sonora, Hermosillo 22–23 March 1985), are useful.
16. Molinar, 'La costumbre electoral', p. 24.
17. Vernon, R. (1965) *The Dilemma of Mexico's Development: The Roles of*

the Private and Public Sectors (Cambridge, Mass.: Harvard University Press) p. 135.

18. The following paragraphs draw on Klesner, J. 'Party System Expansion and Electoral Mobilization in Mexico', (paper presented at the XII Congress of the Latin American Studies Association, Albuquerque, 18–20 April 1985), pp. 20–29; C. Domínguez M., 'Quién es quién en la izquierda mexicana', *Nexos*, 54 (June 1982), 28–32; *Razones*, 58 (22 March– 4 April, 1982), 30–33; Segovia, R. 'Las elecciones federales de 1979'; *Excélsior*, 15 April 1985, 10F.
19. Segovia, 'Las elecciones federales de 1979', p. 407.
20. Discussion of the PAN draws especially on Bartra, R. 'Viaje al centro de la derecha', *Nexos*, 64 (April 1983), 15–23; and Loaeza, S. 'Julio de 86: la cuna y el palo', *Nexos*, 103 (July 1986), 19–27, and *ibid.*, 'Accion Nacional: de la oposicion leal a la oposición electoral' (mimeo, 1986).
21. The term 'foco' comes originally from Marxist theorist Regis Debray, who used it in the context of the insertion of guerrillas in a rural milieu to 'infect' the countryside against the city.
22. *Unomásuno*, 13 January 1984, pp. 1, 5; *Excélsior*, 24 February 1985, pp. 1, 18. 20–A.
23. PAN, *Principios de doctrina* (México: 1980) and 'Anteproyecto de plataforma 85', (mimeo, n.d.), pp. 9–18, set out the main ideas.
24. Data reported by the PRI's electoral action secretary. *Unomásuno*, 10 January 1984, p. 2.
25. *Excélsior*, 27 March 1985, pp. 1, 21–A.
26. CFE, *Federal Electoral Process, 1984–1985*, p. 80.
27. See Gómez Tagle, S. 'Democracy and Power in Mexico: The Meaning of Electoral Fraud in 1979 and 1982' (paper prepared for the XII LASA meeting, Albuquerque, New Mexico, April 1985) for a discussion of fraud and the CFE.
28. The results of the Morelos state elections of February 1985 were not to my knowledge ever published. The party delegate simply asserted that 80 per cent had voted and that the PRI had won 90 per cent of the vote. *Diario de Morelos* (Cuernavaca) 18 March 1985, pp. 1, 4. See also 'Los Intocables', *Excélsior*, 23 May 1985, pp. 1, 15–A.
29. Mexico City poll reported in *Excélsior*, 1 July 1985, and cited in Latell, B. 'Mexico at the Crossroads: The Many Crises of the Political System' (Stanford University, *Hoover Institution Monograph Series* 6, 16 June 1986), p. 16. Sonora poll reported in 'Gente y Cosas', *El Imparcial* (Hermosillo), 8 May 1985.
30. Garza Ramírez, E. (coord.) (1985) *Nuevo León 1985* (Monterrey: Nacional Monumel) p. 140.
31. Klesner, 'Party System Expansion', *Op. Cit.*, p. 32.
32. The President instructed the assembled governors in early January to conduct clean elections, and the Interior Secretary repeated the admonition a few days later. See *Unomásuno*, 10 January 1985, pp. 1, 6; and *Excélsior*, 15 January 1985, pp. 1, 9–A.
33. The report is discussed in *La Jornada*, 8 April 1985, p. 2.
34. *Excélsior*, 25 February 1985, p. 39–A; *ibid.*, 26 February 1985, p. 1–A.
35. Loaeza, S. 'Bursting the Bubble: Mexico's Electoral Process and PAN's Image Were Overblown', *The Arizona Republic*, 28 July 1985, p. C2.

36. *Unomásuno*, 16 March 1984, p. 4.
37. Interview material, Mexico City, March 1985.
38. Interview material. Mexico City, March–April 1985.
39. *Excélsior*, 13 March 1985, pp. 1, 10–A.
40. *La Jornada*, 25 May 1985, p. 3. Emphasis added.
41. See P. Fernandez Christlieb, 'Elecciones federales 1985: los partidos de izquierda ante la "unidad"', *Rev. mexicana de ciencias políticas y sociales*, 31–120 (April–June 1985), 13–48, for a more complete analysis of the left.
42. See the remarks by Jesús González Schmall, *Unomásuno*, 9 January 1985, pp. 1, 6.
43. See the comments about violence by Juan José Hinojosa, *Excélsior*, 11 January 1985, pp. 23, 35–A, and Pablo Madero, *Unomásuno*, 13 January 1985, pp. 1, 5.
44. Sergio Lujambio, for example, observed that the PRI had no intention of allowing free elections. Chihuahua in 1983 was like a thermometer to show the PRI popular attitudes. 'Now they know and it will be difficult to allow such a free game.' *Unamásuno*, 10 January 1984, p. 5.
45. Molinar, 'La costumbre electoral', p. 22.
46. In the Mexican press, see especially the stories in *Proceso*, 454, 15 July, pp. 10–29; and 455, 22 July, pp. 10–13; and also in the Monterrey press, *El Porvenir*, 2 July; and *El Norte*, 6–11 July. In the US press see the coverage by Meislin, R. *The New York Times*, 9, 16 July; Frazier, S. *The Wall Street Journal*, 12 July; Orme, W. *The Washington Post*, 8 July; Volman, D. *The Christian Science Monitor*, 9 July; and Lopez, B. *The Arizona Republic*, 28 July; McCartney, R.J. *The Washington Post*, 11 July, p. A 24, put it most bluntly: 'Several reporters said that less respect was shown for laws and procedures in Sonora than in the elections they covered in El Salvador and Nicaragua.' J.G. Castañeda, 'Mexico at the Brink', *Foreign Affairs*, (Winter, 1985/86), p. 291, concurs: 'According to most accounts [fraud] was so widespread in the northern states of Nuevo León and Sonora that the official results for those states were meaningless.'
47. See *Latin American Monitor*, 2:5 (July 1985), p. 181; and Cornelius, W. and Alvarado, A. *Los Angeles Times*, July 10.
48. Riding, A. (1985) *Distant Neighbors: A Portrait of the Mexicans* (New York: Alfred A. Knopf) pp. 79–82.
49. The nationalistic and aggressive speeches by President De la Madrid (*Excélsior*, 19 July 1985, 1, 10A) and Adolfo Lugo Verduzco (*ibid*, pp. 4, 14A) support this view.
50. J.G. Castañeda, 'Elecciones: tres ideas sin saña', *Proceso*, 451, 24 June 1985, pp. 36–37.
51. See Marquez, P.L. 'Mexico's Opposition Party: El Partido Accion Nacional, A Case Study of the PAN in the State of Chihuahua', (Master's thesis, The University of Texas at El Paso, 1987), pp. 85–117.
52. See Volman, D. *The Christian Science Monitor*, 12 August 1985, p. 9.
53. *Diario Oficial*, 19 June 1986, pp. 2–3, announces the presidential order convening parties and groups for discussion of electoral reform and citizen participation in the government of the Federal District.

8 Conclusions: The Politics of Economic Transformation

1. The argument and the 'nationalist' and 'neo-liberal' categories are developed by Cordera, R. and Tello, C. (1981) *México: la disputa por la nación* (México: Siglo XXI).
2. P.H. Smith gives a useful discussion of these themes in 'Leadership and Change, Intellectuals and Technocrats', in Camp, R.A. (ed.) (1986) *Mexico's Political Stability: The Next Five Years* (Boulder, Colorado: Westview Press) pp. 101–18.
3. Bergsman, J. 'Income Distribution and Poverty in Mexico' (*World Bank Staff Working Paper* No. 395, 1980), p. 41.
4. That President De la Madrid would be scolded by union leaders and hooted down at the inauguration of the World Cup soccer matches of June 1986 illustrates the point.
5. Potter, J.E. 'Mexico: A Model for Success', *Harvard International Review*, 8:4 (March 1986) 33–35.
6. Population estimates are taken from Population Reference Bureau, '1986 World Population Data Sheet' (Washington, D.C.: 1986).
7. Gendell, M. 'Population Growth and Labor Absorption in Latin America, 1970–2000', (mimeo, July 1984) p. 12.
8. Hansen, R. 'The Evolution of US–Mexican Relations: A Sociopolitical Perspective', in Erb, R.E. and Ross, S.R. (eds) (1982) *United States Relations with Mexico* (Washington, D.C.: AEI) p. 42, rightly reminds us that passivity should not be assumed.
9. Experience teaches that religious movements and social delinquency are frequently alternatives to political protest.
10. *The Washington Post*, 23 January 1986, p. A29, reports that 'a Mexican congressional committee recently warned that at its present rate of consumption and development, Mexico could be forced to start importing oil in 15 years, despite its present 50 billion barrels of proven crude reserves'.
11. O'Donnell, G. (1973) *Modernization and Bureaucratic–Authoritarianism: Studies in South American Politics* (Berkeley, Institute for International Studies) fn. 77, pp. 95–97; and 'Tensions in the Bureaucratic–Authoritarian State and the Question of Democracy', in Collier, D. (ed.) (1979) *The New Authoritarianism in Latin America* (Princeton, N.J.: Princeton University Press) p. 312, provides especially interesting comparative insights on the resilience of the Mexican system.
12. See Portes, A. 'Immigration Reform Again: The 1985 Proposals', *LASA Forum*, 16:4 (Winter 1986), 31–34, for a succinct overview.
13. See, for example, Selowsky, M. 'Balancing Trickle Down and Basic Needs Strategies: Income Distribution in Large Middle-Income Countries with Special Reference to Latin America', *World Bank Staff Working Papers*, No. 335 (1979).
14. The single most imaginative piece of thinking on a rural-based strategy of recovery is Barkin, D. 'The War Economy Strategy: An Alternative for Mexico's Debt Management Crisis, (Summary)', (presented at Workshop on Government and the Private Sector in Contemporary Mexico, Center for US–Mexican Studies, University of California, San Diego, 16–18 April 1986).

15. This clearly is another case of ignoring a thorny political issue. The *ejido* remains an especially sensitive topic.
16. One senses that enough 'push' momentum has accumulated in the Mexico City metropolitan area due to difficult living conditions that what remains to promote decentralisation is improved living conditions in the smaller cities.
17. Beltrán del Río, A. 'Problems and Prospects of the Mexican Economy in 1983–88', in *The Mexican Economic Crisis: Policy Implications for the United States*, Joint Economic Committee Print 98–11 (Washington, D.C.: USGPO, 1984), p. 196.
18. A Mexican businessman is quoted as noting that De la Madrid 'should be credited for all the mistakes he hasn't made – for not making wild promises, raising expectations, for example – and argues that a man of caution could prove to be exactly what is needed'. *Wall Street Journal*, 26 September 1985, p. 18.
19. For example, the government's initially inept response after the 1985 earthquakes and the strength of the spontaneous public reaction led some to underestimate the regime's resilience. This has given way to a much rosier assessment of government strength a year later. See *The Miami Herald*, 14 September 1986, pp. 1, 14–A.
20. Given indirect membership, obviously not all those claimed as members turn out to vote, or to vote for the PRI (or even exist, for that matter). But since this option involves essential continuity, we must assume some targeted election-fixing as well.
21. Some Mexican intellectuals comment privately that the US government evidently has concluded that Mexican nationalism has withered and that such gives greater political space for US intervention into Mexican internal affairs. The furore raised by the hearings held by Senator Helms' subcommittee of the Foreign Relations committee on 15–16 May 1986 would suggest otherwise.
22. Summarised from CCE, 'Posición de los organismos empresariales respecto a la liberalización del sector externo de la economía' (Mexico: mimeo, 30 May 1985).
23. This clearly has been the case with agriculture, as shown by Sanderson, S.E. (1986) *The Transformation of Mexican Agriculture: International Structure and the Politics of Rural Change* (Princeton: Princeton University Press).
24. Pablo González Casanova has speculated about this possibility. See Chávez, E. 'El estado tiende a perder sus bases sociales: González Casanova', *Proceso*, 450, 17 June 1985, 20–23.
25. Interview material, Mexico City, January 1985; Washington, D.C., June 1986.
26. On this point one must sympathise with defenders of Mexican presidentialism who hear criticisms of 'hyper-presidentialism' followed by criticisms of weakness, often from the same people, when the incumbent appears less authoritarian.
27. The movement launched by Porfirio Muñoz Ledo in August 1986 to democratise the PRI might be read in this light. See *Unomásuno*, 14 August 1986, pp. 1, 7.
28. In addition, a recent constitutional amendment shifted the date of

presidential elections from the first Sunday in July to the first Sunday in September, in order to cut the lag time between election and inauguration and thus shorten the period of tensions between official power and power-in-waiting. Another reason may be to dampen the lingering temptations the incumbent might experience to use a dramatic exit to seek a place in history.

29. The implicit referent in this line of reasoning is the crucial role played by the CTM president, octagenarian Fidel Valázquez. The scuffle between SNTE and FSTSE in early 1986 hinted at a lapse of discipline that might complicate that year's gubernatorial selections, and perhaps even the succession process. See *Hispanoamericano*, 18 February 1986, pp. 7–8.

Selected Bibliography

Full bibliographical citations are provided in the Notes and References section for each chapter. Also, excellent recent bibliographies on Mexican politics can be found in Levy and Szekely (1987), Newell and Rubio (1984) and Sanderson (1986), cited below. I shall limit the following to recent or less well known works.

Books and Theses

Alisedo, P. *et al.* (1981) *1982: La sucesión presidencial* (México: CISA).

Alonso, J.L. (coord.) (1982) *El estado mexicano* (México: Editorial Nueva Imagen).

Basáñez, M. (1981) *La lucha por la hegemonía en México, 1968–1980* (México: Siglo XXI).

Bossert, T.J. (1968) 'Carlos A. Madrazo: The Study of a Democratic Experiment in Mexico', (Senior Thesis, Princeton University).

Cadena Z., D. (1975) *El candidato presidencial* (México: n.p.).

Camp, R.A. (ed.) (1986) *Mexico's Political Stability: The Next Five Years* (Boulder, Colorado: Westview Press).

Carpizo, J. (1985) *El presidencialismo mexicano*, 3ra edn, (Mexico: Siglo XXI).

Carrillo Castro, A. (1973) *La reforma administrativa en México* (México: INAP).

Cordera, R. and Tello, C. (1981) 2nda edn, *México: la disputa por la nacion* (México: Siglo XXI).

Córdova, A. (1980) *La formación del poder político en México*, 8a edn, (México: Editorial Era).

Cosío Villegas, D. (1975) *El estilo personal de gobernar* (México: Cuadernos de Joaquín Mortiz).

——, (1983) *El sistema político mexicano: las posibilidades de cambio* (México: Cuadernos de Joaquín Mortiz).

De la Madrid, M. (1984) *Ideología y partido* (México: PRI).

——, (1986) *Tres informes de gobierno* (México: n.p.).

——, *et al.*, (1986) *La descentralización de los servicios de salud: el caso de México* (México: Porrúa).

Evers, T. (1979) *El estado en la periferia capitalista* (México: Siglo XXI).

Flores Caballero, R. (1981) *Administración y política en la historia de México* (México: INAP).

Flores de la Peña, H. (1976) *Teoría y práctica del desarrollo* (México: Fondo de Cultura Económica).

Flores Tapia, O. (1983) *López Portillo y yo* (México: Editorial Grijalbo).

Furtak, R.K. (1974) *El partido de la revolución y la estabilidad política en México* (México: UNAM).

Gabbert, J.B. (1963) 'The Evolution of the Mexican Presidency', Ph.D. dissertation, The University of Texas–Austin).

Garrido, J.L. (1982) *El partido de la revolución institucionalizada: la formación del nuevo estado en México (1928–1945)* (México: Siglo XXI).

Garza Ramírez, E. (coord.) (1985) *Nuevo León 1985* (Monterrey: Nacional Monumel).

Gentleman, J. (ed.) *Mexican Politics in Transition* (Boulder, Colorado: Westview Press, 1987).

Godau, R.H. (1976) 'Mexico: A Bureaucratic Polity', (M.A. thesis, University of Texas–Austin).

González Casanova, P. (1982) *El estado y los partidos politicos en México* (México: Ediciones Era).

Granados, O. (1983) *Las organizaciones campesinas* (Mexico: Ediciones Oceaneo).

Grayson, G. (1984) *The United States and Mexico: Patterns of Influence* (New York: Praeger).

Krauze, E. (1986) *Por una democracia sin adjetivos* (México: Joaquín Mortiz).

Levy, D. and Szekely, G. (1987) *Mexico: Paradoxes of Stability and Change*, 2nd edn, (Boulder, Colorado: Westview Press).

Loret de Mola, C. (1984) *El juicio* (México: Editorial Grijalbo).

Marquez, P.L. (1987) 'Mexico's Opposition Party: El Partido Accion Nacional, A Case Study of the PAN in the State of Chihuahua', (M.A. thesis, The University of Texas at El Paso).

Maxfield, S. and Anzaldúa Montoya, R. (eds) (1987) *Government and Private Sector in Contemporary Mexico* (San Diego: UCSD Center for US–Mexican Studies, Monograph Series 20).

México, Presidencia de la República, *Diccionario biográfico del gobierno mexicano* (México: 1985).

——, (1986) Secretaría de Gobernación, Comisión Federal Electoral, *Federal Electoral Process, 1984–1985* (Mexico: Talleres Graficos de la Nación).

——, ——, ——, *Reforma política, gaceta informativa de la Comisión Federal Electoral, Tomo IX* (México: 1982).

——, ——, ——, *Documento definitivo* (México: 1985).

Moreno Rodríguez, R. (1980) *La administración pública federal en México* (México: UNAM).

Newell, R.G. and Rubio F., L. (1984) *Mexico's Dilemma: The Political Origins of Economic Crisis* (Boulder, Colorado: Westview Press).

Pichardo Pagaza, I. (1984) *Introducción a la administración pública de México* (México: INAP) 2 vols.

PRI, (1984) *Documentos básicos* (México: Talleres Gráficos de la Nación).

——, *XII Asamblea Nacional: las grandes cuestiones nacionales; pronunciamentos del partido* (n.p., n.d.).

——, Comisión Coordinadora de Convenciones, 'Consulta directa a la base militante' (México: Secretaría de Divulgación Ideológica, 1985).

——, Instituto de Capacitación Política, *Historia documental del partido de la revolución* (México: Offset Altamira, 1982) 11 vols.

——, Secretaría de Divulgación Ideológica, *Partido Revolucionario Institucional* (n.p., n.d.).
——, ——, *Textos revolucionarios* (México: 1985).
Riding, A. (1985) *Distant Neighbors: A Portrait of the Mexicans* (New York: Alfred A. Knopf).
Rodríguez Araujo, O. (1982) *La reforma política y los partidos en México* (México: Ediciones Era).
Sanderson, S.E. (1986) *The Transformation of Mexican Agriculture: International Structure and the Politics of Rural Change* (Princeton: Princeton University Press).
Segovia, R. (1977) *La politización del niño mexicano* (México: El Colegio de México).
Story, D. (1986) *Industry, the State and Public Policy in Mexico* (Austin: University of Texas Press).
Suarez, L. (1983) *Echeverría en el sexenio de López Portillo*, 3ra edn, (México: Editorial Grijalbo).
Szekely, G. (1983) *Le economía del petroleo en México, 1976–82* (México: Colegio de Mexico).
Weintraub, S. (1984) *Free Trade between Mexico and the United States* (Washington, D.C.: Brookings).
Wyman, D.L. (ed.) (1983) *Mexico's Economic Crisis: Challenges and Options* (San Diego: UCSD Center for US–Mexican Studies, Monograph Series 12).

Articles, Chapters and Occasional Papers

Acevedo de Silva, M.G. 'Crisis del desarrollismo y transformación del aparato estatal: México, 1970–1975', *Rev. mexicana de ciencias políticas y sociales*, 21:82 (October–December 1975).
Arreola Ayala, A. '1981: elecciones en el estado de México', *Estudios políticos (nueva época)*, 1:1 (October–December 1982), 25–32.
Arriola, C. 'Los empresarios tras el estado?' *Nexos*, 14 (February 1979), 3–5.
Baer, D. and Bailey, J. 'Mexico's 1985 Midterm Elections: A Preliminary Assessment', *LASA Forum* (Fall 1985).
Bartra, R. 'Viaje al centro de la derecha', *Nexos*, 64 (April 1983), 15–23.
Beltrán del Rio, A. 'Problems and Prospects of the Mexican Economy in 1983–1988', in *The Mexican Economic Crisis: Policy Implications for the United States*, Joint Committee Print 98–11 (Washington, D.C.: 1984), pp. 181–97.
Booth, J. and Seligson, M. 'The Political Culture of Authoritarianism in Mexico: A Reexamination', *Latin American Research Review*, 19:1 (1984), 106–24.
Camacho, M. 'La cohesión del grupo gobernante', *Vuelta*, 1:11 (October 1977), 28–29.
Camp, R.A. 'Mexico's Presidential Candidates: Changes and Portents for the Future', *Polity*, 16:4 (Summer 1984), 588–605.

——, 'The Political Technocrat in Mexico and the Survival of the Political System', *Latin American Research Review*, 20:1 (1985), 97–118.

Carr, B. 'Temas del comunismo mexicano', *Nexos*, 54 (June 1982), 17–26.

Castañeda, J.G. 'Elecciones: tres ideas sin saña', *Proceso*, 451 (24 June 1985), 36–37.

——, 'Mexico at the Brink', *Foreign Affairs*, 4:2 (Winter 1985/86), 289–303.

Córdova, A. 'El desafío de la izquierda mexicana', *Nexos*, 18 (June 1979), 3–15.

——, 'La larga marcha de la izquierda mexicana', *Nexos*, 9:9 (June 1986), 17–23.

Domínguez Michael, C. 'Quién es quién en la izquierda mexicana', *Nexos*, 54 (June 1982). 28–32.

Fernandez Christlieb, P. 'Reforma política: viejos ensayos nuevos fracasos', *Nexos*, (August 1979), 27–30.

——, 'Elecciones federales 1985: los partidos de izquierda ante la "unidad" ', *Rev. mexicana de ciencias políticas y sociales* 31:120 (nueva epoca) (April–June 1985), 13–48.

Glade, W. 'Mexico: Party-Led Development', in Wesson, R. (ed.) (1984) *Politics, Policies, and Economic Development in Latin America* (Stanford, California: Hoover Institutions Press) pp. 94–160.

Hansen, R. 'The Evolution of US–Mexican Relations: A Sociopolitical Perspective', in Erb R.E. and Ross, S.R. (eds) (1982) *United States Relations with Mexico* (Washington, D.C.: AEI) pp. 39–48.

Kelley, G. 'Politics and Administration in Mexico: Recruitment and Promotion of the Administrative Class' (University of Texas at Austin, Institute of Latin American Studies, *Technical Papers Series*, No. 33, 1981).

Labastida M. del Campo, J. 'Proceso político y dependencia en México', *Rev mexicana de sociología* (1977).

Latell, B. 'Mexico at the Crossroads: The Many Crises of the Political System', (Stanford University, *Hoover Institution Monograph Series* 6, 16 June 1986).

Loaeza, S.(1982) 'Comentario', in PRI, *Perspectivas del sistema político mexicano* (México: Imprenta Madero) pp. 57–59.

——, 'El llamado de las urnas: para qué sirven las elecciones en Mexico?' *Nexos*, 90 (June 1985), 13–19.

Luna, M. 'Los empresarios y el régimen político mexicano; las estrategias tripartitas de los años setenta', *Estudios politicos: nueva época*, 3:1 (January–March 1984), 28–34.

Meyer, L. 'Andamios presidenciales: el todo y sus partes', *Nexos*, 60 (December 1982), 31–37.

Molinar Horcasitas, J. 'La costumbre electoral mexicana', *Nexos*, 85 (January 1985), 17–25.

Needler, M. (1984) 'Mexican Politics and U.S. Concerns', in *The Mexican Economic Crisis: Policy Implications for the United States*, Joint Committee Print 98–11 (Washington, D.C.) pp. 93–98.

Peschard, J. 'Los escenarios del PRI en 1985', *Rev. mexicana de ciencias políticas y sociales*, 31:120 (nueva época) (April–June 1985), 49–64.

Portes, A. 'Immigration Reform Again: The 1985 Proposals', *LASA Forum*, 16:4 (Winter 1986), 31–34.

Potter, J.E. 'Mexico: A Model for Success', *Harvard International Review*, 8:4 (March 1986), 33–35.

Ronfeldt, D.'The Modern Mexican Military: Implications for Mexico's Stability and Security', (Santa Monica, California: RAND Corporation, *A RAND Note*, N–2288–FF/RC, February 1985).

Rorem, M.O. 'Mexico's Organic Law of Federal Public Administration–A New Structure for Modern Administration', *Hastings International and Comparative Law Rev.*, 1:2 (Winter 1978), 367–88.

Sanderson, S.E. 'Presidential Succession and Political Rationality in Mexico', *World Politics*, 35:3 (April 1983), 316–34.

Scott, R.E. (1982) 'Necesidad de actualizar el sistema politico mexicano', in PRI, *Perspectivas del sistema político mexicano* (México: Editorial Madero) pp. 49–52.

Segovia, R. 'Las elecciones federales de 1979', *Foro Internacional*, 20:3 (January–May 1980).

Tirado, R. 'Semblanzas de las organizaciones empresariales mexicanas', *Estudios políticos (nueva época)*, 3:1(January–March 1984), 3–11.

Whitehead, L. 'Mexico from Bust to Boom: A political Evaluation of the 1976–1979 Stabilization Program' (Washington, D.C.: The Wilson Center, Latin American Program, *Working Papers*, No. 44).

Zaid, G. 'Escenarios sobre el fin del PRI', *Vuelta*, 103 (June 1985), 13–21.

Unpublished Documents and Papers

Barkin, D. 'The War Strategy: An Alternative for Mexico's Debt Management Crisis, (Summary)', (presented at Workshop on Government and the Private Sector in Contemporary Mexico, Center for US–Mexican Studies, University of California, San Diego, 16–18 April 1986).

Bath, C.R. and Rodriguez, V.E. 'Mexico's Evolving Decentralization Policy' (unpublished paper, 1985).

Bravo M., L.F. 'Coparmex y la política mexicana', (paper presented at a workshop on Government-Private Sector Relations in Mexico, UCSD, Center for US–Mexican Relations, 16–18 April 1986).

COPARMEX, 'Las elecciones de la crisis (quinta y última parte)', (Mexico: n.d.).

Encinas, R. 'Políticas públicas y grupos de presión', (paper presented at Seminario sobre Procesos Políticos y Elecciones en Sonora, Hermosillo, 22–23 March 1985).

Gentleman, J. 'Mexico after the Oil Boom: PRI Management of the Political Impact of National Disillusionment', (prepared for delivery at the 1985 International Congress of the Latin American Studies Association, Albuquerque, New Mexico, 18–20 April 1985).

Gendell, M. 'Population Growth and Labor Absorption in Latin America, 1970–2000', (mimeo, July 1984).

Gómez Taglia, S. 'Democracy and Power in Mexico: The meaning of Electoral Fraud in 1979 and 1982', (prepared for delivery at the 1985 International Congress of the Latin American Studies Association, Albuquerque, New Mexico, 18–20 April 1985).

Graham, L.S. 'Intergovernmental Relations in Mexico: The View from below', (paper presented at the Annual Meeting of the Southwestern Social Science Association, Fort Worth, Texas, 21–24 March 1984).

Guadarrama, R. and St Clair, A. 'La oposición conservadora en Sonora', (paper presented at Seminario Procesos Políticos y Elecciones en Sonora, Hermosillo 22–23 March 1985).

Klesner, J.L. 'Party System Expansion and Electoral Mobilization in Mexico', (paper presented at the 1985 International Congress of the Latin American Studies Association, Albuquerque, New Mexico, 18–20 April 1985).

Linz, J. 'Notes toward a Typology of Authoritarian Regimes', (paper presented at the Annual Meeting of the American Political Science Association, Washington, D.C., August 1972).

Lugo Verduzco, A. 'Intervención del Presidente del Comité Ejecutivo Nacional del Partido Revolucionario Institucional, en la sesión del Consejo Nacional Extraordinario correspondiente a 1985', (Mexico: mimeo, 10 December 1985).

Luna, M. Tirado R. and Valdés, F. 'Los empresarios y la política en México: 1982–1985', (paper presented at the Workshop on Government and the Private Sector in Contemporary Mexico, Center for US–Mexican Studies, University of California–San Diego, 16–18 April 1986).

Márquez, V. and Godau, R. 'Burocracia y sociedad: una perspectiva desde América Latina' (prepared for Oslak, O. (ed.) (1980) *Teoría de la burocracia estatal: enfoques críticos)*.

Maxfield, S. 'Losing Command of the Heights: Bank Nationalization and the Mexican State' (paper presented at the Latin American Studies Association Meeting, Albuquerque, New Mexico, 1985).

——, 'The Internationalization of Finance and Macroeconomic Management: Mexico and Brazil Compared', (prepared for the Annual Meeting of the American Political Science Association, Washington, D.C., 27 August–September 1986).

México, Secretaría de Gobernación, Comisión Federal Electoral, Registro Nacional de Electores, 'Calendario electoral 1983–88' (mimeo, n.p., n.d.).

Middlebrook, K. 'Political Change and Political Reform in an Authoritarian Regime: The Case of Mexico', (prepared for delivery at the conference on 'Prospects for Democracy: Transitions from Authoritarian Rule', sponsored by the Latin American Program of the Woodrow Wilson International Center for Scholars, Washington, D.C., October 1982).

PRI, 'Proceso interno de consulta a la base militante', (mimeo, 1985).

Newspapers and Periodicals

The Arizona Republic (Phoenix)
Diario de Morelos (Cuernavaca)
Diario Oficial (Mexico City)
El Financiero (Mexico City)
Excélsior (Mexico City)
Hispanoamericano (Mexico City)

Impacto (Mexico City)
El Imparcial (Hermosillo)
La Jornada (Mexico City)
Latin American Monitor (London)
Latin America Political Report (London)
Latin America Weekly Report (London)
Los Angeles Times
Miami Herald
The New York Times
El Norte (Monterrey)
El Porvenir (Monterrey)
Proceso (Mexico City)
Razones (Mexico City)
Unomásuno (Mexico City)
Vuelta (Mexico City)
The Wall Street Journal (New York)
The Washington Post

Index